This book makes Keynes's writings on his General Theory accessible to students by presenting this theory in a careful, consistent manner that is faithful to the original. Keynes's theory continues to be important because the issues it raised, such as the problems of involuntary unemployment, the volatility of investment, and the complexity of monetary arrangements in modern capitalist economies, are still with us. Keynes's method of analysis, which tries to allow for the complications of dealing with historical time, deserves the careful attention given in this book. Keynes's formal analysis dealt only with a short period of time during which changes in productive capacity as a result of net investment were small, relative to initial productive capacity. Roy Harrod and Joan Robinson, the two most prominent followers of Keynes, attempted to extend his analysis to the long period by allowing for the effects of investment on productive capacity as well as on effective demand. The careful examination of their writings on this topic is a natural complement to the presentation of Keynes's General Theory and makes clear the severe limitations on any use of equilibrium concepts in dealing with accumulation in models which try to observe Keynes's warnings about an unknowable future in the type of world we inhabit.

MODERN CAMBRIDGE ECONOMICS

KEYNES'S GENERAL THEORY AND ACCUMULATION

KEYNES'S GENERAL THEORY AND ACCUMULATION

A. Asimakopulos
McGill University

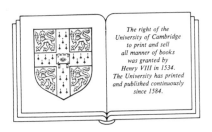

The right of the
University of Cambridge
to print and sell
all manner of books
was granted by
Henry VIII in 1534.
The University has printed
and published continuously
since 1584.

CAMBRIDGE UNIVERSITY PRESS

Cambridge
New York   Port Chester
Melbourne   Sydney

Published by the Press Syndicate of the University of Cambridge
The Pitt Building, Trumpington Street, Cambridge CB2 1RP
40 West 20th Street, New York, NY 10011, USA
10 Stamford Road, Oakleigh, Melbourne 3166, Australia

First published 1991

Printed in Great Britain by Redwood Press Limited, Melksham, Wiltshire

British Library cataloguing in publication data

Asimakopulos, Athanasios 1930–
  Keynes's general theory and accumulation. – Modern
  Cambridge economics).
  1. Economics. Keynes, John Maynard, 1883–1946.
  General theory of employment, interest and money
  1. Title
  330.156

Library of Congress cataloguing in publication data

Asimakopulos, A., 1930–
  Keynes's General theory and accumulation / A. Asimakopulos.
     p.   cm. – (Modern Cambridge economics)
  Includes bibliographical references and index.
  ISBN 0 521 36248 2. – ISBN 0 521 36815 4 (pbk.)
  1. Keynes, John Maynard, 1883–1946.
  General theory of employment, interest, and money.
  2. Keynesian economics. 1. Title. II. Series.
HB99.7.K38A85   1991
330.15'6 – dc20   90–41557   CIP

ISBN 0 521 36248 2 hardback
ISBN 0 521 36815 4 paperback

CE

To my wife, Marika

CONTENTS

Contents

SERIES PREFACE

The Modern Cambridge Economics series, of which this book is one, is designed in the same spirit as and with similar objectives to the series of Cambridge Economic Handbooks launched by Maynard Keynes soon after the First World War. Keynes's series, as he explained in his introduction, was intended 'to convey to the ordinary reader and to the uninitiated student some conception of the general principles of thought which economists now apply to economic problems'. He went on to describe its authors as, generally speaking, 'orthodox members of the Cambridge School of Economics' drawing most of their ideas and prejudices from 'the two economists who have chiefly influenced Cambridge thought for the past fifty years, Dr Marshall and Professor Pigou' and as being 'more anxious to avoid obscure forms of expression than difficult ideas'.

This series of short monographs is also aimed at the intelligent undergraduate and interested general reader, but it differs from Keynes's series in three main ways: first in that it focuses on aspects of economics which have attracted the particular interest of economists in the post Second World War era; second in that its authors, though still sharing a Cambridge tradition of ideas, would regard themselves as deriving their main inspiration from Keynes himself and his immediate successors, rather than from the neoclassical generation of the Cambridge school; and third in that it envisages a wider audience than readers in mature capitalist economies, for it is equally aimed at students in developing countries whose problems and whose interactions with the rest of the world have helped shape the economic issues which have dominated economic thinking in recent decades.

Finally, it should be said that the editors and authors of this Modern Cambridge Economics series represent a wider spectrum of economic doctrine than the Cambridge School of Economics to which Keynes referred in the 1920s. However, the object of the series is not to propagate particular doctrines. It is to stimulate students to escape from conventional theoretical ruts and to think for themselves on live and controversial issues.

PHYLLIS DEANE
GEOFFREY HARCOURT
JAN KREGEL

PREFACE

This book grew out of my lectures to final-year honours economics students and to graduate students, on Keynes's *The General Theory of Employment, Interest and Money*, and on the Keynesian theories of accumulation of Harrod and Robinson. It is not meant to be a substitute for the reading of the original writings, but it should help to make them more accessible to students. Keynes's work continues to be important. The issues he raised, such as the problems of involuntary unemployment, the volatility of investment, and the complexity of monetary arrangements in modern capitalist economies, are still with us. Keynes pointed out that the achievement of full-employment equilibrium is only one of a large number of possible outcomes in a capitalist economy, and such an economy is likely to be operating for substantial periods of time in situations where there is unemployment. His method of analysis, which tries to allow for the complications of dealing with historical time, deserves careful attention. If economic policy is to be effective it must be formulated with an awareness of the need to observe the sequence of real time that cannot be dealt with in a mechanical fashion.

The General Theory is not an easy book to read, in part because the inherently difficult nature of its material does not allow for a simple treatment, and in part because Keynes did not spend (or have) the time necessary to work everything out in a consistent manner. This has given rise to many attempts at exegesis, at finding out what Keynes really meant. This search is complicated by the fact that there are inconsistencies in *The General Theory*, with some statements or definitions that do not follow from the assumptions on which the analysis is based. In addition, there is a simple model, from which Hicks's popular IS–LM analysis draws its inspiration, that has been mistakenly taken to represent the essentials of Keynes's analysis. His analysis contains much more than the simple model that can be distilled from the pages of *The General Theory*, and makes clear the need to allow for institutional arrangements, and for the conventions that are adopted in an attempt to deal with the hazards of a world in which the future cannot be known. With my focus on Keynes's General Theory, it has not been possible to avoid the question of what Keynes really meant. My guides in this quest have been the text, taken as a whole, Keynes's writings at other times, and the recognition that he was a Marshallian economist. The literature on Keynes's General Theory is immense, and no attempt is made to deal with it here.

Keynes's formal analysis dealt only with a period of time sufficiently brief (Marshall's short period of a few months to a year) for the changes taking place in productive capacity over that interval, as a result of net investment, to be negligible relative to the total inherited productive capacity. In this model, investment had an impact on effective demand, but not on productive capacity. It concentrated on the factors determining the level of output and employment in the short period. The determination of output and employment over time could then be analysed by linking adjacent short periods, which have different productive capacities, and allowing for the interdependence of changes in the factors that determine the values for output and employment in the short period. Keynes only briefly sketched this approach at the end of chapter 18 of *The General Theory*, and in his notes on the trade cycle. Even though his formal analysis dealt only with a particular short period, Keynes believed that his conclusions would be valid over a sequence of short periods. The volatility of the factors determining investment is such that there are no reliable forces that would move the economy towards full employment over time.

Harrod's approach to the growth of an economy over time is different because he believed it should be explicitly dynamic. He considered the General Theory, even with its setting in historical time, as static, because it was not focusing on time-rates of change. Our examination of his attempt to develop a dynamic theory, while still remaining faithful to the setting of the General Theory, is thus a natural extension of the presentation of Keynes's theory. Joan Robinson was influenced by Harrod's analysis in her attempt to extend in a formal way the General Theory to the long period, and it is interesting to see the differences between her theory of accumulation and Harrod's dynamic theory. Both Harrod and Robinson came to the realisation that their attempts to give an important role to entrepreneurial equilibrium rates of growth have to be abandoned when Keynes's warnings about an unknowable future are observed.

I have accumulated many intellectual debts in arriving at my interpretation of Keynes, and in the writing of this book. Robinson's writings on the General Theory and on Kalecki started me off on my present road, and the strong impression they had on me was confirmed by personal contacts with her from 1970. An important difference in our approaches is that she wanted to treat the expression 'short period', as well as the expression 'long period', as an adjective and not as a substantive. For her, the short period was not a length of time but a state of affairs, while I consider it, following Marshall, to be an actual interval of time. The historical time analysis that Robinson wanted to see develop must have as its basis an interval of historical time. All my writings have been influenced by a 30-year association with my late colleague, J. C. Weldon. He read drafts of articles that contained early versions of some of the arguments found in the book, and he gave me the hint that led to my criticism of Keynes's definition of the aggregate demand function. G. C. Harcourt has always been most encouraging of my work, and – although I do not want to implicate him in what I have written here – there is a large overlap in our views on Keynes. My participation in the annual sessions of the Trieste International Summer School of Advanced Studies in Economics, and the discussions there with people of diverse views, have also helped me to formulate my ideas. In particular, I would like to mention (again with no implication of agreement with my interpretation of Keynes) some of the regular participants in the School, K. Bharadwaj, P. Davidson, P. Garegnani, J. Kregel, H. Minsky, S. Parrinello, F. Petri, and A. Roncaglia. The 1985 Conference held in Florence to mark the 25th anniversary of the publication of Sraffa's *Production of Commodities by Means of Commodities*, was also an occasion on which I presented and discussed aspects of my approach to Keynes. Mention should also be made of the two Conferences in Perugia, one on Kalecki, and the other on the notion of equilibrium in Keynesian theory, organised by M. Sebastiani, where I had an opportunity to exchange views with others who have published extensively on these topics. I am also grateful to A. Vercelli for the invitation to participate in the Siena Conference on the causes of high unemployment in Europe that took place in July 1989, at which material from a draft of chapter 3 was presented.

Drafts of some parts of this book were read by my former students, L. Ascah, G. Sciadas, and A. Tarasofsky, and I am grateful to them for their comments. Kim Reany, cheerfully and most competently, typed all the versions of this book. Work began on it in 1987 while I was on sabbatical leave that was financed in part by a Leave Fellowship from the Social Sciences and Humanities Research Council of Canada.

1

INTRODUCTION

1.1 THE RELEVANCE OF THE GENERAL THEORY

John Maynard Keynes's *The General Theory of Employment, Interest and Money*,[1] even though it was first published over 50 years ago, is still an important book for understanding current economic problems and theories. Although it is a theoretical treatise, the book was written by an individual who was very active in the world of economic and political affairs. This world has changed in many ways since Keynes's book was first published. Some of the changes have been prompted, at least in part, by the adoption of economic policies that received theoretical support in his book. There have been many developments in economic theory in the intervening years, but an understanding of the General Theory still yields important insights into current questions of economic policy and theory. Keynes had the rare gift that combined an ability to develop theoretical constructs with a sense of the real world, and it is this special combination that keeps the General Theory relevant.

The General Theory spawned a vast literature, and an approach to economics that was labelled 'Keynesian'. This approach still has many adherents, in spite of the development of alternative ways of looking at the operation of the economy, such as the monetarist approach (represented by Friedman 1968), and the new classical theory with its emphasis on rational expectations (represented by Lucas 1981). For example, Blinder (1987) considered eight questions that reveal differences between contemporary macroeconomic theories. He proceeded to provide answers from the writings of Keynes, of Lucas, and of Keynesians. Blinder concluded 'that when Lucas changed the answers given by Keynes, he was mostly turning better answers into worse ones ... ' (136). He also judges modern Keynesian economies to be more 'scientific' than new classical economics.

---

[1] This book will be referred to here as *The General Theory*, while the theory presented in it, and in Keynes's later writings on this topic, will be referred to as the General Theory.

In recent years, there has been the development of 'New Keynesian' models that try to develop the microfoundations for some of the
assumptions made in earlier Keynesian models, such as sticky prices
and wages (e.g. Akerlof and Yellen 1985; Mankiw 1985). Some of this
work can be seen as an attempt to provide a formal theoretical basis
for statements made by Keynes that reflected his understanding of
real-world behaviour, and which affected the way he developed his
theory. For example, Keynes emphasised the importance of relative
money-wage rates in explaining the different attitudes of workers to
equal changes in real-wage rates resulting from changes in their
individual money-wage rates, rather than from changes in the
general level of prices. This difference is not due to money illusion.
Blinder (1988) formalises this insight by postulating workers' utility
functions which include such variables as their relative wage rates, as
well as their real-wage rates.

The continued vitality of the basic ideals in the General Theory
can thus be readily demonstrated, even though they may have been
developed and used in ways that might not have met with Keynes's
approval. In addition, there is a group of economists who are loosely
grouped under the heading 'Post Keynesian', who base their work
directly on Keynes's writings (e.g. Minsky 1975; Davidson 1978)
rather than on the 'Keynesian' literature (e.g. Hicks 1937) that tried
to reconcile Keynes's work with essential elements of neoclassical
theory. The first part of the present book will concentrate on
developing Keynes's General Theory through his writings. The
Keynesian literature is dealt with only briefly in order to point out
important differences in the presentation of Keynes's theory.

1.2 THE GENERAL THEORY AND HISTORICAL TIME

Keynes was a writer of considerable skill, and his exposition of
economic problems and suggestions for policy changes were often
accessible to intelligent laymen. (His *Essays in Persuasion* (1972)
contains many of these writings.) *The General Theory* was, however,
addressed to professional economists, and it is a difficult book to
read. It also contains some minor theoretical errors, as well as
seemingly contradictory statements about key elements of the theory,
such as the determination of investment. A formal model can be
constructed from elements used by Keynes to develop his theory, but
that theory is broader than any such model. Attention should be paid
to the setting of the theory in historical time, and to Keynes's
comments about his theory, both in *The General Theory* and in his later

writings that dealt with criticisms of his theory. There is thus scope for a careful examination of Keynes's General Theory that bases itself on his writings, but that also clears up the minor theoretical slips, and deals with the ambiguities to be found in Keynes's statement of his theory. The development of such a presentation is one of the two main aims of the present book.

Keynes tried to develop a theory that would be relevant to the capitalist economies of his day, economies that existed in historical time. The basic framework for his theory was thus conditioned by his vision of the operation of such economies. Activities occur in a present the technical capabilities of which have been determined by past investment in plant and equipment, and in the education and training of a labour force. The degree of utilisation of the existing productive capacity and the level of employment, depends on the (short-term) expectations of the proceeds to be obtained from the sale of the resulting output. If it is assumed for purposes of simplification, as Keynes generally did, that these short-term expectations are borne out by realised results, then output and employment (in a closed economy with no government economic intervention) can be said to depend on consumption and investment expenditures.

Consumption expenditures were generally taken to be a function of current income, even though it was recognised that a variety of factors, including expectations of future income, could affect this relationship. For investment expenditures, the importance of long-term expectations – expectations of the quasi-rents to be earned over the life of capital equipment produced as a result of current investment decisions – is emphasised. These expectations are taken as given in Keynes's formal model, but their potential variability is underlined. They are concerned with an unknown future, and often they are based on loosely-held group or market sentiments that can change with startling rapidity. It was the unreliability of the factors which help form estimates of future conditions that in historical time are unknown, and on which investment decisions are based, that led Keynes (1973c: 121) to name investment as the *causa causans* of his system. Even though Keynes's theory concentrated on the factors determining the levels of employment and output at a particular point in time – the present – the analysis took place within the boundaries set by historical time. The past provided production opportunities and experience to the present, while the unknown future, through current long-term expectations, affected current production for investment purposes, because this production was undertaken on the basis of hopes of future profitability.

Money entered into Keynes's analysis in an essential way, because the capitalist economies, whose workings his theory was designed to illuminate, were monetary production economies. Money, in such economies, is much more than a unit of account and a convenient instrument for effecting exchanges. It is not simply a neutral link in the transactions between real goods; it 'affects motives and decisions and is, in short, one of the operative factors in the situation, so that the course of events cannot be predicted, either in the long period or in the short, without a knowledge of the behaviour of money between the first state and the last' (Keynes 1973b: 408–9). In a world where the future is unknown money is often held as an asset, as a store of wealth. Most contracts, including wage bargains, are denominated in terms of money, and having immediate command over money can be a sensible way of dealing with situations where the future money-values of real and financial assets may decline. The holding of money is thus, in part, the result of the uncertainty over the future money values of financial (and real) assets. The demand for holding money, or liquidity preference, is thus very much influenced by long-term expectations which, in this way, play an important role in determining the rate of interest.

Long-term expectations are the foundation both for Keynes's liquidity preference function and for his marginal efficiency of capital. This crucial role of long-term expectations is the basis for Keynes's statement in the preface of *The General Theory* that in a monetary economy changing views of the future can affect the level of output and employment, as well as the mix of consumption and investment goods. There is, in Keynes's view of the operations of capitalist economies, no automatic mechanism that tends to keep these economies operating at full employment, so that a change in investment does not necessarily imply an opposite change in consumption. Changes in long-term expectations alter investment expenditures through their effects on the estimates of future quasi-rents from investment outlays and on the rate of interest. These altered values for investment, in turn, change effective demand and, thus, total output and employment.

1.3 THE GENERAL THEORY AND EQUILIBRIUM

Recognition of the observance of the basic features of historical time is necessary for an understanding of the General Theory, but it must be admitted that this feature may be overlooked if attention is concentrated only on the formal model that can be found in *The*

General Theory. This model concentrates on situations of short-period equilibrium, with short-term expectations of proceeds being identical with realised results. This is a 'flow' equilibrium. Note should also be made of the 'stock' equilibrium, which is assumed to hold at each moment of time within the short period. The equilibrium for the demand and supply of money, and of bonds, is seen as a stock equilibrium, with the rate of interest adjusting to equate the demand for money, or bonds, to the existing supply.

Keynes was an economist in the Marshallian tradition – he extended that tradition by developing analytical tools to examine the economy as a whole – and Marshall's short period of a few months to a year, was the 'present' in Keynes's analysis. During that period of time it was reasonable to take as given the skills and size of the labour force, the nature and quantity of plant and equipment, the technical knowledge and managerial skills, the degrees of competition in different markets, the tastes and habits of consumers, etc. The assumption that the values for these factors are given does not mean that changes in them are not occurring within the time span of the short period. What such an assumption reflects is the belief that it is not unreasonable, for analytical purposes, to ignore these changes even when dealing with historical time. The changes in any of these factors over a Marshallian short period are small relative to their average values in the period, and thus it is permissible for a theory – which must always simplify – to abstract from these changes.

Another simplification made by Keynes in this context is the identification with actual values of the short-period equilibrium values that were the focus of his analysis. For example, in the opening sentence of the chapter containing notes on the trade cycle he claimed to have shown the factors determining the level of employment at any time, even though his analysis deals only with short-period equilibrium values. This analysis pays scant attention to the time required for the values of the dependent variables (in particular, employment and income) to reach short-period equilibrium when there is a change in, say, investment. In a 1936 letter to Hawtrey, Keynes (1973c: 27) wrote that 'I am not much interested myself in the brief intermediate period during which the higgling of the market is discovering the facts'. In that same letter, he gave a 'few weeks' as his time estimate for the 'higgling of the market'. In *The General Theory*, it is implicitly assumed that the short-period equilibrium values exert such a strong attraction on actual values that the former can be used to represent the latter. This means that the full multiplier effects of any change in investment were assumed to be completed within the short period. The short period was thus used for two, not necessarily compatible, purposes (cf. Hicks 1965: 64) and an historical time analysis, in which disappointment of expectations could affect outcomes, was not used within the short period. Keynes's justification for this procedure, to be found in the rough notes for his 1937 lectures (Keynes 1973c: 181), is that the effects of disappointed short-term expectations are only of secondary importance, and their inclusion might obscure his conclusion that involuntary unemployment is not necessarily a temporary disequilibrium phenomenon. The introduction of disappointed short-term expectations does not, in this context, add anything of significance to the analysis. Employment decisions are based on short-term expectations of proceeds, and failure of these expectations to be realised would result in a new set of expectations and a new level of employment, etc. In all these cases, however, the aggregate demand and supply conditions that are used to define short-period equilibrium are the controlling influences on output and employment, and Keynes cuts through to the equilibrium position determined by these conditions.

Short-period equilibrium for Marshall was a stepping stone to the consideration of long-period equilibrium, but Keynes stopped at short-period equilibrium and made no significant use of long-period equilibrium in his General Theory. In those parts of *The General Theory* that contain the central core of his analysis, this concept appears only in the nature of an aside. Keynes (1936: 48) defined long-period employment, which is tied to long-period equilibrium, as a special case when he was explaining the role of long-term expectations. This definition was presented simply for purposes of logical completeness. It is possible to deduce long-period equilibrium values that correspond to give technology, the propensity to consume, the rate of interest, and long-term expectations, and this is essentially what Keynes did in defining long-period employment. For this concept to be relevant, the values of the parameters would have to be unchanged over long intervals of time, but Keynes's view of capitalist economies did not contain such intervals. He saw them as exposed to frequent exogenous shocks, and to infectious changes in long-term expectations, so that the economy could not be viewed at any point in time as moving towards long-period equilibrium values. Keynes contrasted the dynamic world (where uncertainty over future conditions, which his theory was trying to illuminate, affected current decisions) with the stationary world of 'static economics' where long-period equilibrium had a role. He was prepared to state that in a dynamic world, long-period equilibrium 'does not properly exist', and it can thus be omitted from a theory that deals with such a world.

I should, I think, be prepared to argue that, in a world ruled by uncertainty with an uncertain future linked to an actual present, a final position of equilibrium, such as one deals with in static economics, does not properly exist. (Keynes 1979: 222)

1.4 SHORT-PERIOD EQUILIBRIUM AND CHANGE

Keynes demonstrated that unemployment could be an equilibrium phenomenon, that there could be no net forces at work in the economy to increase the level of employment, even though workers wanted to supply additional labour at the existing real-wage rates. Employment in this case would be an equilibrium position of rest. In contrast, the output of firms, and consumption and investment expenditures of individuals and firms would all be in chosen positions of equilibrium. The values for these variables were the appropriate ones given the values of the parameters. In this demonstration, Keynes posed a serious challenge to what he called the 'classical theory', which saw unemployment as a temporary, disequilibrium, phenomenon due to cyclical disturbances or to real-wage rates that were too high because workers refused to accept lower money-wage rates.

This focus on short-period equilibrium, a position of rest, appears to be at variance with Keynes's claim in the preface to *The General Theory* that his book was primarily a study of the factors that determine changes in the levels of output and employment. Both equilibrium and change are, however, compatible in Keynes's work, because the determinants of short-period equilibrium are themselves constantly changing, so that the equilibrium position of rest is only a temporary resting place. His analysis gives no reason to expect, however, that these changes will lead to full employment. Full employment is only a characteristic of one of the many possible positions of equilibrium, and Keynes's General Theory thus includes the classical theory outcome as a special case. The long-period implications of Keynes's analysis are that the achievement of full employment is not a special problem of a particular point in historical time, but one that can keep recurring. The knowledge that would lead to some long-period equilibrium does not accrue with the passage of time, because the unpredictable changes that occur during this time make much of past knowledge irrelevant. Many investment decisions turn out to have results different than expected, and new investment decisions are made in a continuing climate of uncertainty.

The independent variables whose values establish the framework for Keynes's short-period equilibrium are: (i) his three fundamental psychological factors, the propensity to consume, the attitude to liquidity, and the expectation of future yields from capital assets on which he bases his marginal efficiency of capital; (ii) the money-wage rates, which are determined by bargaining between employers and workers; and (iii) the quantity of money, which he sees as determined by the action of the central bank. At the end of chapter 18, after Keynes has re-stated the core of his General Theory, he sketches out how changes in these independent variables and their repercussions will, given the framework of his theory, explain the main features of the actual experience of capitalist economies. Another sketch of changes over time developed on the basis of his model, is to be found in his notes on the trade cycle. Keynes does not present a formal model of the cycle, with constant values for the parameters that can be used to trace out a cycle over time. As we shall see below, he did not believe that in the real-world capitalist economies, which were the subject of his study, the values of these parameters would be constant over time. With these changing values for the parameters, short-period equilibrium positions would also be changing. Keynes thus characterised his theory as being one of 'shifting equilibrium' (Keynes 1936: 293) in contrast to theories that were concerned with stationary equilibrium.

Keynes's aim in *The General Theory* was to develop a theory that reflected experience, and which could be used to select those variables that could be manipulated by public policy in order to improve economic performance. His formal model can be set out, as will be done below, in a set of equations that represent the operation of his three fundamental psychological factors, the money-wage rate, and the quantity of money supplied by the banking system. These equations can be 'solved', in the manner of all simultaneous equations, to obtain the short-period equilibrium values of the dependent variables, but Keynes's theory contains more than this formal model. It also points to the possible interdependence between his given factors, where a change in one (e.g. the money-wage rate) can affect another (e.g. the investment function). The equations represent the situation at a given point in historical time, and any change in one of the factors can affect expectations, and thus important characteristics of that point in time. The manipulation of the formal model must thus be handled with great care. It should also be noted that Keynes does not give equal weight to all the equations in his formal model. His attention is focused on those variables and functions that are considered to be mainly responsible for changes in employment, and he accords them a causal role in his theory. The key variable, as noted above, is investment. Keynes (1936: 247) recognises that this attempt to single out those factors in the model which exercise a dominant influence on changes in output from those that have a comparatively negligible influence, is subject to error: 'in a study so complex as economics ... we cannot make completely accurate generalisations'. This isolation of causal factors is very much dependent on Keynes's view of the experience of actual economies, which is reflected in his theory.

1.5 THE GROWTH OF THE ECONOMY OVER TIME

Keynes dealt with intervals of time greater than a short period only in his sketch of the trade cycle, and in his indication of how his model can reproduce actual experiences. Both of these brief outlines lie outside his formal analysis. It was only in these cases that he allowed for the productive-capacity creating effects of investment as well as for its demand creating effects. Any formal attempt to analyse the development of an economy over time would have to deal with both effects. Short periods would be linked, in this attempt, to form a sequence that would be marked by growth and cyclical fluctuations. This linking is a necessary complement to the General Theory, since that theory tries to shed light on the factors determining the changes in output and employment over time. The determination of short-period equilibrium values is only the first stage in the analysis of these factors.

The second main aim of the present book is to examine the attempts by two of Keynes's younger associates, R. F. Harrod and Joan Robinson, to start from Keynes's analysis and to develop theories that deal with the growth of an economy over time. Harrod was the pioneer in this endeavour. He had been trying to develop an analysis of the trade cycle as oscillations around a line of steady growth before the appearance of *The General Theory*. Robinson acknowledged the importance of Harrod's writings on her own efforts to develop a theory of accumulation.

The important differences in the attempts by these two theorists to deal with growth and accumulation will be dealt with below, but two basic similarities should be noted here. Both Harrod and Robinson wanted to set their analyses in Keynes's world where future conditions were unknown, and investment decisions had to be made in a climate of uncertainty about the circumstances that would eventually determine the suitability of these decisions. In spite of this, they both centred their analyses on equilibrium rates of change – Harrod's warranted rate of growth and Robinson's desired rate of accumulation – that were characterised by long-period equilibrium. This assignment of a key role to long-period equilibrium was not in keeping with the Keynes-type world for which these theories were developed, and it will be argued below that neither theory succeeded in fulfilling its ambitious task. Each is, however, a very interesting failure, and worthy of careful study. Our examination of these theories points out the incompatibility between the assumption of a Keynes-type world, and the use of an investment function that leads to long-run equilibrium. An accommodating investment function that results in long-period equilibrium, or in full employment, does not exist in the economies that were the subject of Keynes's General Theory.

TOWARDS *THE GENERAL THEORY*

2.1 INTRODUCTION

The General Theory of Employment, Interest and Money was Keynes's last major work in economics. He referred to the composition of this book as involving 'a struggle of escape from habitual modes of thought and expression' (Keynes 1936: viii). Involved here was not only the radical re-working of economic theory to focus on the factors that determine changes in the scale of output and employment for the economy, but also the presentation of this theory in a clear and convincing manner. Yet soon after the publication of his book Keynes came to feel that his exposition could have been clearer. He went on to re-state the essence of his theory, as he then saw it, by emphasising some of its features in his February 1937 *Quarterly Journal of Economics* article that was written in response to four articles on his book in that journal. In addition, he tried to cover what he came to see as a gap in his treatment of the relationship between investment, money and finance in his 1937 and 1938 articles in the *Economic Journal*. The presentation of Keynes's General Theory must thus deal with these writings as well as with his book.

Keynes's General Theory represents a significant departure from his earlier theoretical writings because of his concentration on the factors determining changes in output and employment, rather than on prices. Keynes also centred his analysis of output on short-period equilibrium rather than the long-period equilibrium, which was the point of reference of his price equations in the book he had only just completed before embarking on *The General Theory*. But the view of capitalist economies as being prone to fluctuations, fluctuations that are largely initiated and fed by changes in investment, underlies both the General Theory and his earlier writings.[1] A brief examination of the transition period between Keynes's completion of *A Treatise on Money* and the publication of *The General Theory*, is useful for an

---

[1] That this was a critical feature of Keynes's vision of the workings of capitalist economies is a main theme in Vicarelli (1984).

understanding of the elements of continuity in his analysis, the problems he faced in formulating his new theory, and the assistance he received along the way. This examination, by indicating how some minor mistakes in the analysis occurred, also helps in the presentation of a statement of Keynes's theory that avoids these errors.

The careful readings of his drafts by Kahn,[2] Joan Robinson, Harrod, Hawtrey and Robertson, and the many suggestions they made, did not eliminate all the minor errors. Keynes never did get all the details of his own analysis straight in his mind, and some of his later statements even contained errors in material that had been presented correctly in earlier drafts. These slips, and various minor criticisms that can be made, do not diminish Keynes's monumental achievement in developing a theory that presents a fundamental challenge to orthodox theory; yet they sometimes obscure the nature of that challenge. Keynes, judging from his writings, was not a meticulous theorist. This could be the result, in part, of the great pressures on his time from his many activities. His concern for producing a theoretical basis for the policy proposals he felt were important in a world economy suffering widespread depression also added to these pressures. On the other hand, this could also be in part a reflection of his mind and his approach to economic theory. In a mid-1934 fragment that could have been intended as a preface to the book then in process, Keynes characterised the writing of economic theory in the following way:

When we write economic theory, we write in a quasi-formal style; and there can be no doubt, in spite of the disadvantages, that this is our best available means of conveying our thoughts to one another. But when an economist writes in a quasi-formal style, he is composing neither a document verbally complete and exact so as to be capable of a strict legal interpretation, nor a logically complete proof. Whilst it is his duty to make his premises and his use of terms as clear as he can, he never states all his premises and his definitions are not perfectly clear-cut.   (Keynes 1973b: 469–70)

This statement is in line with Austin Robinson's comment on Keynes's approach to economic theory. 'I have long felt that Keynes's economic thinking was, in reality, intuitive, impressionis-

---

[2] The written record of suggested changes in volume 13 of the *Collected Writings* (Keynes 1973b) does not do justice to the contributions of Kahn in this regard, because many of his suggestions were made at his meetings with Keynes. For example, Keynes writes to Joan Robinson in March 1934: 'I am going through a stiff week's supervision from R. F. K. [Kahn] on my M. S. He is a marvellous critic and suggester and improver – there never was anyone in the history of the world to whom it was so helpful to submit one's stuff' (Keynes 1973b: 422).

tic, and in a sense feminine rather than precise, ordered, and meticulous' (Robinson 1964: 90).

2.2 THE TRANSITION FROM THE *TREATISE*

Keynes's *A Treatise of Money* was published, after several delays, on 31 October 1930. This was much the most ambitious work on economics that Keynes had undertaken up to that point, and one that left him, as he wrote to his mother, with 'mixed feelings' when it was finished, after being occupied with it 'seven years off and on'. 'Artistically it is a failure – I have changed my mind too much during the course of it for it to be a proper unity. But I think it contains an abundance of ideas and material' (Keynes 1973b: 176). In the theoretical portions of this book, Keynes was primarily concerned with the factors governing the level of prices. The banking system was given a key role in this regard because its response to demand for credit was seen 'to determine – broadly speaking – the rate of investment by the business world' (Keynes 1930a: 153), while changes in the price level were related to the differences between investment and saving.

Keynes centred his analysis in the *Treatise* on long-period equilibrium prices that included normal profits (defined to cover the normal remuneration of entrepreneurs, interest on capital and regular monopoly gains), as well as the efficiency earnings (payments per unit of output) for the other factors of production. Changes that were initiated by 'investment disturbances' are seen as leading to 'an oscillation about an approximately unchanged price-level' (276), while 'monetary disturbances (whenever, that is to say, the monetary change is of a quasi-permanent nature) ... [represent] a passage from one equilibrium price-level to another'. The actual sales proceeds of firms could differ from what the value of the output produced would have been if equilibrium prices prevailed. The differences between these sums represent windfall profits (if positive) or losses (if negative), and Keynes excludes these items from his definition of income. Keynes has a difference between saving and investment in this work because saving is defined as the value of this notional income (income that includes normal profits whether they are obtained or not) minus actual consumption expenditures, while investment is represented by actual investment expenditures. With actual sales proceeds being equal to the sum of investment and consumption expenditures, investment is equal to these proceeds (or actual income) minus consumption. A difference between saving and investment thus arises under these definitions whenever the value of

Keynes's notional income differs from actual sales proceeds. Investment exceeds (falls short of) saving by the amount of the windfall profits (losses) that occur when market forces result in actual prices for output that are higher (lower) than normal prices.

Keynes defines the 'normal' remuneration of entrepreneurs, which is included in his measure of income, in such a way that non-zero values for the windfall items lead, possibly with some time lag, to changes in output. 'For my present purpose I propose to define the "normal" remuneration of entrepreneurs at any time as that rate of remuneration which, if they were open to make new bargains with all the factors of production at the currently prevailing rates of earnings, would leave them under no motive either to increase or to decrease their scale of operations' (124–5). Entrepreneurs also respond to these non-zero values for windfall profits by changing their offers to the factors of production (e.g. 'entrepreneurs will, under the influence of positive or negative profits, be ... willing ... to increase or diminish (as the case may be) the average rate of remuneration ... which they offer to the factors of production' (152)). Fluctuations in prices, as well as in output, thus result from the fluctuations in profits due to differences between investment and saving. Keynes made clear that both the price level and output would tend to change in these circumstances, but he did not consider whether the changes in output would be more important than the changes in efficiency earnings, or vice versa. 'A discussion of the precise circumstances which determine the degree in which a class of entrepreneurs ... pursues the one course or the other over the short-period would, however, lead me too far into the intricate theory of the economics of the short-period' (161). This failure to go more deeply into the question of how cyclical fluctuations are split between output and price changes, as well as the prominence given to his Fundamental Equations for prices in which output was taken to be constant, meant that readers tended to characterise the *Treatise* as dealing only with price changes.[3]

An additional reason for the close attention paid to Keynes's

---

[3] That this tendency still persists is shown by the recent comments of Sir John Hicks (1985: 57) who writes that Keynes in *The General Theory* 'had to abandon the *Treatise* simplification, the study of price-changes without quantity-changes'. In dealing with *The General Theory*, we must be careful not to fall into the opposite error of ignoring the price changes that accompany the output changes that are the focus of Keynes's analysis in that book. Here, too, Hicks oversimplifies. 'Quantity-changes had to be allowed for. He wanted to study them in the same way as the price-changes had been studied; so the natural way to begin was to seek to construct a model in which quantities changed with no effect on prices.'

Fundamental Equations was the causal connection between windfall profits and the purchasing power of money, which he saw as a '*fact* from the real world which gives significance to the particular Fundamental Equations which we have selected and saves them from the character of being mere identities' (156–7). This causal connection arises because of the response of entrepreneurs to non-zero profits. 'It is by altering the rate of profits in particular directions that entrepreneurs can be induced to produce this rather than that, and it is by altering the rate of profits in general that they can be induced to modify the average of their offers of remuneration to the factors of production' (157).

When Keynes did come to deal with 'the intricate theory' of the economics of the short period in *The General Theory*, he made use of elements that had appeared in the *Treatise*, or that he had used in his defence of that work. There is, for example, the role given to short-term expectations (referred to simply as 'anticipations' in the *Treatise*) in determining changes in output and prices: 'it is the *anticipated* profit or loss which is the mainspring of change, and . . . it is by causing anticipations of the appropriate kind that the banking system is able to influence the price level' (159). Further comments on their role, foreshadowing statements in *The General Theory*, appear in a letter to Hawtrey dealing with the latter's comments on proofs of the *Treatise*: 'I certainly agree that the volume of output depends on the anticipated price, not on the actual price' (Keynes 1973b: 144). The definition of saving that Keynes was to use in *The General Theory* appears in his sharp response to Hayek's critical review 'if we define *income* to include profits, and savings as being the excess of income thus defined over expenditure on consumption, then savings and the value of investment are identically the same thing' (251). This definition appears again in some notes on the definition of saving that Keynes sent to Robertson in March 1932 (276). There is also here, as was customary for Keynes, the emphasis on the causal role given to investment rather than to saving, in a form that once more foreshadows *The General Theory*, but the 'dependent' variable is the relation between price and the cost of production rather than output. 'For S' [the definition of saving that makes it identical to investment] always and necessarily accommodates itself to I . . . Not that the virtuous decisions [to save, i.e. the propensities to save] are of no effect. But what they settle is, not the amount of saving, but the relation between the consumption price level and the cost of production . . .' A readiness to give up his *Treatise* definition of saving is announced in a June 1932 letter to Hawtrey. Keynes mentions that 'I am working it out all over again ... that I now put less fundamental reliance on my conception of savings and substitute for it the conception of expenditure ... [in order to] follow up the actual genesis of change' (172–3).

This re-working, which eventually became *The General Theory*, was begun, in Keynes's estimation, soon after the *Treatise* was published. He wrote to his mother on 26 December 1935, in connection with the former: 'I finished my book on Tuesday – it has taken five years' (653). Two important stimuli leading to it were the obvious gap left by his failure to give adequate consideration to the factors determining changes in output, and the world economic situation, where depressed levels of output and employment raised questions as to whether they could be satisfactorily explained by the cyclical fluctuations consistent with orthodox theory. The latter meant that serious consideration had to be given to the possibility that there was no satisfactory 'normal' level of output and employment around which the economy moved. In particular, a self-regulating mechanism that would lead to full-employment levels of output, in the absence of fluctuations, might not exist. It was the examination of this possibility that came to occupy a central place in the new book with cyclical fluctuations hovering in the background. The fact that this, as well as the institutional details on money to be found in the earlier book form part of the setting for *The General Theory* should not be overlooked. Keynes repudiated some of the constructions he had used in the *Treatise*, such as his Fundamental Equations and the 'natural rate of interest', but there were important elements of continuity, as we shall see, in his treatment of the factors determining the rate of interest and the volume of investment. With the *Treatise* available as an expression of his views on many aspects of money, Keynes did not have to repeat himself in *The General Theory*. He could concentrate on presenting the broad factors directly relevant to the determination of the level of employment. References to material in the *Treatise* will be made in later chapters that deal with the role of money and its influence on investment in *The General Theory*.

2.3 THE 'CIRCUS'

Keynes was strongly influenced in embarking on his new work by criticisms of the *Treatise* made by a group of young economists at Cambridge. This group – the most prominent members were Richard Kahn, James Meade, Joan and Austin Robinson, and Piero

Sraffa – met formally during the period January–May 1931.[4] A particular item of contention was Keynes's statements that an increase in entrepreneurs' consumption expenditures will increase the profits of entrepreneurs selling consumption goods by an equal amount, while a decrease in such expenditures will reduce profits by an equal amount. This means that consumption spending by entrepreneurs fails to reduce the wealth of entrepreneurs as a whole – profits as sources of consumption expenditures are inexhaustible (likened by Keynes to 'a widow's cruse' (Keynes 1930a: 139)). But attempts by some entrepreneurs to increase their wealth by cutting down on consumption expenditures, will not lead to an increase in entrepreneurial wealth, because of the lower profits accruing to entrepreneurs selling consumption goods ('a Danaid jar which can never be filled up'). These statements, and Keynes's Fundamental Equations for price levels on which they are based, assume constant output, clearly not a suitable basis for a general theory. As soon as output is allowed to respond to changes in consumption expenditures, the stipulated results do not necessarily follow.[5] As we have seen above, output was not generally held constant in the *Treatise*, but particular attention was directed to those parts that assumed constant output. Keynes's sensitivity on this point is illustrated by his response to an article Joan Robinson had written for *Economica* in 1931 (Robinson 1933) on certain points in the *Treatise*, the proofs of which she sent to Keynes in April 1932. He termed the article 'excellent', but added: 'I think you are a little hard on me as regards the assumption of constant output. It is quite true that I have not followed out the consequences of changes of output in the earlier theoretical part ... [but] it is only at a particular point in the preliminary theoretical argument that I assume constant output' (Keynes 1973b: 270).[6]

Kahn argues in his 1931 article on the multiplier[7] that Keynes's price equations 'apply in their full simplicity ... when the whole of

---

[4] For a discussion of the activities of the 'Circus', based on the memories of these five, see Keynes (1973b: 338–43).

[5] Keynes's treatment of the 'widow's cruse' should not be confused with Kalecki's 1933 explanation (see Kalecki 1971: 12) for the determination of profits, even though in both cases profits increase by the increase in capitalists' consumption expenditures. Kalecki's result is *not* dependent on constant output, it follows from the assumption of short-period equilibrium, with given investment expenditures, and a zero propensity to save out of wages.

[6] Kahn (1984 108) comments, 50 years later, with respect to his group's general characterisation of the *Treatise*: 'I do not see how we – members of the Circus – could have attributed to Keynes the assumption of inelastic supply'

[7] This paper 'was originally conceived in the late summer of 1930' (Kahn 1972: vii).

the factors of production are employed, and continue to be employed, in producing either for consumption or for investment' (Kahn 1931: 10). In the conditions of that time, however, the presence of unemployed labour and unutilised plant, meant that the short-period supply curves of consumption goods had considerable elasticity. It was the demand and supply for these goods that determined their prices, and it was necessary to consider short-period conditions to explain prices as well as output. Kahn showed that the multiplier process would continue until the increase in investment was balanced by an increase in saving that reflects, in later terminology, the economy's propensity to save and the foreign balance. It was this equality between investment and saving as determined by the economy's propensity to save (*not* the definitional equality between saving and investment) that served to define Keynes's short-period equilibrium level of employment. But its use for this purpose had not yet been seen either by Keynes or by Kahn.

Moggridge has concluded that 'within a short time in the winter and spring of 1931 the "Circus" had in its hands most of the important ingredients of the system which was ultimately to appear in the *General Theory*' (Keynes 1973b: 341). But even if this were the case, these 'ingredients' had still to be fitted into place by Keynes. There is no sign of this having been done in his June 1931 Harris Foundation lectures in Chicago that were based on the theoretical framework of the *Treatise*. These lectures feature his emphasis on the rate of investment as the variable that is most likely to cause cyclical fluctuations in output and employment – a constant theme in his writings that was also emphasised, even though he was using a different theoretical framework, in the *Quarterly Journal of Economics* in 1937. In 1931 he writes: 'I shall concentrate on the variability of the rate of investment. For that is, in fact, the element in the economic situation which is capable of sudden and violent change' (354–5). There was also reference in these lectures to 'a reason for expecting an equilibrium point of decline to be reached. A given deficiency of investment causes a given decline of output. Unless there is a constantly increasing deficiency of investment, there is eventually reached, therefore, a sufficiently low level of output which represents a kind of spurious equilibrium' (355–6). Perhaps here, as Moggridge states, there are 'hints of equilibrium at less than full employment' (343), but it could be nothing more than an explanation for the bottoming-out of a slump.[8] A subsequent letter to Kahn shows that in

---

[8] This is how it is interpreted by Patinkin (1982: 23–26).

September of that year Keynes had still not worked out the conditions necessary for a stable equilibrium at less than full
employment.

One of Keynes's interventions during the series of seminars held at
these Chicago meetings deserves mention here. He sketched an
aggregate supply function that related the level of output (for 'the
totality of industries') to the level of prime profit. He prefaced his
remarks with the statement: 'The analysis I shall like to try to outline
is not merely my own; it is due to a young English economist, Mr.
R. F. Kahn. I should like to put his point very shortly' (368).

2.4 DRAFTS OF *THE GENERAL THEORY*

Patinkin, on the basis of lecture notes taken by Keynes's students,
has placed the date for Keynes's development of a key element in his
General Theory 'sometime during 1933' (Patinkin 1982: 22). This
key element is the role of a marginal propensity to consume with a
value less than unity in establishing a stable equilibrium level of
output at less than full employment. This necessary condition for
equilibrium is contained in a handwritten fragment from a chapter
on saving, that has been given a 1933 date: 'it is a necessary condition
of equilibrium that, when aggregate income falls, the aggregate
expenditure on consumption should fall by a lesser amount than the
fall of income' (Keynes 1979: 103). But even with this key element in
place, there was a considerable amount of work to be done in order to
set down his theory in a clear and consistent way, a task that Keynes
never completed. This can be illustrated by considering some of the
drafts of *The General Theory*, and the correspondence between Keynes
and the readers of this material.

Keynes set up models of different types of economies in an attempt
to explain why actual capitalist economies could get 'stuck' in
positions of less than full employment, rather than simply experienc-
ing cyclical downturns. A draft chapter that belongs with a
December 1933 table of contents for Keynes's new book, defines a
co-operative economy as one 'in which the factors of production are
rewarded by dividing up in agreed proportions the actual output of
their co-operative efforts' (77). For this economy 'there is no obstacle
in the way of the employment of an additional unit of labour if this
unit will add to the social product output expected to have an
exchange value ... which is sufficient to balance the disutility of the
additional employment' (78). With production conditions conducive
to the existence of the competitive markets implicitly assumed by

Keynes, the size and number of co-operative production units would be determined by the net marginal product of labour and the marginal disutility of labour. If the marginal product of labour was greater than its marginal disutility, then more labour would be employed in existing production units and/or new units would be established, until equality was obtained. In such an economy total output and employment, as well as the real-wage rate, would be determined in the labour market. All the employment, and thus output decisions, taken on the basis of conditions in the labour market, are then automatically validated in product markets by the payment of output shares to the factors of production.

Keynes surmised that these special labour market conditions would also be fulfilled in an economy where production units are owned and operated by a class of entrepreneurs, as long as total expenditure is always sufficient to purchase, at expected prices, whatever total output is produced. He calls this second type of economy 'a *neutral entrepreneur economy*, or a *neutral economy* for short.' There is no explicit reference to a neutral economy in *The General Theory*, but it appears to underlie his view of classical theory. 'The classical theory assumes, in other words, that the aggregate demand price (or proceeds) always accommodates itself to the aggregate supply price' (Keynes 1936: 26).

In contrast to the co-operative and neutral economies there is what 'we will call a *money-wage* or *entrepreneur economy*' (Keynes 1979: 78). Here, production and employment decisions depend on the expectations of money proceeds relative to variable costs, and 'it is in an entrepreneur economy that we actually live today'. It was this economy that provided the setting for the General Theory, and it is here that employment is determined by independent aggregate demand and supply functions for output, and not by conditions in the labour market.

Keynes's analysis in *The General Theory* is concerned with the factors determining the offers of employment by a large number of competitive firms, offers that must be based on their expectations of prices for their products, since the production processes, even though firms begin with given plant and equipment, take some time to be completed. The prices for these products will be determined, given the firms' supply decisions, by demand conditions in their markets. Keynes's presentation of these features at an aggregate level, for the economy as a whole, was confused and inconsistent with the competitive microfoundations of his theory. He never appeared to get clear in his own mind the distinction between the parameters (expected prices for individual products) on which decisions would be based by his competitive firms, and the parameters (total consumption and investment expenditures) that determine total output from the perspective of the analyst or for a single economy-wide firm. It is only for the latter firm that expectations of aggregate demand can play a role in determining employment.

It is not surprising that Keynes, a pioneer in the formulation of aggregate functions, never got these matters straight, and he would often attach the adjective 'expected' to the aggregate demand function when expectations were fully, and properly, accounted for by decisions based on his aggregate supply function. This continuing confusion in Keynes's thinking could be due, in part, to his use initially of a single firm in trying to define effective demand. His use of such a construct is described in an April 1934 letter[9] to Kahn that will be quoted in full.

I have been making rather extensive changes in the early chapters of my book, to a considerable extent consequential on a simple and obvious, but beautiful and important (I think) precise definition of what is meant by effective demand: –
  Let W be the marginal prime cost of production when output is O.
  Let P be the expected selling price of this output.
  Then OP is effective demand.
The fundamental assumption of the classical theory, 'supply creates its own demand', is that $OW = OP$ *whatever* the level of O, so that effective demand is incapable of setting a limit to employment which consequently depends on the relation between marginal product in wage-good industries and marginal disutility of employment. On *my* theory $OW \neq OP$ for *all* values of O, and entrepreneurs have to choose a value of O for which it *is* equal; – otherwise the equality of price and marginal prime cost is infringed. This is the real starting point of everything.   (Keynes 1973b: 422–3)

In the first part of this letter Keynes is describing the action of a single firm that produces all of the output in the economy, and that decides on the output to produce by equating (as would a competitive firm, one of a very large number selling in a particular market!) its expected selling price to its marginal cost. At the end of the letter he refers to 'entrepreneurs' choosing a value for the same total output, without any indication of awareness that he is being inconsistent.

This lack of awareness that some of his formulations are inconsistent is apparent in drafts, in his correspondence, and in *The General Theory*. In a mid-1934 draft, employment is shown as being deter-

[9] Keynes's use of a single firm for the economy that has expectations concerning total consumption and investment sales proceeds pre-dates this letter, as shown by an early 1933 draft chapter (Keynes 1979: 64).

mined by the intersection of two functional relationships (they are forerunners of his aggregate supply and aggregate demand functions). The former is called the 'employment function' and relates different levels of 'effective demand' to the corresponding quantities of employment to which they would lead. But this effective demand is inappropriately defined for competitive firms, since it is said to be based 'on the expectation of what is going to be consumed and on the expectation of what is going to be invested' (439). In the third proof of *The General Theory*, Keynes had switched use of the term 'effective demand' from the employment function to the aggregate demand function, which is referred to as '*the state of effective demand . . . the schedule relating the sum, for which the current output resulting from the employment of any given number of men can be sold, to the number of men employed*' (Keynes 1973c: 370). The statement of this function is consistent with the microfoundations of his theory because it is not an expectational function, and by the term effective demand he simply means 'the sum for which the current output can be actually sold'. (The 'employment function' in this third proof is, except for its name, the aggregate supply function of *The General Theory*.) This appropriate statement of the aggregage demand function is accidental, because Keynes does not appear to have understood the 'consistency' problem. A few pages later in this same proof he refers to effective demand as relating 'expected sale proceeds' to employment (375).

Hawtrey drew Keynes's attention to this problem when he saw the page proofs of *The General Theory*. He had noted that '[E]ach employer's (hypothetical) expectation is presumably confined to his own product, and I do not see how you are going to aggregate these particular expectations into a total of consumption and a total of investment' (Keynes 1973b: 597). Keynes's defence '[T]he demand which determines the decision as to how much plant to employ must necessarily concern itself with expectations' (602), fails to recognise that expectations of individual product prices, and not of total investment and consumption expenditures, are relevant for his competitive firms. A re-statement of his theory of effective demand that avoids this inconsistency with his microfoundations is given in the next chapter.

Keynes's treatment of the equality between saving and investment did not always distinguish (even after *The General Theory*) between its definitional and its equilibrium form. The definitional and equilibrium equalities are presented correctly in a draft chapter that has been given a 1933 date (Keynes 1979: 102–3). But in a 1935 reply to

Harrod's comments on statements made about the classical theory of interest in proofs of *The General Theory*, Keynes appears to have forgotten that there are two forms of this equality. 'But saving and investment are the *same* thing' (Keynes 1973b: 551). Further evidence of Keynes's failure to remember the equilibrium equality appears in the postscript to that letter, where he writes that '[S]aving and investment are merely alternative names for the difference between income and consumption' (552). He then goes on to incorrectly specify the propensity to save. 'The propensity to save is a curve which relates the amount of *investment* to the amount of income' (italics supplied). (The context makes clear that this is not a typographical error.) Kahn spotted an error of this kind in the proofs, and his comment saved Keynes from error on page 63 of *The General Theory*. Kahn wrote: 'I do not like you saying that saving and investment are "different names for the same thing". They are *different* things (that is the whole point) – they are certainly different acts – but they are equal in *magnitude*' (637). Keynes dropped the identification that Kahn objected to on this page, but that he could still give the same impression is shown by his statement on page 74 of *The General Theory*: '*Saving* and *Investment* have been so defined that they are necessarily equal in amount, being, for the community as a whole, merely different aspects of the same thing'.[10]

Keynes was in a hurry to get his book published. As he wrote to Hawtrey in January 1936, 'I am afraid, indeed, that I did not make some modifications which I would have made otherwise, as I could not face the disturbance and delay of upsetting the pagination except for grave cause' (Keynes 1973b: 626). It should thus not be surprising that Keynes, who was always involved in many activities, did not work out precisely all the details of his general analysis, and that some inconsistencies, as well as inadequate explanations, should have slipped into *The General Theory*. They have often caused problems for students of this book and even Keynes did not always see the full implications of his theory.

2.5 CONCLUSION

Keynes's movement towards *The General Theory* represented an important departure from his earlier writings – he described the composition of this book as 'a long struggle of escape' (Keynes 1936:

---

[10] Hawtrey (1937a: 174) interpreted Keynes as defining saving and investment as 'two different names for the same thing' on the basis of the above-quoted statement (Hawtrey 1937b: 436). The denial by Keynes (1937b: 211) that they are so defined

viii). Instead of the focus of the analysis being on the price level and long-period equilibrium values, it was on the short-period equilibrium levels of output and employment. Keynes's long-time vision of a capitalist economy subject to significant fluctuations that were largely due to variations in investment did not alter during this period or in *The General Theory*, but these fluctuations were no longer seen as occurring around some satisfactory or 'normal' level of output and employment. Keynes, in spite of the considerable assistance of Kahn, and others, never did get all the details of his new analysis straightened out. In particular, his final statement of the aggregate demand function was not consistent with the microfoundations of his theory, and he did not always distinguish between the definitional equality of saving and investment and their functional equality that is a condition of equilibrium.

is not necessarily free of confusion, as pointed out in section 5.8 below, between the definitional and functional equalities of saving and investment.

3

THE GENERAL THEORY OF EMPLOYMENT

3.1 INTRODUCTION

Keynes foresaw that *The General Theory* could create problems for readers, and in his preface he wrote that for the economists of his day the 'difficulty lies, not in the new ideas, but in escaping from the old ones' (Keynes 1936: viii). But obstacles are also placed in the reader's way by Keynes's failure to get clear in his own mind all the elements of his theory. The inconsistencies in his treatment of the equality between saving and investment, and in the use of expectations in the aggregate demand function, discussed in the preceding chapter, illustrate this problem. There is also Keynes's seemingly paradoxical mixing of static analysis with statements and inferences about changes over time, with no explanation of how the former is to be used to derive the latter. He writes in the preface that his book 'has evolved into what is primarily a study of the forces which determine changes in the scale of output and employment as a whole' (vii), but it employs static analysis in its concentration on the short-period equilibrium *levels* of output and employment. Keynes did not deal, in any analytically precise way, with changes over time, and yet his General Theory can be the starting point for their consideration, because it observes essential features of the passage of historical time.

The General Theory is anchored in Marshall's short period, a period of 'a few months or a year' (Marshall 1920: 379), that is, an interval of historical, or actual, time. This short period is part of a sequence. It separates the past, in which decisions and actions were taken that determine present-day production possibilities, from a series of future periods, the economic conditions of which can only be surmised. Keynes did not deal with a sequence of periods. His analysis did not go beyond the present short period, but this analysis cannot be properly understood if its historical setting is overlooked. Keynes's short period is, in Hicks's terminology (1985: 25), not 'self-contained'. The equilibrium values in that period are not determined solely by actual values in that period without reference to values in future periods that could differ from those in the present. These equilibrium values depend in a critical way on current expectations of future conditions, expectations that are, in the nature of things, uncertain, and liable to change. It is this that distinguishes Keynes's theory from the standard static analysis where the single period 'can be examined without reference to anything that goes on outside it (in the temporal sense)'. Keynes pointed out this critical weakness of static analysis, and the 'fact that the assumptions of the static state often underlie present-day economic theory imports into it a large element of unreality' (Keynes 1936: 146). In contrast, he felt that his theory, with its use 'of the concepts of user cost and of the marginal efficiency of capital' that depend on expectations of future conditions, makes possible 'direct account of the influence of the future in our analysis of the existing equilibrium'.

Each short-period equilibrium position is temporary, in Keynes's analytical framework, for two reasons. Changes in the potentially volatile expectations of future conditions will result in different equilibrium positions in successive periods, and they may even be so volatile that they determine more than one equilibrium position in a particular short period. The net investment that is occurring in each of these periods will also change the equilibrium position by altering the technical conditions of production in future periods. This 'temporary' nature of Keynes's short-period equilibrium cannot thus be taken to represent a momentary resting place on the road to a long-period equilibrium that reflects an unchanging state of expectations. Long-period equilibrium has no place in Keynes's analytical framework since the stationary conditions that are required to make long-period equilibrium values centres of attraction for actual values are at variance with Keynes's vision of capitalist economies that are subject to changes from many sources.

In the single-paragraph chapter that opens his book, Keynes justifies the use of the adjective *general* in its title, on the grounds that in his theory, as opposed to the standard theory of his time that he labelled 'classical', there are many possible positions of equilibrium: 'I shall argue that the postulates of the classical theory are applicable to a special case only and not to the general case, the situation which it assumes being a limiting point of the possible positions of equilibrium' (3). Another explanation for the use of the word 'general' is to be found in Keynes's 1939 preface to the French edition of his book. He writes: 'I have called my theory a *general* theory. I mean by this that I am chiefly concerned with the behaviour of the economic system as a whole … rather than with the incomes, profits, output, employment, investment and saving of particular industries, firms or individuals, (Keynes 1973a: xxxii). These two explanations are not contradictory; each refers to a different aspect of his theory. With regard to the first, it is important to be clear on the definition of equilibrium, because Keynes makes selective use of two of the possible definitions of that term. Equilibrium can be defined as a position of 'rest'[1] for the variable of interest, or as a 'chosen' position[2] for the individuals with respect to their actions, given the values of the parameters. It was the level of employment that was in equilibrium according to the former definition in that there was no tendency for it to change given the values of the parameters.[3] Consumption and investment expenditures and the outputs of firms, with their pre-determined productive capacity, were in equilibrium according to the latter definition. Their values were those which were preferable to the possible alternative values in the particular short period.

3.2 THE LABOUR MARKET

Keynes's General Theory is concerned with the operation of a monetary production economy in which contracts and debts are expressed in terms of money. An important category of contracts deals with the payment for the supply of labour services. The terms of

---

[1] A definition of equilibrium along these lines is provided by Hansen (1970: 4): 'if we have an economic model that explains certain variables, and if there is no tendency for these variables to change, given the data of the model, then the system of variables is in equilibrium.'

[2] Hicks (1965: 15) has provided such a definition: 'equilibrium when all the "individuals" in it are choosing those quantities which, out of the alternatives available to them, they prefer to produce and to consume'.

[3] Keynes used the 'rest' definition of equilibrium only with respect to employment, and this did not preclude the possibility of money-wage rates and prices changing in such a situation, as long as these changes do not have any clear effect on the level of employment. Patinkin (1965: 315) used a definition of equilibrium that referred not only to one dependent variable but to the economic system as a whole: '"equilibrium" means that nothing tends to change in the system'. According to this definition, Keynes's unemployment equilibrium is a position of 'disequilibrium' because of the consequent changes in the values of other variables. Patinkin was aware of the implicit definition used by Keynes. 'All, then, that Keynes means by the statement that the system may settle down to a position of "unemployment equilibrium" is that the automatic workings of the system will *not* restore the system to a position of *full-employment equilibrium*. He does *not* mean "equilibrium" in the usual sense of the term that nothing tends to change in the system' (643). Leijonhufvud (1969: 22n) also interprets Keynes's 'unemployment equilibrium' as implying the weakness of the forces 'tending to bring the system back to full employment'.

these contracts are the focus of collective or individual bargaining, whether formal or informal, in labour markets. Before developing his theory of employment that made use of this institutional feature in the labour market, Keynes cleared the ground for it by attacking the 'classical' theory that he wanted to supplant. That theory approached the labour market as though it were a commodity market for which partial equilibrium analysis is appropriate. The price and the quantity exchanged are determined in this case by the intersection of demand and supply curves for the particular commodity. Marshall (1920: 335) had warned that there are, both in theory and in practice, important differences between commodity and labour markets, and Keynes's criticisms of what he called the classical approach encompassed both institutional and theoretical considerations.

Keynes stated that the classical approach to the labour market was based on two 'fundamental postulates' (Keynes 1936: 5). The first, '[T]he wage is equal to the marginal product of labour', is used by that theory to obtain the demand curve for labour. (Both the 'wage' and the 'marginal product of labour' are expressed in real or commodity terms.) The second, '[T]he utility of the wage when a given volume of labour is employed is equal to the marginal disutility of that amount of employment', is a composite postulate. It specifies a supply curve of labour, one that shows the relation between the amount of labour workers want to supply, and the real-wage rate, and then assumes that workers will be on this supply curve since the volume of labour employed is that shown by this curve. The first part of this second postulate, which specifies a causal relation between the amount of labour available for employment and the real-wage rate for that labour, was accepted by Keynes, and he used it in his definition of full employment. But Keynes rejected the second part (and thus the composite postulate as a whole), because it did not allow for the 'involuntary unemployment' that Keynes saw as a major problem of capitalist economies in the 1930s. He said that involuntary unemployment existed when the aggregate supply of labour in the economy would be greater than the volume currently employed, even at a slightly reduced real-wage rate (15).

Keynes saw the classical theory as assuming, in effect, that through the arrangements they make with employers, workers are in a position to set their real-wage rates. In this case, they would also be responsible for determining the level of employment (and unemployment). Employers, faced with diminishing returns from the operation of given plant and equipment, would only be willing to increase employment if the real-wage rate were lower. Any unemployment that exists must thus either be 'frictional', that is, temporary for individuals as they briefly search for, and find and move to, new jobs, or 'voluntary' due to the unwillingness of individuals to accept the lower real-wage rates at which they can find work.

Keynes denied that workers are in a position to set their real-wage rates. He pointed to the institutional arrangements where labour-market bargains are made in terms of money-wage rates. He also observed that employment arrangements are not generally disturbed when the prices of wage goods rise, even though workers react strongly when attempts are made to lower money-wage rates that would produce similar effects on their real-wage rates. This does not mean that workers suffer from 'money illusion', but that relative as well as real, wage rates are important in determining workers' responses to possible changes in their remuneration. It is through their money-wage bargains that workers try to protect their relative positions. 'In other words, the struggle about money-wages primarily affects the *distribution* of the aggregate real wage between different labour-groups, and not its average amount per unit of employment, which depends, as we shall see, on a different set of forces' (14). This does not mean that money-wage rates cannot be reduced when there is a considerable amount of unemployment or when particular industries are in difficult economic circumstances – they were reduced during the Great Depression while *The General Theory* was being written – but only that attempts to reduce them can be very disruptive to labour relations. The uneven pattern of wage cuts that results will upset established patterns of wage relativity and may introduce changes in the distribution of income that cannot easily be justified.

Keynes did not base his theory of employment on the assumption of rigid money-wage rates. He first developed his theory using the assumption of given money-wage rates, and then in chapter 19 he examined whether the introduction of flexible money-wage rates would require a change in conclusions. This examination will be considered in chapter 6 below, but we can note here that in a brief preview of his theory Keynes stated that it would be unaffected by the introduction of changing money-wage rates (27). Keynes did not provide a detailed explanation of the factors determining the money-wage rate. In the working out of his model, the money-wage rate was taken as given exogenously, 'as determined by the bargains reached between employers and employed' (247). There was recognition that changes in the demand for labour would affect the relative strengths of the bargaining positions of the two sides, and thus the money-wage rate. For example, he observed that 'the wage-unit itself will tend to rise as employment improves' (249), and '[W]hen there is a change in employment, money-wages tend to change in the same direction as, but not in great disproportion to, the change in employment' (251). These observations were not part of the formal model, which was left open at this point. There was no equation that set out the factors involved in the determination of the money-wage rate. This rate was regarded as one of 'our ultimate independent variables' (246). Treating it in this way was both an analytical convenience, and a reflection of his general approach which saw the determination of money-wage rates as being very much affected by particular historical and institutional circumstances. There was no suitable general functional form relating changes in money-wage rates to changes in the level of employment.

The unsatisfactory results from attempts to reduce money-wage rates was not a new theme in Keynes's writings. An important reason for his strong opposition to the United Kingdom's 1925 return to the pre-war gold parity, was that it would require money-wage reductions that would be difficult to achieve, and result in undesirable distributional consequences. When he considered the transition from one long-period equilibrium price level to a lower one, in the *Treatise*, he noted that 'in the systems of Capitalistic Individualism' (Keynes 1930a: 273) it is not possible for the monetary authorities to act directly to lower efficiency earnings. They must work indirectly 'to involve entrepreneurs in losses and the factors of production in unemployment, for only in this way can the money-rates of efficiency-earnings be reduced'. Further, '[T]he effect of contraction is not to secure an equal reduction all round, but to concentrate the reduction on those particular factors which are in the weakest bargaining position or have the shortest contracts governing their rate of money earnings. It may be a very long time before *relative* rates of efficiency-earnings are restored to their former proportions' (271).

It is important to keep in mind that although reference is often made in macroeconomics to a 'labour market', this term really comprises a very large number of labour markets. The bargaining positions of workers in each of these markets is very much influenced by money-wage rates in the other markets. Even though Keynes often refers to the money-wage rate, he is well aware that it represents a very large number of money-wage rates. It is this awareness, plus the importance of wage-relativity to workers, that leads Keynes to make the empirical observation that workers respond differently to a given decrease in their real-wage rate depending on whether it is the result of a higher price for wage goods or a lower money-wage rate. This observation has been formalised by Blinder (1988), who makes use of a worker's utility function the variables of which include relative wage rates, as well as the real-wage rate. As long as a worker's relative wage matters, then a given decrease in the real wage due to a higher price level will have a smaller effect on utility than the same decrease brought about by a lower (relative) money-wage rate.[4] This result can be contrasted with that implied by the 'classical approach' (as presented, for example, by Modigliani (1944: 188)) which has the labour supply curve as a function only of the real-wage rate. In such a case an equal percentage change in the real-wage rate will have the same effect on utility whether brought about by a change in prices or in money-wage rates.[5]

A fundamental theoretical objection is added in *The General Theory* to Keynes's criticism of proposals to reduce money-wage rates in order to establish full employment. 'There may exist no expedient by which labour as a whole can reduce its *real* wage to a given figure by making revised *money* bargains with the entrepreneurs' (Keynes 1936: 13). This objection follows from his theory that employment and the real-wage rate are both determined, given the money-wage rate, by the aggregate demand and the aggregate supply conditions in commodity markets. This difference from the 'classical theory' thus had nothing to do with the existence of 'money illusion' or with the downward rigidity of money-wage rates, but with the workings of labour markets in a monetary production economy. In that economy only money-wage rates were set in these markets, with employment being dependent on conditions in goods markets.[6] It is this critical feature of such an economy that Keynes tried to make clear by his contrast between 'co-operative' and 'money-wage or entrepreneur'

---

[4] The belief in the strong resistance to changes in wage relativity was the reason for New York's Mayor Koch's rejection of an advisory panel recommendation that police officers' pay be increased by 42 per cent ('Koch Rejects Call to End Police-Fire Wage Parity', *The New York Times*, 24 September, 1987, p. B4). Attempts to change relative wage rates in the 1960's proved to be unsuccessful, and very costly to the city, as firemen (and other workers) were able to regain parity (or their traditional ratio) with police officers' pay at higher levels.

[5] Chick (1983: 149) adopts the position taken here and argues that for Keynes, in contrast to the classical approach, the effects of changes in wages and prices on labour supply would not be symmetrical.

[6] Fender (1981) interprets Keynes's treatment of the labour market in a manner that is very similar to the one presented here. He does, however, use the term 'stability' in a manner that might be misleading. 'Keynes's discussion of the wage bargain's being in money terms . . . is a discussion of the stability of the labour market' (34). Keynes's discussion was not concerned with the stability of the labour market, but with what was decided on such markets.

economies in the 1933 draft of *The General Theory*, referred to in section 2.4 above.

The money-wage rate adjustments that occur as a result of unemployment may not move the economy towards full employment. The 'clearing' of the labour markets requires that conditions in the goods markets be such as to result in demands for labour sufficient to employ the labour-hours available at the prevailing real-wage rates. Keynes's position was often misinterpreted because of the economic theorists' standard approach to any market in terms of demand and supply equations that are supposed to be sufficient to explain the equilibrium quantity transacted as well as the equilibrium price. In order to fit Keynes's conclusion about employment into the standard vision, use was made of an appropriately defined supply curve of labour. For example, Modigliani (1944: 189) assumed that in the Keynesian system 'the supply of labour is assumed to be perfectly elastic at the historically ruling [money-] wage rate . . .' up to the point of full employment. This then leads to the statement that Keynesian theory reaches the conclusion that unemployment equilibrium is possible only because of 'rigid wages' (211), which refers to this assumed infinite supply curve of labour. Keynes did not, as we have seen, assume 'rigid wages' in this, or in any other sense.

3.3 INVOLUNTARY UNEMPLOYMENT

The emphasis in the preceding section on the nature of labour markets in Keynes's theory should make it possible to draw aggregate labour supply and demand curves, in order to illustrate his definition of involuntary unemployment, without any implication that the real-wage rate and employment are determined by the intersection of these curves. Keynes accepted, as noted above, the notion of an aggregate supply curve of labour, with the real-wage rate as the independent variable. The supply curve of any particular sub-group of workers depends on their relative money-wage rates as well as on the real-wage rate, *but given relative wage rates* it is possible for purposes of macroeconomic analysis to depict the total supply curve of labour for Keynes's model by the curve labelled N_s in figure 3.1 (cf. Trevithick 1976). It shows the maximum amount of labour hours workers would be prepared to supply at different real-wage rates.[7]

---

[7] Chick (1983: 136) refers to this labour supply curve 'as a frontier: all positions to the left of it are acceptable to workers lucky enough to get a job, while positions to the

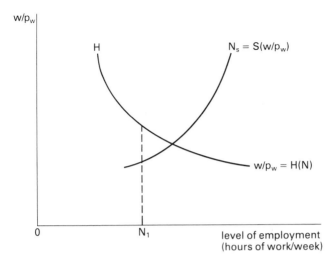

Figure. 3.1

There is also in Keynes's model a negatively-sloped curve that shows the inverse relation between the level of employment and the real-wage rate. It is illustrated by the curve that is labelled H in figure 3.1. Keynes saw its presence in his model as 'an important point of agreement' (17) with the classical system, but he does not attribute any causal significance to it. It does *not* show the real-wage rate as determining the level of employment, or vice versa. In a draft chapter belonging to the last 1933 table of contents, when he had already worked out the main elements of his theory, we find 'we may well discover empirically a correlation between employment and real wages. But this will occur, not because the one causes the other, but because they are both consequences of the same cause' (Keynes 1979: 100). This inverse relation is, he states, 'simply the obverse of the familiar proposition that industry is normally working subject to decreasing returns in the short period during which equipment etc. is assumed to be constant; so that the marginal product in the wage-good industries (which governs real wages) necessarily diminishes as employment is increased. So long, indeed, as this proposition holds, *any* means of increasing employment must lead at the same time to a diminution of the marginal product and hence of the rate of wages

right are unacceptable'. This 'frontier' aspect is not a special property of a labour supply curve, it is true of all supply curves.

measured in terms of this product' (Keynes 1936: 17–18). Keynes gives two separate reasons for this inverse relation. The first draws on diminishing returns in agriculture when more labour that is, presumably, homogeneous is employed with a given amount of land (17n). The second refers to the additional labour employed in industry as being 'less suitable' and having the effect of 'leading to a diminishing return from the capital equipment in terms of output as more labour is employed on it' (42).

The negatively-sloped curve drawn in figure 3.1 can be referred to as a demand curve for labour, as long as it is kept in mind that it is a derived demand curve that reflects short-period equilibrium conditions in good markets. It does not, in conjunction with an aggregate labour supply curve, determine the real-wage rate and the level of employment. It shows the consequences for employment of competitive firms being on their short-period supply curves. For example, consider the situation of producers of wage goods, where the output produced by a typical firm is determined by the intersection of the price of wage goods (P_w) and its marginal cost of production (MC_w). Marginal costs at any rate of output are equal to the sum of incremental wage costs ($w \triangle N_w$, where w is the money-wage rate and $\triangle N_w$ is the marginal increment in employment) and other prime costs ($\triangle OPC_w$), divided by the increment in output ($\triangle Q_w$).[8] That is,

$$P_w = MC_w = (w \triangle N_w + \triangle OPC_w)/\triangle Q_w \qquad (3.1)$$

Re-arranging this expression we derive

$$w/P_w = \triangle Q_w/\triangle N_w - \triangle OPC_w/P_w \triangle N_w \qquad (3.2)$$

With competitive firms on their short-period supply curves, the real-wage rate is equal to the short-period marginal product of labour in the wage-goods industry minus the ratio of the increment in other prime costs to the product of the price of wage goods and the increase in employment. Keynes assumed that the short-period marginal product of labour decreases with higher employment, and therefore the latter must be accompanied by a lower real-wage rate. (There is no reason to expect that the decline in the short-period marginal product of labour will be offset by a greater decline in other prime costs, costs that are likely to be increasing in these circumstances.)

---

[8] The explicit introduction of other prime costs in Keynes's model is justified by his statement that 'we are not so foolish in practice as to refuse to associate with additional labour appropriate additions of other factors' (Keynes 1936: 273n).

This conclusion can be readily extended to other industries, given the ratios of the prices of their products to the price of wage goods.[9]

The two curves in figure 3.1 can be used to illustrate Keynes's definition of involuntary unemployment. With ON_1 as the level of employment that is determined (as shown in the next section) by conditions in the commodity markets, then even with a slightly lower real-wage rate due to 'a small rise in the price of wage-goods relatively to the money-wage' (15), the 'aggregate supply of labour willing to work for the current money-wage ... would be greater than the existing volume of employment'. The aggregate demand for labour would also be greater in such a situation because firms would want to increase output and employment when prices rise relative to costs of production.

The explanation given here about involuntary unemployment can be compared with some statements that have attracted considerable attention in the economics literature. There is Clower's (1965: 119) observation – based on his 'dual decision hypothesis' – that 'the other side of involuntary unemployment would seem to be involuntary under-consumption' (see also Leijonhufvud (1968: 69) where this statement is repeated and emphasised). This observation contains an element of truth. The consumption levels of unemployed workers could be adversely affected by lower incomes resulting from unemployment, but this does not mean that involuntary unemployment would disappear if unemployed workers successfully communicated their potential demand to producers. For employment to be

---

[9] Consider a non-wage goods industry where in short-period equilibrium the price of its output (P_{nw}) is equal to the marginal cost of production (MC_{nw}). This equality can be written as

$$P_{nw} = MC_{nw} = (w \triangle N_{nw} + \triangle OPC_{nw})/\triangle Q_{nw} \qquad (3.1n)$$

or as,

$$w/P_{nw} = \triangle Q_{nw}/\triangle N_{nw} - \triangle OPC_{nw}/P_{nw}\triangle N_{nw} \qquad (3.2n)$$

Multiplying both sides of equation (3.2n) by the relative price of non-wage and wage goods (P_{nw}/P_w), we derive

$$w/P_w = (\triangle Q_{nw}/\triangle N_{nw} - \triangle OPC_{nw}/P_{nw}\triangle N_{nw})(P_{nw}/P_w) \qquad (3.3n)$$

With a constant value for the relative price of these two types of goods there is an inverse relation between employment in this non-wage good industry and the real-wage rate, because of decreasing returns in that industry. Each value for the real-wage rate translates into a value for the wage in terms of its product for the non-wage good, and from equation (3.2n), given the technical conditions of production, it is possible to deduce the value for employment at which this equation is satisfied. It is the summation of these values for employment over all industries, given different values for real-wage rates, that gives rise to the 'labour demand curve' drawn in figure 3.1.

increased, prices obtained must increase relative to marginal cost curves. The equilibrium equalities between prices and marginal costs that would then be attained at higher levels of output (and employment) require total expenditures on goods to increase by more than the wages of the additional labour hired. A higher level of employment can only be made effective if expenditures from non-labour incomes, for example, investment expenditures, are higher, thus making possible the increase in quasi-rents that are a necessary accompaniment of higher prices relative to marginal costs.

Malinvaud (1977: 31) refers to 'Keynesian unemployment' as being the result of a buyers' market in the goods market. With positive excess supply at the (sticky) prevailing price for the single good in the model, firms do not hire as much labour as they otherwise would at the prevailing wage in terms of their product. The fact that they are off their supply curve for goods, means that they are not on their (unrestrained) demand curve for labour. As we have seen in presenting Keynes's theory, it is only the labour market that may not clear, for the reasons mentioned above.[10] Involuntary unemployment for Keynes is a result of the extent of demand for goods, given the supply curves of goods and the labour supply curve, rather than the result of sticky prices or of sticky money-wage rates.[11]

The inverse relation between the level of employment and the real-wage rate that Keynes made part of his theory was the subject of empirical investigation by Dunlop (1938) and Tarshis (1939). They did not find the predicted relation, and many others who followed in their footsteps tended to confirm their results. A study by Geary and Kennan (1982) that reviews these empirical investigations of the employment-real wage relationship – and contributes to it – concludes that it is not possible to reject the hypothesis that movements in employment and real wages are independent. In spite of its incorporation into *The General Theory*, the negative correlation between employment and the real-wage rate is not a necessary element in Keynes's theory. Its removal would give even greater force

---

[10] Cf. Bliss (1975: 208): 'it does look as though the particular view which Keynes took of the operation of the labour market, which view was in sharp contrast to the neoclassical idea that factor markets are just like any other markets subject to exactly the same laws of supply and demand, is a very essential component of his theory.'

[11] Malinvaud (1977: 32n) does recognise that his specification of 'Keynesian unemployment' may not give a good representation of Keynes's position. 'The name "Keynesian unemployment" which I shall be using here, should thus be understood to refer to the views of post-war Keynesians rather than to those of Keynes himself.'

to his policy proposals, as Keynes noted (Keynes 1939: 401), in responding to the Dunlop and Tarshis articles. The H curve in figure 3.1 would be horizontal if the level of employment and the real-wage rate were independent as employment is increased.[12] In this case, as in the one of a negative correlation, neither employment nor the real-wage rate is determined in the labour market. Their determinants are effective demand, the technical conditions of production, and the degree of competition in commodity markets.

To conclude this discussion of the labour market, it might be useful to set out the equations that are implicit in Keynes's treatment of this market. (Although reference is made here to a market, it should be understood from the statements made above that this is a macro-economic representation of many labour markets. They are aggregated into a single market for this purpose by the assumptions that relative money-wage rates and relative prices are constant.) They are:

$$N_s = S\ (w/P_w),\quad S' > 0 \tag{3.3}$$

$$w/P_w = H\ (N),\quad H' < 0 \tag{3.4}$$

$$w = \bar{w} \tag{3.5}$$

Equation (3.3) shows that if *relative money-wage rates* are given, the labour supply (N_s) is a positive function of the real-wage rate. Equation (3.4) shows the short-period inverse relation between employment (N) and the real-wage rate that follows from Keynes's assumption that firms are on their short-period supply curves. There is also a constraint on the possible values for N, given the nature of equations (3.3) and (3.4), because workers can refuse to work if the real-wage rate is insufficient. Thus we have, $N_s \geq N$. The final equation (3.5) states that the money-wage rate is exogenous. There are 4 unknowns, N_s, N, w and P_w, in the 3 equations, and these equations are thus not sufficient to complete the system. Keynes completed it by bringing in effective demand, to which we now turn.

---

[12] This independence would hold in the case of oligopoly with mark-up pricing, since variations in output in response to effective demand do not, over some range of output, lead to changes in the price of the product relative to money-wage rates. The setting of the price of the wage good can be represented by $P_w = (1 + \mu)\ MC_w = (1 + \mu)(w \triangle N_w + \triangle OPC_w)/\triangle Q_w$, where μ is the mark-up on marginal costs that are assumed to be constant in the relevant range. Re-arranging terms, we find $w/P_w = (1/1 + \mu) \triangle Q_w/\triangle N_w - \triangle OPC_w/P_w \triangle N_w$. With a constant mark-up, and the assumed constancy of marginal costs, the real-wage rate is constant even though employment is varied.

(Classical theory would close the system by assuming that the labour market clears, and it would thus add a fourth equation, $N_s = N$, to the three above.)

3.4 EXPECTATIONS, TIME AND REALISED RESULTS

With its setting in a period of historical time where future conditions cannot be known with any certainty, Keynes's theory of effective demand must be developed in terms of current expectations of the future values of parameters that are relevant for current decisions. Some preliminary observations on his treatment of expectations will help in the presentation of his theory of effective demand.

Keynes distinguishes between two main categories of expectations, short-term and long-term. Production (and thus employment) decisions at any point in time, given plant and equipment, depend on the short-term expectations of prices at the time when the output resulting from those decisions will be ready for sale. Realised results, actual prices, are only relevant for production decisions in so far as they influence expectations. Keynes's analysis tended to ignore differences between short-term expectations of prices and the actual prices that were received for the goods produced as a consequence of those expectations. He argued that 'it will often be safe to omit express reference to *short-term* expectation, in view of the fact that in practice the process of revision of short-term expectation is a gradual and continuous one, carried on largely in the light of realised results; so that expected and realised results run into and overlap one another in their influence' (Keynes 1936: 50). The effect of leaving out references to short-term expectations is to treat short-period decisions as though they were determined in a static context where there is no need to distinguish between results and expectations. This static context is out of keeping with the historical-time setting of the General Theory, as Keynes implicitly recognised in the surviving rough notes from his 1937 lectures. 'The *expected* results are not on a par with the *realised* results in a theory of employment. The *realised* results are only relevant in so far as they influence the ensuing expectations in the next production period' (Keynes 1973c: 179). The justification for treating them 'on a par', for placing this part of the theory of employment in a static context, is that explicit recognition of the difference between short-term expectations and realised results would not change the general tenor of the theory's conclusions: 'eventually I felt it to be of secondary importance, emphasis on it obscuring the real argument. For the theory of effective demand is substantially the same if we assume that short-period expectations are always fulfilled' (181).

Keynes's treatment of long-term expectations is always consistent with the historical-time setting of the model. The relevant results for long-term expectations will be the returns to investment expenditures over future intervals of time, and there is no suggestion that these expenditures will, in general, turn out to be justified by these results. There is, similarly, no suggestion that the long-term expectations held in the past that gave rise to current productive capacity have been borne out by current events. Long-term expectations are usually assumed to be exogenous in *The General Theory* (e.g. in chapter 11). But it is also recognised that 'the facts of the existing situation enter, in a sense disproportionately into the formation of our long-term expectations' (148). In the latter case, long-term expectations could be affected by changes in the current short period. The assumption of exogenously given long-term expectations allowed Keynes (as noted by Kregel 1976: 212) to specify functional relations for the determination of investment and consumption, while avoiding any presumption that future conditions are foreseen with any degree of precision. But the basis of knowledge for these expectations was seen as being extremely precarious, and thus liable to sudden change. The definite investment demand schedule that Keynes derived with exogenous, and unchanging, long-term expectations in chapter 11 becomes, as we shall see in the following chapter, a shifting and unreliable function in chapter 12.

Keynes develops his theory of effective demand on the assumption of given money-wage rates, even though there is the recognition noted above that money-wage bargains would be affected by the level of employment. He then, after the introduction of all the factors in his analysis, considers the effects on his conclusions about involuntary unemployment, if money-wage rates are reduced in response to continuing unemployment. Keynes explains the determination of employment, in any short period, as the result of the interaction of aggregate demand and supply curves. As a pioneer in this work, it is not surprising that he did not succeed in working out a consistent statement of all the basic relations in his model, but his slips do not affect the main conclusions of his analysis. Keynes built on, and adapted, the Marshallian tools of analysis that he took for granted, in order to derive these aggregate relations. They require units of measure common to all industries, that would allow for the summation of demands and supplies over all industries, even though these are initially expressed in terms of specific products. For this purpose he makes use 'of only two fundamental units of quantity, namely, quantities of money-value and quantities of employment' (Keynes 1936: 41). He assumes that the many different types of labour can be 'homogenised' for his purposes, with relative wage rates used to allow for the relative efficiency of these different types of labour. Therefore, 'the quantity of employment can be sufficiently defined for our purpose by taking an hour's employment of special labour in proportion to its remuneration; *i.e.* an hour of special labour remunerated at double ordinary rates will count as two units'. Further, the quantity of output in the short period examined is indicated by the amount of employment associated with the given plant and equipment.

Production decisions made by Keynes's competitive firms must be based on expectations of prices, because of the gap between the time when these decisions are made, and the time when the resulting output is ready for sale.[13] Keynes also notes that some time must elapse before firms can revise their production decisions. This interval of time is denoted by the adjective 'daily', and he refers to it as 'the minimum effective unit of time' (47n). He does not discuss its relation to the short period in which his analysis is set, but clearly the daily interval is more brief than the short period. In the latter there is time for firms to revise their short-term expectations, and the resulting production decisions, thus providing the justification for the close relation between these expectations and realised results that is assumed in the theory. These expectations are referred to as 'short-term' to distinguish them from the expectations (labelled 'long-term') that are concerned with the possible patterns of future returns from investment in capital equipment. The realised results in the present, from the sale of output produced because of production decisions taken earlier, are important in so far as they condition subsequent short-term expectations. Keynes often uses, as we have seen, the realised results to represent these expectations, because the 'test' of short-term expectations is not long-delayed, and the revisions that appear to be necessary are based on realised results. There is no such 'early' test for long-term expectations that are concerned with conditions over intervals of future time. Keynes generally takes these expectations to be exogenous in the particular short period of his analysis, and notes that 'they are liable to sudden revision' (51).

---

[13] '... the entrepreneur ... has to form the best expectations he can as to what the consumers will be prepared to pay when he is ready to supply them ... and he has no choice but to be guided by these expectations if he is to produce at all by processes which occupy time' (Keynes 1936: 46).

From brief comments made by Keynes, it is possible to distinguish the relevant orders of magnitude he implicitly assumes for the different intervals of time that appear in his analysis. The daily interval, during which a firm is committed to a decision on how much employment to offer, is the shortest of these time intervals. The length of the production period clearly varies with the nature of the goods produced, and it could be very long for some capital goods. Keynes implicitly assumed that the interval for the production period is always greater than the daily interval when he noted that a change in short-term expectations will only produce its full effects on employment over some time.

this is because changes in expectation are not, as a rule, sufficiently violent or rapid, when they are for the worse, to cause the abandonment of work on all the productive processes which, in the light of the revised expectation, it was a mistake to have begun ... (48)

The above statement makes clear that firms could have abandoned work in progress, if it were in their economic interest to do so. The production period is thus assumed to occupy more time than the daily interval. The relative lengths of the short period and the production period obviously depend on the nature of the goods being produced, but Keynes's practice of identifying short-term expectations and realised proceeds is consistent with a short period longer than a production period. This allows production to be adjusted to coincide with short-term expectations within the short period. Finally, there is the long period which, when used as a substantive, occupies an interval of time that encompasses many short periods. Keynes also refers to market equilibrium situations for bonds and money, in which the stocks available are taken as given, and demand factors based on long-term expectations determine bond prices and the associated rates of interest. No interval of time is explicitly associated with this equilibrium, but adjustments to changing demand appear to take place instantaneously.

3.5 EFFECTIVE DEMAND

The output of (and thus the employment provided by) a competitive firm is determined (given the standard profit-maximising criterion) from the point of intersection of the expected price for its product and its marginal cost curve. The latter is positively-sloped in the relevant range, and it shows the increased costs arising from increasing output. These costs include extra payments to the factors of production resulting from higher output, the increase in costs of inputs purchased from other firms, and the costs incurred because equipment (Keynes includes stocks of raw materials under this heading) is used more intensively. The sum of the latter two types of cost is called the user cost. The sacrifice involved in using equipment in the present is based on estimates of what that equipment could have earned in future periods if it had been used less intensively in the present. This is one of the ways in which Keynes sees that his analysis takes account of the influence of the future on current activity (146).

The total expected revenue of the firm (the product of the expected price for its output and the amount of that output as shown by the point of intersection of the price and its marginal cost curve) is reduced by Keynes to an expectation of 'proceeds' by subtracting user costs. The higher the expected price for its product, the higher the firm's expectation of proceeds, and therefore the latter can be used as a proxy for the former, even though it should never be forgotten that output decisions by his competitive firms are made primarily on the basis of expected prices and not on expected proceeds. The advantage of dealing with the expectation of proceeds rather than prices is that the former, being in identical money-value units, can be aggregated over all industries, while the latter are product-specific. This relationship between expected proceeds and output can be turned into a relationship between the expectation of proceeds and employment, because the level of employment is used by Keynes as an index of the level of output. It is the latter relationship that provides the basis for Keynes's aggregate supply function. (See the appendix to this chapter for the conceptual derivation of this aggregate supply function.)

Keynes defines 'the aggregate supply price of the output of a given amount of employment [as] the expectation of proceeds which will just make it worth the while of the entrepreneurs to give that employment' (24). The functional relation between the two is formally stated as: 'Let Z be the aggregate supply price of the output from employing N men, the relationship between Z and N being written $Z = \phi(N)$, which can be called the *Aggregate Supply Function*' (25). In spite of Keynes's unconventional notation, it is clear that it is the expectation of proceeds which is the independent variable, while the employment offered is the dependent variable. These proceeds cover the earnings of the factors of production (earnings that are made 'actual' if the entrepreneurs hire on the basis of these expectations), as well as the expected earnings of firms. The latter will *only* be realised if *actual* demand conditions turn out to be the same as *expected* conditions, but entrepreneurs can only act on the basis of expectations they know may be mistaken.[14] The employment that is established thus depends on their expectations of proceeds and the aggregate supply function. If the term 'effective demand' is used to indicate the point of determination of the level of employment (and this is how Keynes uses it), then it is the point on the aggregate supply function corresponding to the entrepreneurs' expectations of proceeds.[15] This is *not* Keynes's definition of effective demand; as noted in chapter 2 he mistakenly attached expectations to the aggregate demand function, but the definition given here is consistent with his model, in which employment is determined by short-term expectations and supply conditions. Actual demand conditions (that can be represented by an aggregate demand function) enter the picture through their effects on realised results, which in turn influence short-term expectations. It is this sequence that Keynes jotted down in the rough notes that survive from his 1937 lectures (Keynes 1973c: 179). (Keynes's statement on this point is given in the preceding section in the discussion of the static context of his short-period equilibrium.) Before turning to the definition of short-period equilibrium effective demand that is a key element in Keynes's theory, it is necessary to consider the aggregate demand function in more detail.

Keynes's definition of the aggregate demand function assumes that individual entrepreneurs see a relation between the employment they each offer and the market demand for their own output, a relation that does not hold for Keynes's competitive firms. Such a relation would only hold, as pointed out in section 2.4 above, for a giant firm whose employees' incomes are the source of demand for its output of consumption goods. In working out his theory, Keynes at times assumed a single firm that produced the economy's total output, and traces of that assumption are found in his definition of the aggregate demand function:[16] 'let D be the proceeds which entrepreneurs

---

14 Keynes noted that an entrepreneur 'who has to reach a practical decision as to his scale of production, does not, of course, entertain a single undoubting expectation of what the sale-proceeds of a given output will be, but several hypothetical expectations held with varying degrees of probability and definiteness. By his expectation of proceeds I mean, therefore, that expectation of proceeds which, if it were held with certainty, would lead to the same behaviour as does the bundle of vague and more various possibilities which actually make up his state of expectation when he reaches his decision' (Keynes 1936: 24n.3). This footnote was added as a result of criticisms by Hawtrey (Keynes 1973b: 596).

15 This definition for effective demand is suggested in Asimakopulos (1982: 20).

16 This giant firm is implicitly assumed in the passage that states that its entrepreneur will offer 'the volume of employment which will maximise his profit [and it] depends

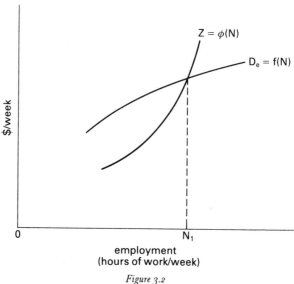

Figure 3.2

expect to receive from the employment of N men, the relationship between D and N ... can be called the *Aggregate Demand Function*'[17] (Keynes 1936: 25). Fortunately for Keynes's analysis, it is only his definition of the aggregate demand function, and not the way that it is utilised, that is at variance with the microfoundations of his model.[18] He uses it to show the total expenditures that would result, given the level of employment, from consumption expenditures that are in line with current incomes and tastes, and investment expenditures that reflect current investment intentions.[19] Employment is the indepen-

on the aggregate demand function given by his expectations of the sum of the proceeds resulting from consumption and investment respectively on various hypotheses' (Keynes 1936: 77).

[17] The inconsistency between Keynes's aggregate demand function, and the microfoundations of his theory has been pointed out by Parrinello (1980), Casarosa (1981), and Asimakopulos (1982).

[18] Robertson noticed that Keynes used 'aggregate demand price' in two different senses. He pointed to Keynes's (1936: 30) statement about what entrepreneurs 'can expect' to receive, as indicating 'what they can legitimately expect to receive, because that, whether they expect or not, is what they *will* receive' (Robertson 1936: 169).

[19] In this form the aggregate demand function is analogous to Marshall's demand curve for a commodity. The latter illustrates the 'demand price for each amount of the commodity, that is, a price at which each particular amount of the commodity can find purchasers ...' (Marshall 1920: 342), while the former shows the proceeds

dent variable in this function, and the realisation of equilibrium proceeds is the dependent variable. This version of the aggregate demand function is represented in figure 3.2 by the curve D_e, while the aggregate supply function is indicated by the curve Z. The point of intersection of the two curves illustrates a position of short-period equilibrium, with ON_1 being the short-period equilibrium level of employment, and the corresponding value of proceeds is the equilibrium effective demand.

The aggregate demand and supply curves in figure 3.2 are drawn up on the basis of the same money-wage rate at all the levels of employment shown. Keynes recognised, as we have seen, that when there is a change in employment money-wage rates tend to change in the same direction. He would thus not expect to use the same set of curves if a fairly wide range of employment was being considered. The curves would have to be re-drawn on the basis of the appropriate schedule of remuneration for each level of employment. The position and shape of the aggregate supply function depend, given the money-wage rate, on the technical conditions of production that underlie the individual firms' marginal cost curves. The position of the aggregate demand function depends on the value of investment planned for and carried out in the period, and on the economy's consumption function. This function's slope reflects the assumption that the economy's marginal propensity to consume is less than one. The curves in figure 3.2, and the short-period equilibrium level of employment, ON_1, illustrate Keynes's statement about the 'essence' of his General Theory of Employment: 'the volume of employment in equilibrium depends on (i) the aggregate supply function ... (ii) the propensity to consume ... and (iii) the volume of investment ...' (29).

To each level of employment and demand for consumption goods, there is a corresponding marginal product of labour in the wage-goods industries that determines the real-wage rate. Keynes's assumption of diminishing marginal productivity means, as we saw in the preceding section, that the real-wage rate is inversely related to the level of employment. The supply curve of labour that appears in Keynes's theory relates labour supply to the real-wage rate, and thus limits the volume of employment that can be determined by conditions in the commodity markets that underlie the aggregate demand and supply curves. There may be no additional labour available, at the slightly lower real-wage rate that would be associ-

(aggregate demand price) corresponding to each volume of employment (output) under equilibrium conditions.

ated with higher employment. This possibility leads to Keynes's definition of full employment (the absence of 'involuntary unemployment'): 'a situation in which aggregate employment is inelastic in response to an increase in the effective demand for its output' (26).

The introduction of the aggregate supply function and the aggregate demand function (whose components will be examined in the next chapter), allows Keynes to determine the short-period equilibrium level of employment. With this level of employment, the simple economic system, part of which is represented by the 3 equations for the 'labour market' in section 3.3, can now be completed. Three new equations are involved:

$$Z = \phi(N) \quad (3.6); \quad D = f(N) \quad (3.7); \quad D = Z \quad (3.8)$$

These equations add only two new unknowns, Z and D, and together with the 3 in section 3.3, they are, in principle, sufficient to solve for the 6 unknowns in the system (N, N_s, w, P_w, Z and D), subject to the constraint, noted above, $N_s \geq N$. Equation (3.6) states that employment (N) is a function of the short-term expectations of proceeds (Z), while equation (3.7) shows total expenditures on the firms' outputs as a function of total employment. (These are equilibrium expenditures, those that result from consumption that is in the desired relation to income, and from investment that is planned for this period.) Finally, equation (3.8) states the equilibrium condition for effective demand, that the expectations of proceeds are equal to the level of expenditures from the level of employment determined by those expectations. Alternatively, it can be seen as showing that the expected value of total output or income (the sum of factor costs plus profits on the aggregate supply function) becomes the actual value as a result of the total expenditures shown by the aggregate demand function.

3.6 THE STABILITY OF EQUILIBRIUM

In Keynes's theory of employment, there are many possible positions of short-period equilibrium, each corresponding to different values for the volume of investment and/or the economy's consumption function. These equilibrium positions are stable, given the volume of investment and the consumption function, because the marginal propensity to consume is assumed to have a value smaller than unity. If, for example, in the situation depicted in figure 3.2 entrepreneurs' short-term expectations are optimistic and the employment they give rise to is greater than ON_1, then the realised results will fall short of expectations. The realised results need not lie on the D_e curve at the point corresponding to this 'optimistic' level of employment, because that curve shows the *equilibrium* consumption and investment expenditures. It takes time for consumption to adjust fully after a change occurs, so that it regains its normal relation to income. In situations where mistaken short-term expectations lead to an increase in employment, proceeds will tend to lie below the corresponding point on the D_e curve, because of this time lag. Conversely, they tend to lie above the corresponding point on the D_e curve, when pessimistic short-term expectations lead to a lower level of employment (and incomes) than that justified by actual conditions. In either case though, the realised results will lead to a revision of short-term expectations that moves the employment offered in the direction of the short-period equilibrium level of employment, ON_1. This equilibrium position (at which there may be involuntary unemployment) is thus stable, given Keynes's implicit assumption of a given volume of investment that is built into the aggregate demand function, and a value for the marginal propensity to consume of less than one.

The difference between Keynes's view that an equilibrium position at less than full employment is stable, and classical theory, thus depends on the response of aggregate demand to an increase (or a decrease) in employment. The behaviour of investment expenditures is crucial here, because they must fill the gap between income and consumption expenditures. This point will be considered in some detail after Keynes's theory of the determination of investment is considered in the following chapter, but it can be noted here that Robertson, in his review of *The General Theory*, saw this as a challenge to be faced. He raised the possibility that the expectations that led to an increase in output, which would appear to be mistaken when an equilibrium aggregate demand function with a given volume of investment is compared with the aggregate supply function, may turn out to be correct when allowance is made for induced investment. If this is the case, then the initial equilibrium position would not be stable. 'But perhaps, as output grows ... consumption breeds investment, as well as investment consumption. The mistake will turn out not to have been a mistake after all' (Robertson 1936: 170). Robertson's possible outcome requires, in effect, that the marginal propensity to spend (out of wages and other factor incomes) on consumption and investment goods be equal to unity, with entrepreneurs increasing their expenditures to match the increases in their gross profits that they foresee as a result of higher short-term expectations of proceeds relative to money-wage costs.

Keynes concentrates on positions of short-period equilibrium, in his theory of employment, because of his belief that such positions are stable and they serve to attract actual values. Implicit in this attitude is the view that the time interval for which such a position exists is considerable relative to the time required for entrepreneurs to adjust to it as a result of trial and error. In the surviving rough notes for his 1937 lectures, Keynes contrasts his position with that of Hawtrey on this point.

Entrepreneurs have to endeavour to forecast demand. They do not, as a rule, make wildly wrong forecasts of the equilibrium position. But, as the matter is very complex, they do not get it just right; and they endeavour to approximate to the true position by a method of trial and error. Contracting where they find that they are overshooting their market, expanding where the opposite occurs. It corresponds precisely to the higgling of the market by means of which buyers and sellers endeavour to discover the true equilibrium position of supply and demand.

Now Hawtrey, as it seems to me, mistakes this higgling process by which the equilibrium position is discovered for the much more fundamental forces which determine what the equilibrium position is. . . .

The main point is to distinguish the forces determining the position of equilibrium from the technique of trial and error by means of which the entrepreneur [sic] discovers where the position is.   (Keynes 1973c: 182)

Keynes paid scant attention in *The General Theory* to the difference between short-term expectations and realised results, because the equilibrium positions where the two coincide are sufficiently general for his purposes. 'I began, as I have said, by regarding this difference as important. But eventually I felt it to be of secondary importance, emphasis on it obscuring the real argument. For the theory of effective demand is substantially the same if we assume that short-period expectations are always fulfilled' (181). But in order to prevent misunderstandings concerning the critical features of his analysis he stated: 'I now feel that if I were writing the book again I should begin by setting forth my theory on the assumption that short-period expectations were always fulfilled; and then have a subsequent chapter showing what difference it makes when short-period expectations are disappointed'. It is clear that he felt this difference would not be significant. The attraction of short-period equilibrium values for actual values was taken to be so strong that he claimed his theory 'to have shown . . . what determines the value of employment at any time' (Keynes 1936: 313).

3.7 SAY'S LAW

Keynes uses his aggregate demand and supply functions to interpret Say's law, or the doctrine that supply creates its own demand. He sees it as implying that the aggregate demand function must coincide with the aggregate supply function throughout its whole length. It is in this way that the expectations of proceeds that give rise to any particular level of employment are self-fulfilling because the equilibrium expenditures corresponding to that employment will validate these expectations. If this is the case, then there is a large number of possible equilibrium positions for employment – there is a large number of values for equilibrium effective demand, even with one pair of curves: 'the amount of [equilibrium] employment is indeterminate except in so far as the marginal disutility of labour sets an upper limit' (26). Keynes goes on to state that under these circumstances competition between employers would lead to an expansion of employment, until this upper limit of full employment is reached. In making this statement, Keynes mistook the forces that would push the economy to full employment. It is the competition for jobs, with unemployed workers putting pressure on those employed, that leads to this result. The competition between entrepreneurs has been allowed for fully in the assumption of perfectly competitive markets used to arrive at Keynes's aggregate supply function. The lower money-wage rates that ensue as labourers try to secure employment lead to a fall in production costs, and given unchanged expectations of prices, they induce entrepreneurs to increase output and employment. These increases then turn out to be justified because of accommodating increases in demand. This process can continue until full employment is reached, an equilibrium position that is stable because there is then no incentive for workers to offer their labour services at wages below prevailing rates.

Keynes's analysis, amended in this way, also makes clear the implicit assumption made by 'classical-type' theories that assume labour markets could clear if money-wage rates would fall in situations of unemployment. This assumption is that the aggregate demand function would accommodate itself to the aggregate supply function, and that, in particular, investment expenditures would take the values required for full employment. Demand in the labour market is a derived demand, a reflection of conditions in commodity markets. If it is seen as resulting in full employment, it can only be because demand conditions in commodity markets are such as to lead to this outcome.

3.8 LONG-PERIOD EMPLOYMENT

When explaining the roles of short- and long-term expectations in determining output and employment, Keynes refers briefly to 'long-period employment', a concept that plays no role in his analysis, but that deserves some attention in order to forestall possible misunderstanding of his work. As the presentation of Keynes's theory of effective demand in the preceding sections has emphasised, it is centered around positions of short-period equilibrium, and the employment it focuses on can be called 'short-period equilibrium employment'. This employment depends on all the factors that determine the technical conditions of production in the given short period, with their values being taken as pre-determined in that period, as well as on the economy's consumption function, and on the volume of intended investment for the period, investment that is made 'actual' in an equilibrium situation. Keynes steps outside his formal model to observe that when short-term expectations have been changing, employment at any point in time will not reflect fully the changes in expectations because it takes time to bring employment into line with these expectations. It would be too costly to abandon all production started under short-term expectations that subsequently appear to have been too optimistic. Similarly it takes time to make appropriate provisions for an increase in employment justified by improved short-term expectations. These adjustment problems are noted for purposes of completeness but they are generally ignored, given Keynes's identification of actual employment with the short-period equilibrium level of employment.

The time lags that are involved before employment is brought into line with changes in long-term expectations cannot be so readily ignored. They involve not only the time required to produce and install capital goods, but also their economic lifetimes once installed. Even though the long-term expectation that led to the construction of some equipment turns out to have been mistaken, that equipment will continue to contribute to the economy's productive capacity for a considerable amount of time after long-term expectations have changed. The level of employment in the economy at any time, one of whose determinants is available productive capacity, will thus usually reflect a series of past, as well as current, long-term expectations. It is only in the very special case, where long-term expectations have been unchanged for a substantial interval of time (presumably because they turn out to be in accord with eventual outcomes), that all employment in the current short period would reflect the same state of expectations. Keynes calls this level of employment 'the long-period employment corresponding to that state of expectations' (48).[20] Keynes adds a footnote here that extends the scope of this term to include, as well as stationary conditions, the very special dynamic conditions of a steady-state. 'It is not necessary that the level of long-period employment should be *constant, i.e.* long-period conditions are not necessarily static. For example, a steady increase in wealth or population may constitute a part of the unchanging expectation. The only condition is that the existing expectations should have been foreseen sufficiently far ahead' (48n). This footnote indicates the conditions that would have to be satisfied on an equilibrium growth path for Keynes's type of model where future conditions can never be known with certainty. An unchanging state of long-term expectations of steady growth is needed, but these expectations must be justified by events in each short period in order to be held over time. The Keynesian models of accumulation developed by Harrod and Robinson made use, as we shall see in the second part of this book, of this special equilibrium growth path.

Keynes's brief excursion into 'long-period employment' is in the nature of an aside, the indication of a special item in a taxonomy of possible equilibrium situations.[21] It is tossed into a discussion of expectations, and then disappears from view because it represents an outcome that is not, even to a very modest degree, compatible with his understanding of the behaviour of capitalist economies. Even though what has been called here 'short-period equilibrium employ- ment' is also an equilibrium construct that does not hold for any actual period of time in these economies, it is given a central role in Keynes's theory, because of his implicit assumption that it serves as a centre of attraction for actual values.

3.9 CONCLUSION

Keynes uses aggregate demand and supply functions for the economy to get an overall view of the factors determining both the level of employment and the real-wage rate. These functions represent

---

[20] This could also be called the 'long-period equilibrium level of employment', because it would be the level of employment in a situation of long-period equilibrium.

[21] This taxonomic nature of the reference to long-period employment is implicit in the statement Keynes makes after he defines the term. 'It follows that, although expectations may change so frequently that the actual level of employment has never had time to reach the long-period employment corresponding to the existing state of expectation, nevertheless every state of expectation has its definite corresponding level of long-period employment' (Keynes 1936: 48).

conditions in commodity markets. Labour market arrangements in his analysis can only establish money-wage contracts and not, in contrast to his interpretation of the position of classical theory, real-wage rates. He argues that there may be no way for workers as a group to determine their real-wage rates, because of the macro-economic consequences of changes in their money-wage rates. The competitive firms in Keynes's model must base their output and employment decisions on their expectations of the prices for their individual products, because of the time that must elapse, even with given plant and equipment, between decisions to produce and the time when output is ready for sale. These short-term expectations of prices are turned into expectations of proceeds in order to derive the aggregate supply function for the economy. This function shows the employment that would be offered, given the firms' expectations of proceeds. This aggregate supply function is purely an analytical construct that Keynes found useful in pointing out the factors that determine employment in the economy. It is not a decision function for anyone, or for any group of individuals. Entrepreneurs make their output and employment decisions on the basis of expected prices for their products, given their short-period marginal cost curves.

The aggregate demand function shows the total proceeds that would result under equilibrium conditions from different levels of employment. Its position and shape depend on the economy's consumption function and the volume of investment (intended and actual) in the short period of the analysis. Equilibrium effective demand is shown by the point of intersection of the aggregate demand and supply functions, which indicates a position of short-period equilibrium. This equilibrium position is stable, given the volume of investment, because the value for the economy's marginal propensity to consume is less than unity. The volume of investment is determined on the basis of long-term expectations. It does not adjust in such a way as to validate the short-term expectations of proceeds that result in a particular level of employment, when they are different from the proceeds shown by the equilibrium aggregate demand function for this level of employment.

APPENDIX: THE DERIVATION OF THE AGGREGATE SUPPLY FUNCTION

Keynes's aggregate supply function is based on the industry short-period supply curves to be found in Marshall. In reply to a query from Robertson on this function as it appeared in the first proof of *The General Theory* (it was called the 'employment function' in that proof (Keynes 1973c: 370)), Keynes stated that '[T]he employment function ... can be derived from the ordinary supply function, or rather from the family of ordinary supply functions corresponding to different hypotheses' (Keynes 1973b: 513). This Marshallian under-pinning is reflected in Keynes's choice of words for the definition of aggregate supply price. His statement that 'the aggregate supply price of the output of a given amount of employment is the expectation of proceeds which will just make it worth the while of the entrepreneurs to give that employment' (Keynes 1936: 24), echoes Marshall's definition of the supply price for a particular commodity: 'the normal supply price of any amount of that commodity ... is the price the expectation of which will just suffice to maintain the existing aggregate amount of production' (Marshall 1920: 342–3). For Keynes, as well as for Marshall, the 'expectation' that is controlling the situation is an expectation of price that is held by individual entrepreneurs deciding on their individual rates of output (and employment). Where Marshall limited his aggregation to an industry and thus to an industry supply curve, Keynes went on to define an aggregate supply curve for the economy as a whole.

The expected proceeds at the industry level, which Keynes then aggregates, can be derived from the industry short-period supply curve as illustrated in figure 3.3. The product of the expected price and the corresponding output from the industry supply curve gives the expectation of proceeds shown in panel B of figure 3.3. On the abscissa are shown the levels of employment required to produce different amounts of output. For example, the expectations of proceeds $OP_1 \cdot Oq_1$ will lead to the employment of On_1 man-hours per week. This procedure can be repeated for each industry, before user costs are deducted from expected sale-proceeds, as a preliminary step in obtaining Keynes's aggregate supply function. The shape and position of the latter depend on how its constituent elements are

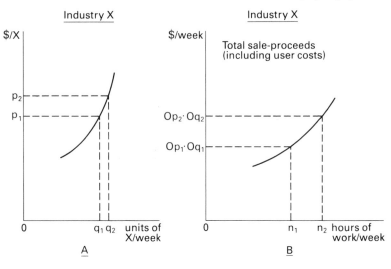

Fig 3.3

combined, a matter that Keynes touched on only briefly, since it 'belongs to the detailed analysis of the general ideas here set forth, which it is no part of my immediate purpose to pursue' (Keynes 1936: 43n).

Keynes did, however, briefly indicate two possible methods of aggregation. The first assumes 'that a given volume of effective demand has a particular distribution of this demand between different products uniquely associated with it'. In this case we begin with an assumed value for the expected proceeds of a particular industry, and its corresponding employment, and then using the assumed fixed proportions, we obtain the expected proceeds for each of the remaining industries, and their corresponding levels of employment. The summation of these proceeds, and the summation of the corresponding levels of employment, then determine a point on the aggregate supply function. Each point on such a function can then be obtained by repeating this process, starting with a different assumed value for the expected proceeds of the first industry. The proportion of total employment in each industry will not be the same at each point on this curve, because the proceeds-employment relationship is not the same for each industry. This also means that the aggregate supply function will differ for each assumed distribution of effective demand between industries.

The second method of aggregation mentioned by Keynes (1936:

45), takes the distribution of aggregate employment to be the same at each point on the aggregate supply function. The conceptual derivation of this function begins, in this case, with an assumed value for employment in a particular industry, and finds the expected proceeds that would lead to this employment. The unique distribution of employment can then be used to derive the corresponding levels of employment in each of the other industries. The expected proceeds that would lead to these levels of employment can be obtained from their respective proceeds curves. The summation over all industries provides a point on the aggregate supply function. This procedure can then be repeated in order to obtain other points on this function. Asimakopulos (1982: 25) noted two other possible methods of aggregation. One assumes that the relative expected prices for the different industry outputs are constant along an aggregate supply function. The other assumes that the relative quantities of each product produced are constant. All four methods, even though they begin with the same industry 'expected proceeds-employment' curves, will result in somewhat different aggregate supply functions. This difference, however, does not affect the broad outlines of Keynes's analysis.

The aggregate supply function is positively-sloped, and it has been shown that there is a relation between the elasticity of that curve and the change in factor shares if employment is changed: 'this elasticity value is less than unity, unity or greater than unity, as the labour share is decreased, constant, or increased, respectively, when employment is higher' (26).

One point that is implicit in the conceptual derivation of the aggregate supply function should be pointed out because of confusion in the literature. Each point on the aggregate supply curve represents a position where the model's competitive firms are maximising their profits, given the short-term expectations of prices and their marginal cost curves. The proceeds, the expectations of which give rise to particular levels of employment, thus include expected profits as well as expected wage costs. This interpretation is consistent with Keynes's response to Robertson about the aggregate supply function that 'it is only a re-concoction of our old friend the supply function' (Keynes 1973b: 513). He also noted that at the point of effective demand 'the entrepreneurs' expectation of profits will be maximised, (Keynes 1936: 25). But the implicit assumption of a giant firm controlling the economy's output that led to the error noted above in Keynes's first definition of the aggregate demand function also led to errors in some of his comments about the aggregate supply function.

These comments misled readers (for example, Patinkin 1982: 143–50) into concluding that expected profits are not included in the aggregate supply function. He interprets this function to include only variable costs. There is, for example, the footnote about the aggregate supply function on p. 55 of *The General Theory*, which is attached to a paragraph in which Keynes is implicitly assuming a single economy-wide firm that equates 'the marginal proceeds (or income) to the marginal factor cost.' With the aggregate supply curve then implicitly treated as a variable cost curve for this non-existent giant firm, profits are not included in that footnote's treatment of this curve. (For a more detailed examination of this footnote, see Asimakopulos 1982, 1983a.)

The interpretation of the aggregate supply function presented here implies that each point on the curve of that function is a potential position of equilibrium from the point of view of producing firms. Which of these points represents the actual position of equilibrium can only be determined after demand conditions are introduced. If it is assumed that actual expenditures are shown by the equilibrium aggregate demand function drawn in figure 3.2 (or set out in equation (3.7)) then the equilibrium position is indicated by the point of intersection of the curve representing this function and the aggregate supply curve. At this point on the aggregate supply function, not only is gross national product (the sum of incomes, including profits) equal to gross national expenditure, as it must by definition, but it is the expectation of this value for the sum of incomes that led to the employment that gave rise to this expenditure. If employment is at any other level, for example, below the short-period equilibrium level, then the expenditures give rise to proceeds (price) greater than those required to justify this level of employment, and firms tend to increase output. The reverse holds if employment is greater than the equilibrium level.

The same considerations apply for the equilibrium aggregate demand function. It is based on the assumption of a given and planned investment, with consumption in the desired relation to the income that corresponds to the employment shown. This means that not only is saving equal to investment, as it must if it is defined as the difference between total income (equal to total expenditure) and consumption, but this saving is in the desired relation to income. By itself, this condition is not sufficient to determine the equilibrium for the economy, it only indicates a potential position of equilibrium on the demand side. The actual position of equilibrium must also satisfy the requirements for equilibrium on the supply side, and it is thus shown by the point where the aggregate supply function intersects the equilibrium aggregate demand function. Short-period equilibrium in the economy requires equilibrium on both the production and expenditure sides.

It is possible to conceive of a wide range of aggregate demands that are not equilibrium functions, even if they each incorporate the planned level of investment for the period. They would differ in showing different degrees of lack of full adjustment of consumption to income. The point of intersection of the aggregate supply function with any one of these functions would not indicate a position of equilibrium even though the proceeds at that point are those, the expectation of which leads to the employment at that point. Saving must be equal to investment, but this saving is not in the desired relation to income, and individuals try to adjust their expenditures to more closely conform to the desired relations to income. The equilibrating effects of these adjustments will be examined in the next chapter after the presentation of the consumption function.

Keynes's aggregate supply function is built up, as we have seen, from the short-period supply curves of competitive firms whose individual rates of output have negligible effects on market prices. Large firms whose markets are not perfectly competitive, for example oligopolistic, set the prices for their products. Their short-term expectations of proceeds then depend on the amounts they expect to be able to sell at these prices. In an economy of such firms, the aggregate supply function would be replaced by what can be called an 'aggregate proceeds function' that shows the total proceeds that *would* result *if* various amounts of output, corresponding to the various levels of employment on the abscissa, could be sold at the prices set by the firm. This aggregate proceeds function would be distinct from the aggregate demand function for such an economy, since the latter shows the proceeds that *do* result from different levels of employment, given the assumptions about money-wage rates and prices used to construct the aggregate proceeds function. Effective demand and the short-period equilibrium level of employment for this non-perfectly competitive economy would be indicated by the point of intersection of the two curves representing these functions. No new principles would be introduced into the theory of effective demand by this introduction of oligopolistic markets and pricing. It should be noted that there is a change in one of the implications that Keynes drew from his presentation. For variations in aggregate demand in the range in which prices relative to unit wage costs can be taken to be constant, employment would be altered without any consequent change in real-wage rates.

4

CONSUMPTION AND INVESTMENT

Production decisions that determine the current level of employment and output are based on short-term expectations of proceeds in the near future. These expectations can never stray very far from actual conditions because they are soon subject to verification by realised results. Keynes thus felt justified, as noted in the preceding chapter, in using realised results to represent short-term expectations. Total receipts are made up of consumption and investment expenditures in a model of a closed economy in which government expenditures are excluded. Keynes used such a model to develop his theory. His usual procedure was to treat these expenditures as though they satisfied the requirements for short-period equilibrium. Current consumption expenditures were implicitly assumed to be in the desired relation to current income, and actual investment expenditures were assumed equal to those intended for this period.

Keynes did not always make clear the special assumptions that he was using in working with consumption and investment expenditures, and some of his statements are at variance with the 'historical time' setting of his analysis. Keynes sometimes treats the definitional equality between saving and investment as though this saving also satisfies the equilibrium requirement that saving be in the desired relation to income. The marginal propensity to consume that he uses in presenting the logical theory of the multiplier is *not* related to the consumption function that he developed to justify the relation between consumption expenditures and employment that is an important element in the aggregate demand function. There are also potential inconsistencies between the treatment of investment as determined from the schedule of the marginal efficiency of capital and the rate of interest, as developed in chapter 11 of *The General Theory*, and statements that point to the unreliability of the factors that determine investment. The latter seem to be raising serious questions about the feasibility of a stable schedule that can be used to indicate the rates of investment that would take place, given different rates of interest. There is also the temporal sequence between investment decisions and the consequent investment expenditures to be considered, because Keynes did not make explicit allowance for the time taken by the investment process.

The rush to get *The General Theory* into print gave rise to inconsistencies that pose problems of interpretation. There was not enough time for the reflection, and the necessary re-writing, that Keynes needed to ensure that all the elements of his theory were presented in a manner that is consistent with his own final understanding of the outcome of his 'long struggle of escape'. Some indication of this final understanding on the role, and determinants, of investment can, perhaps, be obtained from his reply to reviews of *The General Theory* in the 1937 *Quarterly Journal of Economics* that placed particular emphasis on the volatility of the factors determining investment. As well, the surviving rough notes for his 1937 lectures contain comments on the difficulty of establishing a stable relationship between current consumption and current income that serve to emphasise factors that were not given prominence in *The General Theory*.

4.2 THE CONSUMPTION FUNCTION

The consumption function is an important element in Keynes's theoretical structure because it provides the equilibrating mechanisms in his theory. Its assumed properties result, given the values for the other determinants of employment, in a unique and stable equilibrium position. Keynes uses the two terms, consumption function and the propensity to consume interchangeably, to represent the functional relation between consumption and income.[1] This relation is influenced by various factors that are labelled as 'objective' or 'subjective'. The subjective factors are psychological characteristics and social practices and institutions that can be taken to be constant for a short period of time 'except in abnormal or revolutionary circumstances' (Keynes 1936: 91), and thus no further attention need be devoted to them in setting out Keynes's theory. In contrast, the values for the objective factors may change even within a short period of time, and explicit account of them must be given.

The income concept that Keynes thinks is most relevant for the consumption function is real income, but he is precluded from using

---

[1] Keynes often refers to the consumption function as the 'propensity to consume.' This term should not be confused with the average and marginal propensities to consume, which refer to particular aspects of the consumption function.

real income by his distrust of index numbers. It is this distrust which led to his decision 'to make use of only two fundamental units of quantity, namely, quantities of money-value and quantities of employment' (41). Keynes thus uses income measured in wage-units (that is, the money-value of income (Y) divided by the wage-unit (w)), as a proxy for real income. Consumption is also measured in wage-units, and the resulting consumption function can be written as $C_w = C_w (Y_w)$. The money-value of total consumption expenditures (C) is thus equal to $w \cdot C_w$. The changes in income expressed in wage-units is not a precise indicator of changes in real income as employment changes in Keynes's model, because of the assumed inverse relation between real-wage rates and employment. Real income increases as employment increases, but it increases by less than income measured in wage-units, because of the effect of prices that rise relative to money-wage rates. Keynes judged, however, that a consumption function that shows the relation between consumption and income measured in wage-units would be a useful approximation to a real-income consumption function for the purposes of deducing the money-value of consumption expenditures. Keynes also recognised that some allowance might have to be made for the changes in the consumption function that result from a change in the money-wage rate that produces a 'change in the distribution of a given real income between entrepreneurs and rentiers' (92). This possible variation in the money-wage rate is listed by Keynes as one of the objective factors which influence the propensity to consume. (Its presence also serves to make clear that the assumption of given money-wage rates, used by Keynes as a convenient device for setting out his model, was not considered by him to be an essential feature of short-period conditions in that model.)

There is a further approximation involved in his treatment of the contribution of consumption expenditures to the aggregate demand function. In that function employment (N) is the independent variable, and consistency would require Keynes to relate consumption expenditures to employment. The functional relation between consumption and income measured in wage-units can be transformed into one between consumption and employment, only if income in wage-units is a unique function of employment. Keynes recognises that such a function does not exist and that a different distribution of employment between different industries, even with given capital equipment, could lead to different values for income in wage-units. This difference is not considered to be significant for the purposes of presentation of the theory, and Keynes proceeds on the assumption that 'in general it is a good approximation to regard Y_w as uniquely determined by N' (90). With this approximation, N can be substituted for Y_w in the consumption function, which can now be written as $C_w = N_{cw}$ (N). When this function is multiplied by the money-wage rate, consumption expenditures can be shown to be a function of employment, as required for the aggregate demand function.[2] Keynes appears to accept these various approximations as the prices that have to be paid for a simple analytical structure that makes it possible to relate total consumption expenditure to total employment in the economy.

There are five objective factors, in addition to the change in the wage-unit mentioned above. Changes in accounting or management procedures, or a large burst of investment, that result in a change in the difference between income and net income could affect the function that relates consumption to total income because consumption is responsive to net income. This factor is not considered to be of 'practical importance' save 'in exceptional circumstances' (92). Windfall changes in the money values of assets owned by 'the wealth-owning class' might affect the propensity to consume of this class, and thus alter the relation between consumption and income. Keynes classifies these changes 'amongst the major factors capable of causing short-period changes in the propensity to consume' (93).

No mention was made by Keynes of the possible effects on the propensity to consume of changes in the real value of money balances that were given a prominent place in the later literature under the heading of the 'Pigou' or 'real balance' effects (see, for example, Patinkin 1965). There are two possible reasons, within the context of Keynes's model, why the real balance effect would not be given a significant role. The first has to do with the type of money in the model, and the second with the effects of changes in a historical time context. The money in *The General Theory* is bank money ('I shall . . .

---

[2] It is clear that in his development of the consumption function Keynes is referring to *actual* consumption expenditures. For example, he begins by considering 'what sum will be spent on consumption when employment is at a given level' (Keynes 1936: 90), but the 'expectational' error in his statement of the aggregate demand function, mentioned in chapters 2 and 3 above, reappears in the paragraph that precedes the above quotation. 'The aggregate demand function relates any given level of employment to the "proceeds" which that level of employment is expected to realise' (89). There is no sign of Keynes's recognition of the incompatibility between this use of the adjective 'expected' that refers in his model to a very large number of competitive entrepreneurs concerned with their individual products, the demands for which are independent of their individual offers of employment, and an economy-wide function relating total consumption expenditures to total employment.

assume that money is co-extensive with bank deposits' (167n.1)), that is, 'inside' money, which consists of debts of private institutions, while it is only 'outside' money, the currency, or IOU's created by the government, which provides the basis for the real balance effect. For the real balance effect to operate in a noticeable manner, even with outside money, there would have to be a substantial fall in prices (and wages), but Keynes saw that such decisions would lead to bankruptcies and disruptions in the economic system. These would tend to swamp any beneficial effects on the propensity to consume of higher real money balances. Kalecki wrote a comment on the Pigou effect, which Keynes published in the *Economic Journal*, that expressed views which Keynes would probably endorse. 'The adjustment required [to result in an automatic adjustment to full employment] would increase catastrophically the real value of debts, and would consequently lead to wholesale bankruptcy and a "confidence crisis". The "adjustment" would probably never be carried to the end: if the workers persisted in their game of unrestricted competition, the Government would introduce a wage stop under the pressure of employers' (Kalecki 1944: 132).

Another of the objective factors mentioned by Keynes as influencing the propensity to consume is the rate of time-discounting, the weighing up of present versus future consumption, which is identified, approximately, with the rate of interest. It can also be affected by expected changes in the purchasing power of money. Not too much importance was accorded by Keynes to changes in the rate of interest in altering the short-period relation between consumption and income because changes in interest have an income as well as a substitution effect: 'the short-period influence of the rate of interest on individual spending out of given income is secondary and relatively unimportant, except, perhaps, where unusually large changes are in question' (94). Changes in fiscal policy are added to the list of objective factors, because when they result in high taxes on incomes from investment, death duties, etc., they are seen as capable of altering the propensity to consume. Finally, note is taken of the possible influence of changes in expectations of the relation between present and future levels of income. This factor is seen as something that could be considered important for individuals, but Keynes thought that it is likely to average out for the community as a whole. In making this judgement, he appears to have ignored the changes in expectations of the relation between present and future incomes that often occur during cyclical periods, and that cannot be eliminated by averaging out over the community. In his 1937 lecture notes and in other comments, as we shall see below, Keynes was very much aware of the potential importance of this factor.

From his consideration of consumption, Keynes concluded that 'given the general economic situation, the expenditure on consumption in terms of the wage-unit depends in the main, on the volume of output and employment' (96). The possible influence on the propensity to consume of variations in the objective factors 'must not be forgotten', but 'the aggregate income measured in terms of the wage-unit is, as a rule, the principal variable upon which the consumption-constituent of the aggregate demand function will depend'. When he uses the aggregate demand function, as we saw, he assumes that current consumption is in the desired, or equilibrium, relation to current income.

Having satisfied himself 'that the propensity to consume is a fairly stable function', Keynes goes on to consider the question, 'what is the normal shape of this function?' Keynes's treatment of this question is very cautious, and it displays concern with the complicating factors that could effect the relations between changes in income and changes in consumption that were generally neglected in the subsequent Keynesian literature. He recognises that habits are important, and that over the relatively short periods of some cyclical fluctuations, consumption will not respond very readily to changes in income. But he uses for his theory the general proposition 'that men are disposed, as a rule and on the average, to increase their consumption as their income increases, but not by as much as the increase in their income'. It is this proposition, with its consequence of a value for the marginal propensity to consume of less than unity, which provides Keynes with the basis for the stability of his short-period equilibrium level of employment. It also follows that the higher the level of income, the higher the absolute value of the gap between income and consumption – this gap must be filled by investment if the higher level of income is to be maintained.

The gap between the increase in income and the increase in consumption is the only feature of his consumption function that has an integral role in Keynes's General Theory.[3] Its existence is not dependent on any particular relationship between the average and marginal propensities to consume; all that it requires is that the value

---

[3] In a 1936 letter to Harrod, Keynes underlines the importance of this 'gap' in his own thinking as he moved away from the *Treatise on Money*. 'One of the most important transitions for me, after my *Treatise on Money* had been published . . . only came after I had enunciated to myself the psychological law that, when income increases, the gap between income and consumption will increase' (Keynes 1973c: 85).

of the latter be less than unity. These two propensities could, for example, be equal in value, even though Keynes felt that once 'the immediate primary needs of a man and his family' were satisfied, and 'a margin of comfort has been attained ... [they] will lead, as a rule, to a greater *proportion* of income being saved as real income increases' (97). In the latter case, the marginal propensity to consume would decline as income increased, and its value would fall below that of the average propensity to consume. This purported relationship between the two propensities has not been found in data that cover substantial intervals of time (with cyclical fluctuations averaged out), and where changes in real income have been significant.[4] This negative finding does not affect, for the reason previously mentioned, any of the critical elements of the General Theory.

Keynes's recognition of the potential influence of expectations of future income on the propensity to consume was noted above. It is interesting to observe that even though he tended to dismiss this factor as something mentioned in *The General Theory* 'for the sake of completeness' (95), he would use it in analysing a situation where there could be important changes in expectations of future income. This was reflected in his 1937 correspondence with Kalecki on the latter's theory of taxation paper that Keynes had accepted for publication in the *Economic Journal*. Kalecki (1937b: 36) had assumed that the capitalists' propensity to consume depends only on current income and was insensitive to the expectations of a subsequent change in income. Keynes (1983: 797) took the opposite position that news of the imposition of the increase in tax would alter the current consumption function because of its adverse effects on expectations of future income.

Keynes's reference to consumption behaviour in the rough notes for his 1937 lectures also shows this increased emphasis on the influence of these expectations. It displays considerable scepticism about the possibility of relating consumption to current income. His revised position is compatible with subsequent approaches to this topic, such as the permanent-income hypothesis of Friedman (1957), and the life-cycle hypothesis of Modigliani and Brumberg (1954). Keynes notes: 'Propensity to consume is determined *solely* by a psychological composite of actual and expected income and is determined neither by effective demand at a definite date nor by income at a definite date' (Keynes 1973c: 180). He did not get around to considering the implication of this view for the formulation of the

---

[4] The study by Kuznets (1946) found that the ratios of consumption to income in the years during the very long interval 1869–1938, were relatively constant.

equilibrium aggregate demand function that he used to determine the short-period equilibrium level of employment that figures prominently in his General Theory. In so far as it makes the relation between consumption expenditures and current income less definite, this revised approach also makes the aggregate demand function less responsive to changes in employment. It would also affect the difference in income between equilibrium positions that are based on the same consumption function, but have different values for planned investment. This will be dealt with in the next section on the multiplier.

Keynes's treatment of the consumption function is representative of much of his book. There is a core that is straightforward, and that has provided the material for Keynesian theories and textbooks. Consumption in real terms (or wage-units) is an increasing function of current income in real terms (or wage-units), with the marginal propensity to consume being less than one. But Keynes's book contains more than this core, there are also qualifications and limitations that could be significant in an historical time setting, in which economic policy measures would have to operate. In some of these settings, consumption expenditures would be rather unresponsive to fluctuations in employment. In other circumstances, where unemployed workers are sharply constrained in their expenditures by lack of liquidity, consumption expenditures may be very responsive. It is necessary to assess the particular historical circumstances, as Keynes's comments and qualifications make clear, before a particular policy is implemented.

4.3 THE MULTIPLIER

With consumption an increasing function of income, any change in investment that changes income will also affect consumption, and thus the initial change in investment will have indirect as well as direct effects on income and employment. When two equilibrium positions that differ because of different values for investment are compared, the differences in income (or employment) between the two situations can be shown to be some multiple of their difference in investment (or in employment in the investment sector). The value for this multiple, or multiplier, can be derived from the marginal propensity to consume. The term *investment multiplier* is used if differences in income are related to differences in the value of investment, and *employment multiplier* is used if differences in employment are related to differences in employment in the investment sector. In his pioneer article on the multiplier, Kahn (1931) developed the employment multiplier, while Keynes concentrated on the investment multiplier.

Keynes's treatment of the multiplier is confusing because he uses the term the 'marginal propensity to consume' to refer both to the result of differentiating the consumption function that shows the normal relation between consumption expenditures and income, and to the ratio of the increment of consumption to the increment of income. When the latter usage is adopted, the time interval over which these changes occur could be very short, much too short to allow for the normal relations between consumption and income to be re-established after changes in income. Very little attention is paid, in any case, to the time occupied by the multiplier process, and Keynes's analysis of the multiplier is essentially static and concerned with the comparison of two positions with different values for investment.

Keynes, after his discussion of the consumption function, uses the derivative of this function, dC_w/dY_w, to define the marginal propensity to consume. He comments that this 'quantity is of considerable importance, because it tells us how the next increment of output will have to be divided between consumption and investment' (Keynes 1936: 115). The implication is that this 'next increment of output' will be divided in the normal relation between consumption and investment (saving), which means that the time interval over which this increment occurs will be characterised by short-period equilibrium. The multiplier formula is deduced as follows: for this 'next increment of output', we have by definition, $\triangle Y_w = \triangle C_w + \triangle I_w$, and assuming the normal relation between consumption and income with respect to this increment, $\triangle C_w = (dC_w/dY_w) \triangle Y_w$. By substitution, and the rearrangement of terms, we find $\triangle Y_w = k \triangle I_w$, where k, which is equal to $1/(1-dC_w/dY_w)$, is the investment multiplier, and therefore the marginal propensity to consume for the economy, dC_w/dY_w is equal to $1-1/k$. What keeps this formulation from being simply definitional is the interpretation given to the marginal propensity to consume, with this term representing a normal relationship between increments of consumption and income. The multiplier will not attain the value indicated under this interpretation, as Keynes observes, 'until the new level (and distribution) of incomes provides a margin of [desired] saving sufficient to correspond to the increased investment' (117), and equilibrium is re-established.

There is explicit recognition of the time occupied by the multiplier process when Keynes writes about the consequence of an increase in investment that was not fully foreseen. 'It is obvious that an initiative of this description only produces its full effect on employment over a period of time' (122). From this point, however, he goes on to consider 'the logical theory of the multiplier, which holds good continuously, without time lag, at all moments of time', and the marginal propensity to consume, without warning from Keynes, takes on a different meaning. It becomes equal to the ratio of the increments of consumption and income that happen to have occurred in the interval of time considered, and that may not even approximate some underlying basic relationship. The multiplier formula in this case becomes definitional, a re-arrangement of the saving-investment identity. 'But in every interval of time the theory of the multiplier holds good in the sense that the increment of aggregate demand is equal to the product of the increment of aggregate investment and the multiplier as determined by the marginal propensity to consume' (123). This use of one term to represent two different things is a potential source of error, and it may have contributed to Keynes's failure to distinguish in some of his writings between the definitional and equilibrium equalities of saving and investment.[5]

Keynes appears to provide a justification for the lack of attention in *The General Theory* to the time required for the multiplier to operate when he notes that his comparative static analysis is concerned with 'the total benefit to employment to be expected from an expansion in the capital-goods industries' (124). In contrast, '[T]he fact that an unforeseen change only exercises its full effect on employment over a period of time is important ... in the analysis of the trade cycle (on lines such as I followed in my *Treatise on Money*)'. In any case, Keynes believes the time lag in the multiplier to be short: 'there is no reason to suppose that more than a brief interval of time need elapse before employment in the consumption industries is advancing *pari passu* with employment in the capital-goods industries with the multiplier operating near its normal figure' (124–5). No empirical estimate is provided in *The General Theory* to confirm this supposition. Kahn (1984: 102–3) considers that Keynes estimated the time lags in the multiplier process in the American edition of his 1933 essay, 'The Means to Prosperity'. Although Keynes concluded in this work 'that the time-lags involved are not unduly serious' (Keynes 1972: 342), the analysis supporting it lacked substantial empirical content.

---

[5] Shackle (1967: 162) notices the potential danger in this version of Keynes's multiplier that was 'a trivial, truistical manipulation of the marginal propensity to consume .... [that] confuses equilibrium and identical equality'.

Keynes assumed that only 70 per cent of any increase in expenditures would result in higher income and employment, because of adverse repercussions caused in other areas. He also, quite arbitrarily, uses 70 per cent as the economy's marginal propensity to consume, and thus deduces an 'effective' (in terms of changes in output and employment) marginal propensity to consume of 0.49 (=0.7 × 0.7), or roughly one-half. If the effect of the initial increase in expenditure is represented by 1, then the multiplier sequence is $1 + 1/2 + 1/4 + \ldots = 2$. Seven-eighths of the total multiplier effect is accounted for by the primary expenditure and the first two rounds, and this is the basis for Keynes's conclusion. But there is no investigation of the length of time occupied by these rounds.

Keynes's treatment of the multiplier is thus incomplete. It is always necessary to keep in mind that the passage of time is not dealt with in comparative static analysis, and this time element must be introduced in any application of the analysis that is concerned with the effects of changes. Keynes's language in referring to the multiplier sometimes gives the impression that he is dealing with changes, but his treatment of it is confined to comparative statics. For example, in introducing the investment multiplier, k, he writes: 'It tells us that, when there is an increment of aggregate investment, income will increase by an amount k times the increment of investment' (115). The word 'increase' implies change, but Keynes's multiplier is concerned with the comparison of two positions of static equilibrium. He implicitly assumes when referring to any change in investment that the equilibrium position corresponding to the new level of investment will be achieved within the given short period. Hicks has observed that Keynes, with the addition of his multiplier analysis makes two, not necessarily compatible, uses of the short period. The short period represents an interval of time sufficiently brief so that the changes during this interval in productive capacity that occur continuously in any economy with positive net investment, are small relative to the initial productive capacity so that they can be legitimately ignored. This interval, however, must also be sufficiently long for most of the multiplier effects of a change in investment to have been completed within that period.

It is one of the major difficulties of the Keynes theory ... that it works with a *period* which is taken to be one of equilibrium (investment being equal to saving, saving that is a function of *current* income), and which is nevertheless identified with the Marshallian 'short period', in which capital equipment (now the capital equipment of the whole economy) remains unchanged. The second seems to require that the period should not be too long, but the first requires that it should not be too short; for the *process* of getting into the equilibrium in question (the multiplier process) must occupy a length of time that is by no means negligible. It is not easy to see that there can be any length of time that will adequately satisfy both requirements.

(Hicks 1965: 64–5)

Hicks (1974: 9–30) subsequently pointed out the implicit assumption made by Keynes about the availability of stocks of raw materials that were prerequisites for the increase in output and employment due to an increase in demand for investment goods. When stocks of raw materials were very low, an expansion of total output (and employment) could not be readily brought about by increasing investment demand, because of the unavailability of necessary materials. The multiplier story could not be told without explicit reference to conditions in the primary goods sector, as well as to conditions in the manufacturing sector. Unutilised productive capacity in the latter, and unemployed labour, might thus not be a sufficient basis for an increase in output following an increase in investment demand. The split between the price and output effects of an increase in investment will also be affected by the size of stocks of raw materials, and the terms at which merchants are prepared to allow variations in their holdings of these stocks. The value of the multiplier and the time required for the full multiplier effects to be developed, thus depend on the particular conditions in the economy being analysed.

The value for the multiplier, as well as the length of time required for it to operate, is relevant for policy purposes. As we saw in the presentation of the consumption function in the preceding section, the responsiveness of consumption expenditures to changes in income depends on historical circumstances. This responsiveness is very much affected by expectations of future incomes, and the ability of those who are unemployed to maintain customary standards of expenditures. The level of unemployment benefits and the length of time over which they are available are obviously important. In situations where individuals have experienced substantial spells of unemployment, consumption expenditures may be more responsive to an increase in employment resulting from, say, an increase in government expenditure than when these spells have been short. In the former situations the unemployed would have sold and pledged many of their assets in order to maintain themselves and their families, while in the latter they would still own assets that together with unemployment benefits permit them to keep consumption at previous levels. Leijonhufvud (1969: 42–5) has argued that the multiplier is an illiquidity phenomenon, because unemployed workers are prevented from keeping up consumption expenditures in line with 'wealth' (in which he includes the value of human capital), only if liquidity constraints are important. His examination of empirical studies suggests that during the depression of the 1930s the consumption expenditures of the unemployed reflected their lower current incomes. These expenditures were much less responsive to changes in current incomes during other, less-pronounced, cyclical declines.

4.4 THE MARGINAL EFFICIENCY OF CAPITAL

Before going into the details of Keynes's explanation of the determination of investment, it is important to emphasise again the pervasive role of money, and monetary institutions and arrangements, in Keynes's vision of the operations of a capitalist economy. The existence of a large variety of financial assets, some of which are traded in highly organised and active markets, allows individuals to keep adjusting the forms in which their wealth is held. Many of these assets owe their existence to the raising of funds by firms for the purpose of financing the purchase of capital goods. In ordering these goods the firms expected that the returns from their ownership, in spite of the risk and uncertainty of investment in physical assets whose profitability depends on future conditions that may turn out to be unfavourable, would outweigh the interest and other costs incurred to obtain the funds needed for their purchase.[6] These funds are collected through some combination of income (retained earnings), short and long-term borrowing, and the issue of new shares. Each of these methods has an explicit and/or implicit cost. For example, the opportunity cost of retained earnings is the rate of interest that could have been obtained on these earnings, while the cost of borrowed funds includes both the explicit interest cost on the obligations assumed and the implicit cost of possible loss of control of the firm if the scheduled payments cannot be covered at some future time. In his formal model Keynes abstracted from these institutional details, with only bonds and physical capital appearing explicitly as the non-money assets, but his General Theory contains more than this formal model. Keynes referred to 'the rate of interest' as a factor that determines in conjunction with the prospective yield, the volume of investment, but he noted that more than one interest rate is involved:

---

[6] Minsky (1975: 89) sees this activity as 'the fundamental speculation of a capitalist economy ... the acquisition of capital assets and the putting out of commitments to pay cash embodied in the liabilities used to finance such capital acquisitions'.

'I have slurred the point that we are dealing with complexes of rates of interest' (Keynes 1936: 137n).

Even when note is taken of the need to supplement the very abstract formal model contained in *The General Theory* in order to understand the full extent of Keynes's General Theory, there still remain potentially contradictory elements in his treatment of investment. There is, on the one hand, the presentation of a seemingly calculable investment demand schedule that is used with the market rate of interest to determine the volume of investment for the short period of his analysis. On the other hand, there is the strong emphasis on the unreliability of the factors determining investment that raises doubts about the existence of a stable investment demand schedule that can be used in conjunction with the rate of interest for this purpose in Keynes's model. The apparent difference between these two approaches has been vividly expressed by Shackle (1967: 130): 'Chapter 11 shows us the arithmetic of the marginal efficiency of capital and its relation with interest-rates a matter for actuaries and slide-rules. Chapter 12 reveals the hollowness of all this. The material for the slide-rules is absent, or arbitrary.' In part, this difference reflects the relative importance Keynes gives, in each of these chapters, to 'enterprise' and to 'speculation'. He defines the former as 'the activity of forecasting the prospective yield of assets over their whole life' and the latter as 'the activity of forecasting the psychology of the [stock] market' (Keynes 1936: 158).

Keynes also is vague about the time element in the investment process, i.e., the length of the interval from the making of an investment decision on fixed capital, through the investment expenditures that are a consequence of this decision, to the delivery of the capital goods. His investment demand schedule appears to give him, at one and the same time, both investment decisions in the period, and actual investment expenditures.

Keynes defines the marginal efficiency of capital by assuming a given state of long-term expectations about future conditions that provides potential purchasers of capital goods with a basis for estimating the prospective yield from the ownership of each type of such goods: 'I define the marginal efficiency of capital as being equal to that rate of discount which would make the present value of the series of annuities given by the returns expected from the capital-asset during its life just equal to its supply price' (135). The marginal efficiency of capital, in general, is the value of the greatest of these individual marginal efficiencies of capital. In the short period of his analysis the change in productive capacity that occurs is small relative to the existing capacity, so that the expected yield would not be adversely affected by higher investment because of noticeable changes in factor proportions, changes that can only occur over longer periods of time. Keynes points to the rising supply price of capital goods when investment is increased, due to the positively-sloped short-period supply curves for these goods, as the basis for the downward-sloping marginal efficiency of capital curve that is his investment demand schedule. He then states 'it is obvious that the actual rate of current investment will be pushed to the point where there is no longer any class of capital-asset of which the marginal efficiency exceeds the current rate of interest. In other words, the rate of investment will be pushed to the point on the investment demand schedule where the marginal efficiency of capital in general is equal to the market rate of interest' (136–7).[7]

This relationship between the marginal efficiency of capital and the rate of interest that determines the volume of investment is also expressed by Keynes as an equality between the demand and supply prices for the capital goods that are ordered and produced in the short period of the analysis. In chapter 11 this demand price for a particular capital good is seen as being arrived at by using the current rate of interest as the discount rate in calculating the present value of the prospective yields from the ownership of that capital good. Since the marginal efficiency of capital for this good is that rate of discount that equates the present value of its expected quasi-rents with its supply price, equating the marginal efficiency of capital and the rate of interest is equivalent to equating the demand and supply prices for this good.[8] In chapter 12, in contrast, the daily revaluations of equity prices on stock exchanges are important elements in determining investment – they 'inevitably exert a decisive influence on the rate of current investment' (151) – because these valuations are taken to represent the demand prices for the capital goods owned by a firm.

[7] Keynes (1936: 180) draws an investment demand schedule in the single diagram of *The General Theory*, in connection with his criticism of the classical theory of interest. It has the amount of investment on the vertical axis, and the rate of interest on the horizontal axis.

[8] This identification of these two statements of the equilibrium conditions for the determination of investment is in line with Keynes's assertion that they are expressing the 'same thing' (Keynes 1936: 137). Minsky, who considers the approach to the determination of investment in chapter 12 and in the 1937 *Quarterly Journal of Economics* article with its emphasis on financial relations, sees this reference to capitalising prospective yields as a move toward that approach. 'The capitalising formula is a more natural format for the introduction of uncertainty and risk preference of asset holders into the determination of investments than is the marginal efficiency schedule' (Minsky 1975: 99–100).

This identification is a carry-over from Keynes's *Treatise on Money*, where the consideration of the factors of investment goods (e.g. Keynes 1930a: 140–6). Keynes drew attention to this similarity, where the only difference is one of terminology. Instead of following the earlier practice of considering a high quotation for a company as equivalent to its being able to borrow at a lower rate of interest, 'I should now describe this by saying that a high quotation for existing equities involves an increase in the marginal efficiency of the corresponding type of capital' (151 n.1). The marginal efficiency of capital in this chapter is thus subject to 'speculation' rather than to 'enterprise'.[9]

Keynes considered the marginal efficiency of capital to be a critical element in his General Theory, because of its dependence on expectations of future conditions that provide an important avenue through which the future affects current activity.[10] 'The schedule of the marginal efficiency of capital is of fundamental importance because it is mainly through this factor (much more than through the rate of interest) that the expectation of the future influences the present' (145). It is the possibility of sudden revision, due to exogenous factors, in the long-term expectations that are crucial elements in his marginal efficiency of capital, that led Keynes to ignore the potential conflict, made vivid by Shackle in the quotation above, in his treatments of the determination of investment in chapters 11 and 12 of *The General Theory*. But his argument for a downward-sloping investment demand schedule is not consistent with important features of his own model. Keynes's description of that schedule invites constructs, such as Hicks's IS curve (Hicks 1937) that camouflage the potential volatility of the long-term

---

[9] Keynes (1936: 156) uses 'the term *speculation* for the activity of forecasting the psychology of the market, and the term *enterprise* for the activity of forecasting the prospective yield of assets over their whole life'.

[10] The importance Keynes attached to the marginal efficiency of capital is indicated in a letter to Harrod, dated 30 August 1936, that spoke 'of my own progress of mind from the classical position to my present views .... And last fall, after an immense lot of muddling and many drafts, the proper definition of the marginal efficiency of capital linked up one thing with another' (Keynes 1973c: 84–5). The importance to him of this concept had also been emphasised in a 27 August 1935 letter to Harrod when the latter was reading galley proofs of *The General Theory*: 'the discovery of the definition of marginal efficiency of capital looks very slight and scarcely more than formal, yet in my own progress of thought it was absolutely vital' (Keynes 1973b: 549). (The August 1935 letter indicates that Keynes was mistaken in his 1936 recollection of when he had arrived at 'the proper definition of the marginal efficiency of capital.' This definition had been formulated sometime before August 1935.)

expectations that is an essential ingredient of Keynes's vision of the likely behaviour of a capitalist economy.

Kalecki, whose work on the business cycle (first published in Polish in 1933) made use of the main elements incorporated in Keynes's theory of effective demand, pointed to 'two serious deficiencies' in Keynes's determination of investment, in his 1936 review of *The General Theory* (reprinted in English in Targetti and Kinda-Hass 1982). The first concerns the lack of distinction in *The General Theory* between investment decisions and actual investment in his short period, and the second is the result of the use by Keynes of 'an approach which is basically static to a matter which is by its nature dynamic. Keynes takes as given the state of the expectations of returns and from this he deduces a certain determined level of investment, overlooking the effects that investment will have in turn on expectations' (252).[11]

Keynes argued, as we saw, that 'in the short run' – the period of his analysis – the inverse relation between the marginal efficiency of capital and the level of investment is due to the rising supply price of capital goods, while long-term expectations of future revenues are implicitly assumed to be unaffected by increased investment. The investment demand schedule that is based on this declining marginal efficiency of capital is an *ex ante* schedule; it shows the investment firms will try to carry out, given the rate of interest. Keynes's terminology makes it appear analogous to a market demand curve for a commodity, but there is a fundamental difference. An individual's demand curve for a good is downward-sloping because he *anticipates* his own diminishing marginal utility as more of that good is consumed. Keynes has to introduce an *ex post* element, the *experience* of rising prices for capital goods as total investment is increasing, in order to obtain a negatively-sloped investment demand schedule. This schedule is thus an unsatisfactory analytical device because of its hybrid nature.

There is as well the point referred to by Kalecki, that Keynes can only obtain his downward-sloping marginal efficiency of capital by carefully selecting, from among the *ex post* effects of higher investment, the one that produces the desired result. Keynes ignores an important consequence of an increase in current investment activity, the higher profits that go hand-in-hand with higher prices, and that could have a favourable impact on current long-term expectations. In chapter 11, Keynes tended to treat these expectations as indepen-

---

[11] On this point, see also Robinson (1964) and Asimakopulos (1971).

dent of current conditions, with his insistence that 'the meaning and significance of the marginal efficiency of capital ... depends on the *prospective* yield of capital, and not merely on its current yield' (Keynes 1936, 141). Some of his statements were even stronger on this point (e.g. 139), and denied any direct relationship between current aggregate profits and the marginal efficiency of capital. This independence was also seen as a factor in the substantial variations in the rate of investment that occur, because being 'free', long-term expectations could experience sudden changes. 'It is important to understand the dependence of the marginal efficiency of a given stock of capital on changes in expectation, because it is chiefly this dependence which renders the marginal efficiency of capital subject to the somewhat violent fluctuations which are the explanation of the Trade Cycle' (143–4). Keynes also points to this independence as an important dynamic element in his analysis. 'The mistake of regarding the marginal efficiency of capital primarily in terms of the *current* yield of capital equipment, which would be correct only in the static state where there is no changing future to influence the present, has had the result of breaking the theoretical link between to-day and tomorrow' (145). But Keynes recognised that these expectations cannot be isolated from what is happening in the economy at present, and in chapter 12 he goes some way to tying them to current conditions.

It would be foolish, in forming our expectations, to attach great weight to matters which are very uncertain. It is reasonable, therefore, to be guided to a considerable degree by the facts about which we feel somewhat confident, even though they may be less decisively relevant to the issue than other facts about which our knowledge is vague and scanty. For this reason the facts of the existing situation enter, in a sense disproportionately, into the formation of our long-term expectations; our usual practice being to take the existing situation and to project it into the future, modified only to the extent that we have more or less definite reasons for expecting a change. (148)

The presentation by Keynes of the marginal efficiency of capital is thus, quite apart from the technical problems noted above, not consistent with his statements about the factors affecting long-term expectations and investment.[12] He should have made some allowance for the influence of the higher current profits that result from

12 This criticism of Keynes's presentation of his investment demand schedule should not be confused with the mistaken view that Keynes incorrectly specified the stock-flow relation between capital and investment, but otherwise presented a neoclassical theory of investment based on the marginal productivity of capital. Leroy (1983) shows that a careful reading of Keynes's writings makes these neoclassical interpretations untenable.

increased investment, even though this could have led to the scrapping of his downward-sloping investment demand schedule. A move in the direction of Kalecki's (1971: 6–7) double-sided relation between profits and investment would have provided more scope for the inclusion of factors that appear in Keynes's analysis. One side of this relation is provided by the influence of current investment expenditures on current profits. The other shows the influence of current profits on long-term expectations and thus on current investment decisions that result in investment expenditures in future periods. Such a move would also have provided a clear demarcation between current investment decisions and current investment expenditures, a demarcation that is blurred in Keynes's presentation. Kalecki's approach also has the virtue of showing the determination of investment as part of a process going on through time, with decisions in the relatively-recent past determining current investment, and current investment decisions being added to those that have not yet been fully executed, to determine investment in succeeding periods.

A different explanation for the negatively-sloped investment demand schedule in *The General Theory*, is given by Pasinetti (1974: 36–7):

In any given short-run situation (with a given technology and a given capital structure), the total amount of investment depends on the expected profitability of all possible investment projects and on the rate of interest. We may imagine entrepreneurs ranking all possible investment projects in order of decreasing profitability and then carrying out investments up to the point at which the expected rate of profit from the last project (called the 'marginal efficiency of capital') is just higher than, or equal to, the rate of interest, as expressing the cost of borrowing.

This is not Keynes's marginal efficiency of capital because, as we have seen, it is the rising supply price of capital goods as investment increases that is the reason he gives for the declining expected profitability of investment projects. In the absence of these higher prices, Keynes saw no reason why, in a particular short period, all investment expenditures would not be directed to the most profitable type. The approach suggested by Pasinetti appears to concentrate only on current investment decisions, and not on the investment that Keynes uses, along with consumption, to explain the determination of current income. It does not readily provide the notion of the investment process as a link between different periods that is to be found in Kalecki's theory.

4.5 INVESTMENT DECISIONS, INVESTMENT AND TIME

The relationship in Keynes's model between investment decisions and investment in a particular short period, already mentioned in the preceding section, deserves more detailed examination. One of the unsatisfactory features of Keynes's analysis of the determination of investment, is his failure to distinguish between the two. The point on the investment demand schedule that corresponds to the current rate of interest, seems to show both the current volume of investment decisions and the current volume of investment. The identification of these two items might be acceptable in either one of two situations. If static conditions are assumed, then the 'dating' of variables is unnecessary, since past, present and future conditions are essentially the same, with investment decisions and investment (both measured in gross flows) identical, in any period. Alternatively, it might be argued that the time lags between investment decisions and investment are small relative to the basic time interval of the analysis, allowing current investment to be brought into line with current investment decisions, even under changing conditions. Keynes's statements make it very clear that he does not see his theory as being concerned with static conditions. He contends that the assumption of static conditions by the 'present-day economic theory' that he wants to supplant, 'imports into it a large element of unreality' (Keynes 1936: 146). Keynes's position on the time lag between investment decisions and the resulting investment is less clear. A significant time lag can be inferred from statements in *The General Theory*, but Keynes seems to deny its significance in correspondence with Kalecki in 1937.

The introductory comments to Keynes's brief consideration of long-term employment (see also section 3.8, above) recognised that 'a *change* in expectations (whether short-term or long-term) will only produce its full effects on employment over a considerable period' (47). Projects planned and started under one set of long-term expectations tend to be carried out, even though expectations have since changed, because of commitments undertaken that would be very costly to undo. The value of current investment decisions made in a particular short period can thus differ from the value of investment being undertaken in that period, when conditions have been changing over time. Keynes, with his strictures against the assumption of a static state, would appear to see his short period as part of a sequence of intervals over which substantial changes can occur. There would thus be no reason to expect that current investment decisions and current investment would be identical in the short period of Keynes's analysis.

The difference between current investment decisions and current investment should not be confused with that between intended investment for a period and actual investment in that period. This latter difference arises from mistaken short-term expectations (Keynes 1973c: 181), and is reflected in unplanned changes in inventories. In Keynes's short-period equilibrium, this difference does not arise, because short-term expectations are confirmed by realised results. A difference between investment decisions and investment can exist in a position of short-period equilibrium because this position can change over time with changing invest-ment. The conclusion Keynes draws from his analysis about the possible persistence over time of involuntary unemployment requires only that there be no reason to expect that changes in investment will be such as to bring about full employment.

Keynes played down the significance of the time lag between investment decisions and investment in correspondence with Kalecki about the latter's article on the incidence of taxation (Kalecki 1937b). (In another connection, when Keynes discussed the role of finance in facilitating increases in investment, investment decisions were seen as being taken 'well in advance of the actual process of investment' (Keynes 1937c: 216)). (See below, section 5.7.) Kalecki had assumed that capitalists' expenditures were unaffected by the announcement of tax changes, and only responded to changes in after-tax incomes as experienced in the new short-period equilibrium. When challenged by Keynes, Kalecki defended his assumption on investment, as follows: 'After the introduction of new tax the entrepreneurs even if they expect their incomes to fall *cannot* immediately reduce their investment because it is the result of previous investment decisions which require a certain time to be completed. Thus their savings [investment expenditures?] remain unaltered in the first period of new taxation regime' (Keynes 1983: 794). Keynes replied ('As a private critic ... though please take no notice of this' (797)) that 'I regard the assumption that investment is fixed as unplausible. Firstly, because it ignores the possibility of fluctuation in stocks. Secondly, because it ignores the possibility of altering the pace at which existing investment decisions are carried out, and thirdly, because at best it can be overcome after a time lag, which may be very short indeed'. The first of the reasons given concerns unanticipated changes in inventories due to mistaken short-term expectations, but when dealing with short-period equilibrium it is only the last two reasons that are relevant. They give the impression that Keynes did not, at times, consider it unreasonable to assume that current investment expenditures are largely determined by current conditions and current investment decisions. If this assumption underlies 'the volume of investment' that appears in his statement of 'the essence of the General Theory of Employment' (Keynes 1936: 29), then the investment in his short-period equilibrium is the 'chosen' amount, given long-term expectations and the rate of interest in that period.

Kalecki had sent Keynes, for comment, a copy of his article on the business cycle (Kalecki 1937a) in which he repeated the criticisms of Keynes's investment demand schedule that had first appeared in his review of *The General Theory*. Keynes initially misinterpreted Kalecki as assuming that expectations of future prices would be changed in exactly the same proportion as changes in current prices (Keynes 1983: 793). When Kalecki pointed out that only a positive relation between current changes and current long-term expectations was involved, Keynes then turned to a position that ignored the significance of the time lags in the investment process. In Kalecki's theory of the business cycle, investment orders exceed (fall short of) investment expenditures in each short period during the upswing (downswing) of a cycle, with the two becoming equal only in the periods that mark changes in the phases of the cycle. Keynes took this equality – which he referred to as 'a version of Achilles and the tortoise' (798) – as justification for his own identification of investment orders and investment expenditures in the short period. The two are not, of course, comparable because this equality does not hold generally in Kalecki's theory, and the investment orders are for expenditures in a subsequent period.

Keynes's position on the time lags separating investment decisions and the subsequent investment is, at least for fixed capital, less soundly based than Kalecki's. Reddaway, writing almost thirty years after the publication of *The General Theory* that he had reviewed in 1936, drew attention to the lack of a clear distinction in *The General Theory* between investment decisions and investment. He considers that the investment demand schedule, and the rate of interest, show only 'the expenditure which would seem, at some one time, to be worth incurring over a very ill-defined period' (Reddaway 1964: 121). He drew on a 1958 inquiry by the Royal Institute of British Architects into the time required for the completion of building projects, to indicate that very substantial lags were involved in the investment process. The average time for the completion of a building (including allowance for the drawing-up of plans) in this study, was 38 months. Even with considerable variation around this average, Reddaway concluded that '[T]he length of these lags has a convenient result for short-term analysis: to a reasonable approximation the level of fixed investment over the next six months or a year can be treated as *given* "for better or worse" by past decisions, and only in small degree influenced by events within that period' (122). The short-period equilibrium in *The General Theory* should, on this basis, be seen as determined by investment planned in the past and carried out in the present. The investment expenditures currently being planned could be different from those currently taking place. If they are different, then the corresponding short-period equilibrium in a future period will be different for this reason, quite apart from the effects of different productive capacities.

4.6 THE VOLATILITY OF INVESTMENT

The determination of investment in the General Theory, as mentioned above, involves more monetary and financial elements than are found in the formal model of that theory.[13] Keynes undermines the apparent solidity of his investment demand schedule developed in chapter 11, by his emphasis in chapter 12 on 'the extreme precariousness of the basis of knowledge on which our estimates of prospective yield have to be made' (Keynes 1936: 149). The calculations that culminate in a marginal efficiency of capital are not, in this view, decisive in determining whether an investment project will be undertaken, because they are subject to such wide margins of error. 'If human nature felt no temptation to take a chance, no satisfaction (profit apart) in constructing a factory, a railway, a mine or a farm, there might not be much investment merely as a result of cold calculation' (150).

The nature of the marginal efficiency of capital then appears to undergo a change, with its values being determined by stock exchange quotations through their effects on the demand prices for capital goods. 'Thus certain classes of investment are governed by the average expectation of those who deal on the Stock Exchange as

[13] Minsky has repeatedly emphasised this in statements such as the following: 'In the part of *The General Theory* that was lost to standard economics as it evolved into the neoclassical synthesis, Keynes put forth an investment theory of fluctuations in real demand and a financial theory of fluctuations in real investment. Desired portfolio composition and thus financial relations in general are most clearly the areas of decision where changing views about the future can most quickly affect current behavior' (Minsky 1975: 57).

revealed in the price of shares, rather than by the genuine expectations of the professional entrepreneur' (151). With these stock exchange valuations subject to considerable variation due to speculation, the marginal efficiency of capital becomes rather volatile. But even for professional entrepreneurs the forecasts of prospective yields are subject to considerable error, and the feelings of confidence with which they are held can change substantially over brief intervals, with important consequences for investment decisions. It is in this connection that Keynes points to the importance of 'animal spirits' for major investment activity.

Even apart from the instability due to speculation, there is the instability due to the characteristic of human nature that a large proportion of our positive activities depend on spontaneous optimism rather than on a mathematical expectation, whether moral or hedonistic or economic. Most, probably, of our decisions to do something positive, the full consequences of which will be drawn out over many days to come, can only be taken as a result of animal spirits – of a spontaneous urge to action rather than inaction, and not as the outcome of a weighted average of quantitative benefits multiplied by quantitative probabilities. Enterprise only pretends to itself to be mainly actuated by the statements in its own prospectus, however candid and sincere. Only a little more than an expedition to the South Pole, is it based on an exact calculation of benefits to come. Thus if the animal spirits are dimmed and the spontaneous optimism falters, leaving us to depend on nothing but a mathematical expectation, enterprise will fade and die; – though fears of loss may have a basis no more reasonable than hopes of profit had before.   (161–2)

The critical point that Keynes keeps returning to is that decisions affecting the future are not only based on mathematical expectations. This is a point that blurs, to put it mildly, the picture of investment determined from an investment demand schedule based on such expectations. Keynes (144–5) had noted that borrower's and lender's risks must also be allowed for in using this schedule to determine investment, and when these magnitudes depend on the confidence with which estimates of prospective yields are made, the use of this schedule appears to be, in Robinson's words 'in the nature of a fudge'. She goes on to elaborate:

For a scheme of investment to be undertaken, the profit expected from it must exceed its interest-cost by a considerable margin to cover the risk involved. The prospective rate of profit on the finance to be committed can be reduced to equality with the relevant rate of interest only by subtracting a risk premium equal to the difference between them. To say that the required risk premium is low or high is then no more than saying that the propensity to invest is high or low.   (Robinson 1962: 37)

When Keynes tried to express 'the fundamental ideas which underlie my theory' (Keynes 1973c: 111), in his 1937 *Quarterly Journal of Economics* article, he emphasised the absence of reliable knowledge about future conditions, conditions that will determine the profitability of investment projects planned today. Without a secure foundation in knowledge that is held with a high degree of confidence, long-term expectations can be volatile. This is the reason Keynes gives for taking investment as the *causa causans* of his theory. 'But of these several factors [which determine aggregate output] it is those which determine the rate of investment which are most unreliable, since it is they which are influenced by our views of the future about which we know so little' (121).

4.7 CONCLUSION

There is a need to sift through Keynes's statements in order to separate out those that are directly relevant to his theory from those that are asides, that relate to a much broader inquiry, or that may be misleading. This is particularly evident in his treatment of consumption and investment. The essence of his theory, according to Keynes, is the demonstration that there is a very large number of potential (stable) short-period equilibrium positions, with only one displaying full employment of labour. The relevant position is determined by the economy's consumption function and the investment planned for the particular short period. The consumption function shows that consumption expenditures are positively related to income, with the marginal propensity to consume being less than unity. The value for this propensity determines the value of the investment multiplier, the change in the equilibrium aggregate output due to a unit change in investment. Keynes's ambiguous presentation of the multiplier, with its inclusion of the logical theory of this construct that makes use of the marginal propensity to consume in a definitional sense, does not pay sufficient attention to the time required for the multiplier process to be completed. This inconsistency in the use of the marginal propensity to consume – at times, it is a property of a functional relation, while at others it is definitional – may be a reflection of the confusion in Keynes's writings over the nature of the equality between saving and investment. These two flows must always be equal, given their definition in *The General Theory*, but there is also the further 'equality' that only holds in short-period equilibrium, where saving is in the desired relation to income.

Keynes appears to set out a definite functional relation between investment and the rate of interest, on the basis of the prospective yields from the use of capital goods in production. There are technical problems with his formulation of this investment demand schedule. It uses a mixture of *ex ante* and *ex post* elements, and is selective in its choice of the latter in order to arrive at a strong presumption that this schedule is negatively-sloped in the short period of the analysis. Insufficient attention is paid by Keynes to the time lag between investment decisions and investment in his analysis. With this time lag significant in real economies, the actual investment taking place in Keynes's short-period equilibrium is best seen as the investment planned in earlier periods for the present. Keynes's statements that long-term expectations are volatile because of the absence of reliable knowledge of future conditions, raise serious doubts about the adequacy of his own investment demand schedule as a vehicle for explaining the determination of investment.

There is an underlying tension in the exposition of *The General Theory* between the formal analysis that deals with short-period equilibrium positions, and the specific historical setting of a capitalist economy that is subject to cyclical behaviour – to booms and crises. This tension is also reflected in the different approaches used by Keynes in his consideration of the determination of investment. On the one hand there is a determinate investment demand schedule that, given alternative values for the rate of interest, shows the corresponding volumes of investment. On the other hand, there is a view of investment being determined by factors so potentially volatile, and subject to changes in mood induced by current events, that different values for the rate of interest cannot be assumed necessarily to leave the investment demand schedule unaffected.

One reason why Keynes's formal analysis ended with the consideration of equilibrium conditions in a particular period – even though he gives as the aim of his book 'the study of the forces which determine changes in the scale of output and employment as a whole' (Keynes 1936: vii) – may be that there was no way, given his vision of a capitalist economy, in which this analysis can be extended in any precise way to trace a path over time. The parameters which determine the values of the dependent variables are subject to unpredictable changes over time.[14] The formal attempt to show that

---

[14] This concern with the lack of constancy of parameter values over time surfaced, as Rowley (1988) has pointed out, in Keynes's comments on the proofs, and his review, of Tinbergen's study of the statistical testing of business cycle theories (Tinbergen 1939). In his comments on the proofs, Keynes observed: 'The coefficients arrived at are apparently assumed to be constant for 10 years or for a larger period. Yet, surely we know that they are not constant. There is no reason at all why they should not be different every year' (Keynes 1973c: 286).

an economy can generally be trapped in situations where there is considerable involuntary unemployment, without forces being released to move it towards full employment, thus leads to and ends with the consideration of short-period equilibrium positions. Changes over time are then dealt with in a suggestive manner, as in his notes on the trade cycle (313–32).

MONEY, FINANCE AND THE RATE OF INTEREST

5.1 INTRODUCTION

The General Theory is concerned with the operations of a monetary production economy, and the existence of money affects the analysis in an essential way. The technical details of money – details that had occupied considerable space in the *Treatise on Money* – are ignored, but the importance of money in the General Theory should not be underestimated. Its presence pervades the analysis, and it complements the historical setting of the particular short period considered by linking uncertain expectations about an unknown future to current employment. 'A monetary economy . . . is essentially one in which changing views about the future are capable of influencing the quantity of employment and not merely its direction' (Keynes 1936: vii). Money is held not only to facilitate transactions, but also as a store of value, as one of the assets in which wealth is held. It can serve this function, even though it earns little or no interest, because there are advantages to holding a part of wealth in money or near-monies when contracts are written in terms of money, as long as the purchasing power of money is expected to be relatively stable. The prices that will be obtained for bonds and physical assets, if they have to be sold at some future time, cannot be known because of the inescapable uncertainty over future conditions.

Equilibrium in the money market at any point in time requires that the money prices of financial assets be such that individual decision-making units in the economy are prepared to hold the mix of existing financial assets and money. The equilibrium rate of interest (or rather, equilibrium rates of interest, since they can differ for bonds of different maturities) at that point in time can then be calculated from these prices. Keynes shows this equilibrium rate of interest as being determined by the (stock) demand for money and its (stock) supply, where the term liquidity preference was used to represent the demand for money. Alternatively, it can be calculated from the money prices of bonds that equate the (stock) demand for bonds with their (stock) supply. The supplies of bonds and money can be changing at each point in time due, for example, to a difference between the creation of new financial securities and the expiry of old ones, and to the creation of money. Similarly, the demand for these assets would be increasing when net saving is positive. The demand for them would also be affected, of course, by changes in expectations. Competition in financial markets keeps the prices of, or rates of interest on, new and old securities, of equal maturity and reliability, identical. But since the changes in the available supplies of securities in any short period are small relative to the existing supplies, it is the public's attitude to the holding of these stocks of securities (or money) that determines the rates of interest. The rates of interest on new securities must, of course, conform to the rates on existing securities. Keynes's position on this point and his emphasis on the overwhelming importance of the stock relation in determining the prices of securities, had already been stated in the *Treatise on Money*: 'the decision as to holding bank-deposits or securities relates, not only to the current increment to the wealth of individuals, but also to the whole block of their existing capital. Indeed, since the current increment is but a trifling proportion of the block of existing wealth, it is but a minor element in the matter' (Keynes 1930a: 141).

The focus of attention in *The General Theory* on the stock demand for the holding of money is a logical outcome of the setting of its model in historical time, where the uncertain knowledge of future conditions cannot be ignored, and there is a role for money as a store of wealth. This attention also serves the polemical purpose of denying a key postulate of the classical theory that has the rate of interest determined by the demand for, and supply of, current saving. According to classical theory the rate of interest would adjust so as to equate saving and investment, where both these variables are functionally related to the rate of interest. This adjustment in the rate of interest, which would increase investment if the propensity to save increased, was an important element in the analytical argument that strong forces would be set in motion to move the economy back towards full employment under these conditions. With the rate of interest being determined in the money market, independently of current investment and saving, the basis for such a force is taken away. It is the variation in output that is given the role of restoring the equilibrium equality between saving and investment. The resulting equilibrium output may be too low to provide full employment of labour and productive capacity.

Keynes assumed in *The General Theory* that the money supply is exogenously determined by the monetary authority, even though he had observed in the *Treatise* (e.g. Keynes 1930b: 211) that the amount of bank money was very much influenced by the decisions of individuals in the economy. Keynes returned to this *Treatise* position in his 1937 and 1938 papers on finance, when he saw the need to sketch the mechanism that allowed investment to be independent of saving. It was the flexibility of the banking system, with its readiness to meet an increased demand for credit, that made it possible for firms to obtain the finance needed to increase investment prior to an increase in saving. These papers on finance were part of an exchange with Ohlin, Robertson and Hawtrey in which Keynes was determined not to allow the determination of the rate of interest to be seen as the outcome of the equilibrium adjustment of saving and investment, dressed up in the guise of the supply and demand for loanable funds. Some of the problems with Keynes's formulation of his theory that we have noted in previous chapters: the neglect of the time required for the multiplier process to be completed, and the confusion between an identity and an equilibrium equality, reappear in his responses to critics of his theory of interest.

5.2 THE DEMAND FOR MONEY

A monetary economy is one where transactions are made, and contracts are written, in terms of money. By this means firms try to control their costs of production, and where possible their sales revenues, in a world where knowledge of many future conditions is uncertain. It is the writing of contracts in which money is used to meet commitments and extinguish debts that marks for Keynes the essential difference between a barter and a money economy (Keynes 1930a: 3–5). Under the category of 'contracts' he includes debts, which are acknowledgements of obligations to make payments in some future intervals of time, and price lists that specify the terms at which goods and services may be bought and sold until some specified time in the future, or until further notice. We have seen in the preceding chapter that monetary considerations played an important role in Keynes's treatment of the determination of investment, because the production and purchase of capital goods involves the assumption of debts with their attendant obligations. (This same choice between capital goods and financial assets is also made when a firm uses its retained earnings to finance capital goods, because these earnings could have been used to purchase debt instruments.) The rates of interest that holders of these debt contracts obtain are affected by long-term expectations. The uncertainty over future conditions that influence these expectations may, at times, lead to levels of the rate of interest that result in rates of investment which are insufficient to provide full employment.

The economic model in *The General Theory* contained a banking system, supervised by a central bank, that provided the money supply in the economy. Keynes noted that '[a]s a rule, I shall, as in my *Treatise on Money*, assume that money is co-extensive with bank deposits' (Keynes 1936: 167n). A person holding a sum of money has immediate command over goods equal to the purchasing power of that sum. An individual holding some other assets, whether financial such as bonds, or physical, such as buildings, also has potential command over goods, but it is not immediate command, because these assets must first be sold in order for such command to be obtained. Keynes uses the term 'liquid' to signify 'immediate' in this context. He writes that an individual who has saved must decide whether he wants to hold his savings, or a portion of them, 'in the form of immediate, liquid command' (166). There is a definitional problem here, because 'immediate' need not be the same as 'instantaneous'. Financial assets do exist, such as 30-day treasury bills, that can be turned into cash with no capital loss, within a very short period of time. If they are not 'money', then they are certainly 'near-monies' that can serve many of the purposes of the former. Keynes, before adopting his 'rule' on what is covered by the term 'money', recognised this problem:

we can draw the line between 'money' and 'debts' at whatever point is most convenient for handling a particular problem. For example, we can treat as *money* any command over general purchasing power which the owner has not parted with for a period in excess of three months, and as *debt* what cannot be recovered for a longer period than this; or we can substitute for 'three months' one month or three days or three hours or any other period; or we can exclude from *money* whatever is not legal tender on the spot. It is often convenient in practice to include in *money* time-deposits with banks and, occasionally, even such instruments as (e.g.) treasury bills.   (167n)

Once the line between money and debts has been drawn, then the demand for money, or for liquidity (the two terms are used synonymously by Keynes) is analysed by means of a liquidity preference function. The arguments that make an explicit appearance in this function are the rate of interest and the level of income. The rate of interest can be seen as the opportunity cost of holding money, while the level of income indicates the demand for money for transactions purposes.[1] It is convenient to have money on hand for personal and business expenses. Keynes calls this the 'transactions-motive' for holding cash. In addition, there is a demand for money as a store of wealth, a demand whose 'necessary condition is the existence of *uncertainty* as to the future of the rate of interest, *i.e.* as to the complex of rates of interest for varying maturities which will rule at future dates' (168). An individual who switches some of his money assets into the holding of bonds will gain interest income, but if at some time in the future before they mature additional immediate command over goods is required, then these bonds will have to be sold. If interest rates have increased in the interval, the prices they fetch may be sufficiently low to have made the holding of cash a preferable course of action in the circumstances. Uncertainty over future conditions – a double uncertainty in this case, since it involves the possibility of the need for additional cash at some unknown time and the prevailing interest rate at that time – thus gives rise to a 'precautionary-motive' for holding money. Keynes attaches particular importance to another reason for holding money when the uncertainty over future conditions leads to different views about the behaviour of interest rates. Individuals who have expectations about future interest rates that differ from those reflected in current bond prices, switch from holding bonds to holding money, and vice versa, depending on how their expectations differ. If they expect future rates of interest to be higher (and thus bond prices to be lower) than those assumed by the market (as reflected in current bond prices), they have an incentive to sell bonds and hold cash. Conversely, individuals who feel that interest rates will fall, and bond prices will rise, have an incentive to borrow short-term funds and use them to purchase bonds. This is the basis for Keynes's 'speculative-motive' for holding money, 'the object of securing profit from knowing better than the market what the future will bring forth' (170).

When no adjective is used to qualify the rate of interest, Keynes is referring to 'the complex of the various rates of interest current for different periods of time, *i.e.* for debts of different maturities' (167). These are all long-term rates, and their explanation requires consideration of the terms at which the public is prepared to hold long-term securities, while short-term rates are said to be 'easily controlled by the monetary authority' (203). The term structure of interest rates can thus be changed by changes in the public's demand

---

[1] Keynes often describes this liquidity preference function with only the rate of interest being given explicit recognition. It is not always clear in such cases that the level of income is constant (e.g. Keynes 1936: 205).

for securities. Keynes noted that if the central bank was prepared to deal extensively in the markets for long-term securities, then it could determine, subject to certain limitations, this term structure. But '[T]he monetary authority often tends in practice to concentrate upon short-term debts and to leave the price of long-term debts to be influenced by belated and imperfect reactions from the price of short-term debts' (206). His theory of interest is thus concerned with these long-term rates. In the *Treatise* Keynes used the term 'Bank-rate' for 'the complex of interest rates effective in the market at any time for the borrowing and lending of money for short periods' (Keynes 1930a: 200). The term 'Bond-rate' was used 'to designate the complex of interest rates effective in the market for the borrowing and lending of money for longer periods; and we shall use the term "market rate of interest" for the complex of bank-rate and bond-rate' (201). Keynes in *The General Theory*, given his *Treatise* terminology, is concerned with the factors determining the 'Bond-rate' of interest.

In *The General Theory*, Keynes usually combines the precautionary and transactions motives into a single function with only the level of income as an explicit argument (e.g. Keynes 1936: 199). His observation in the 1937 *Quarterly Journal of Economics* article that 'our desire to hold money as a store of wealth is a barometer of the degree of our distrust of our own calculations and conventions concerning the future' (Keynes 1973c: 116), casts doubt on the usefulness of this procedure, since the precautionary motive is not only related to the level of income. With its source in uncertain knowledge of future conditions, the precautionary motive has important similarities to the speculative motive. The difference Kahn sees between them is that 'in principle the precautionary motive can be said to operate in so far as some persons think that the rate of interest is likely to move; the speculative motive in so far as some persons think that on balance it is likely to move one way rather than the other' (Kahn 1954: 81). In practice though, this distinction is blurred, and Kahn finds it impossible 'to identify the quantity of money held on account of the speculative motive as something different from the quantity of money held on account of the precautionary motive. The two motives do not act additively: the demand for money is a complicated outcome of their interplay' (85).

Shackle combines the precautionary motive with the speculative motive, by redefining the latter to make it coextensive with the reason that allows money to serve as a store of wealth. That reason is uncertainty over future interest rates, or 'doubt about how their price [i.e. the price of bonds] may behave. But *that* doubt is merely the speculative motive. When we have properly conceived and expressed the transactions motive and the speculative motive for holding a stock of money, no separate precautionary motive remains' (Shackle 1967: 205). Harrod keeps these two motives separate, but he considers the precautionary motive to be both important and dependent on the rate of interest, so that there are important similarities between his position and those of Kahn and Shackle. 'I would suggest that ... there is at any time a large amount of money held for the precautionary motive ... There will be a much stronger case for caution if the loss of interest is moderate (owing to its rate being low) and the risk of a loss of capital value, if securities are bought, correspondingly high' (Harrod 1969: 173).

The demand for money to satisfy each of the three motives is inversely related to the rate of interest, given expectations and the level of income. The higher the rate of interest, the higher the opportunity cost of holding money for transactions purposes, and the velocity of circulation can vary to mitigate the effects of this increase. There could also be a cutback on cash held for precautionary purposes, as the higher cost of such funds is weighed against a given degree of uncertainty. The speculative motive for holding cash would also be weakened, because with expectations of possible future interest rates unchanged, the higher the current rate, the lower the expected gain from delaying the purchase of bonds until some future time. Even though an argument can be made, in this way, for the effects of the rate of interest on each of these motives for holding money, it was to the speculative motive that Keynes looked for significant responses to changes in the rate of interest:[2] 'experience indicates that the aggregate demand for money to satisfy the speculative-motive usually shows a continuous response to gradual changes in the rate of interest' (Keynes 1936: 197). This statement refers to situations where there is no change in long-term expectations. These expectations are generally diverse, and they could differ substantially from individual to individual. The gradual change in the rate of interest, say a fall, means that fewer persons now expect a further fall, while more expect this rate to rise. As a consequence the speculative demand for money increases. Those individuals who expect the rate of interest to fall (the price of bonds to rise) were referred to as 'bulls' in the *Treatise on Money*, while those who expect

---

[2] Even though Kahn, as noted above, found it impossible to distinguish the money held for the precautionary motive from that held for the speculative motive, he concluded that only the latter was responsive to changes in the rate of interest (Kahn 1954: 87).

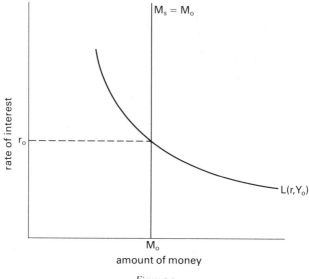

Figure 5.1

the rate of interest to rise (the price of bonds to fall) were referred to
as 'bears' (Keynes 1930a: 250). In an equilibrium position, the rate of
interest is such that the two conflicting views, those of the bulls and
bears, offset each other. 'The market price [of bonds] will be fixed at
the point at which the sales of the "bears" and the purchases of the
"bulls" are balanced' (Keynes 1936: 170).

Keynes noted that at very low levels for the rate of interest, the
small income gains from holding bonds, would be outweighed by the
fears of large capital losses. In this case, 'liquidity preference may
become virtually absolute in the sense that almost everyone prefers
cash to holding a debt which yields so low a rate of interest. In this
event the monetary authority would have lost effective control over
the rate of interest. But whilst this limiting case might become
practically important in future, I know of no example of it hitherto'
(207). This possibility is, of course, the 'liquidity trap', of which
much was made in the Keynesian literature, but it played no role in
Keynes's analysis.

The shape of the liquidity preference function is illustrated in
figure 5.1. The level of income is Y_0 for the particular function shown,
and there would be a different curve for each level of income. The
schedule shifts to the right for higher income, and to the left for lower
income. Keynes's usage in this regard leaves something to be desired,

because in certain places his analysis was concerned with shifting schedules, even though he only referred to a single schedule. For example:

As a rule, we can suppose that the schedule of liquidity-preference relating the quantity of money to the rate of interest is given by a smooth curve which shows the rate of interest falling as the quantity of money is increased. For there are several different causes all leading towards this result. In the first place, as the rate of interest falls, it is likely, *cet.par.*, that more money will be absorbed by liquidity-preferences due to the transactions-motive. For if the fall in the rate of interest increases the national income, the amount of money which it is convenient to keep for transactions will be increased more or less proportionately to the increase in income; whilst, at the same time, the cost of the convenience of plenty of ready cash in terms of loss of interest will be diminished ... In the second place, every fall in the rate of interest may, as we have just seen, increase the quantity of cash which certain individuals will wish to hold because their views as to the future of the rate of interest differ from the market views. (171–2)

The first consideration mentioned by Keynes in the above quotation refers to a shift in the liquidity preference schedule, and not to its shape. It is only the second point that deals with the shape of the curve that is obtained from this schedule.

The equilibrium rate of interest in Keynes's theory is determined by the intersection of the stock demand and supply curve for money, as in figure 5.1.[3] The rate of interest 'is the "price" which equilibrates the desire to hold wealth in the form of cash with the available quantity of cash' (167). Alternatively, it can be seen as 'the reward for parting with liquidity for a specified period', because it is earned by exchanging liquid command over goods for the deferred command represented by a bond. As with all exchanges of this type the equilibrium equality can be restated in terms of the item exchanged for money, that is, with reference to the demand and supply of debts.

---

[3] Keynes's theory of interest can, alternatively, be presented in terms of the prices for bonds (securities) that equate the aggregate demand for bonds with their total supply. It is from this perspective that Kahn (1954: 80) states the 'essence' of this theory.

The extent to which the banks hold securities, finance the holders of securities, and finance the holding of physical assets, is equal to the quantity of money. The quantity of money is the means by which the public hold that part of their wealth which is looked after by the banking system. The prices of securities are such as to secure a home for all of them with the public, apart from what the banking system looks after itself. That is the essence of the Keynes liquidity preference theory of the rate of interest, the supply and demand for money being the obverse of the supply of securities in the hands of the public and the demand for securities by the public.

It is equality between the demand and supply of loans of money, *i.e.* of debts, which is brought about by the rate of interest (186n).

Keynes implies in *The General Theory* that the supply of money is exogenously determined. For example, he writes that 'an increase in the quantity of money will have to lower the rate of interest almost forthwith' (171), an increase that has obviously not been brought about by an increase in the demand for money. He later states that 'the quantity of money is not determined by the public' (174). This represents a position quite different from the one he took in the *Treatise*, where the savings deposits portion of money was seen to depend 'upon the comparative attractions, in the mind of the depositor, of this and of alternative securities' (Keynes 1930a: 38). We shall see below (section 5.7) that Keynes in his post-*General Theory* writings gives an important role in determining the money supply to the demands by firms for finance to help cover the cost of investment expenditures. In *The General Theory* there was recognition that changes in the supply of money could affect the demand for money, through repercussions on the expectations that help determine the position of the liquidity preference schedule, such as the one drawn in figure 5.1. Changes in the supply of money might thus not have the effects on the rate of interest that can be deduced from such figures, since they assume that the liquidity schedule is independent of the supply of money. 'circumstances can develop in which even a large increase in the quantity of money may exert a comparatively small influence on the rate of interest. For a large increase in the quantity of money may cause so much uncertainty about the future that liquidity-preference due to the precautionary-motive may be strengthened' (Keynes 1936: 172).

A careful reader of *The General Theory* would not have been surprised to find that in the late 1970s and early 1980s, publication of data showing substantial increases in the money supply resulted in higher interest rates because of their effects on expectations. The monetary authorities were not in a position to determine the rate of interest by increasing the supply of money along an *unchanged* liquidity preference function. The experience of very low and even negative real rates of interest in the period 1973–80, as the rate of inflation exceeded the rate of interest, disrupted bond markets. This eroded the ability of the monetary authorities to determine the rate of interest by increasing the supply of money. It was not only the increase in uncertainty about the future mentioned by Keynes that shifted the liquidity function, but also the belief that substantial increases in the money supply would have inflationary consequences for the future that would lead to higher interest rates. This belief, whether justified or not, meant that the announcement of increases in the measures of monetary aggregates would result in interest rate changes in the same direction. Bond prices would fall until they reached lower levels at which fears of possible future capital loss were sufficiently dulled, given interest income, to permit the continued holding of the mass of existing bonds.

There are important similarities between the liquidity preference function and the marginal efficiency of capital. They have the appearance of serviceable functions that between them, with the addition of the money supply, determine the rate of interest and the level of investment. Keynes uses them in this way, at times, to suggest a neat self-contained model, but lurking beneath the surfaces of both are expectations of an unknown future, expectations that are volatile and that can shift these functions erratically.[4] It is these shifts, as much as, or even more than, the functions themselves, that are of importance in determining the rates of interest and investment. This was emphasised by Keynes in his 1937 *Quarterly Journal of Economics* article when he wrote:

It is not surprising that the volume of investment ... should fluctuate widely from time to time. For it depends on two sets of judgments about the future, neither of which rests on an adequate or secure foundation – on the propensity to hoard and on opinions of the future yield of capital assets ... Indeed, the conditions which aggravate the one factor tend, as a rule, to aggravate the other. For the same circumstances which lead to pessimistic views about future yields are apt to increase the propensity to hoard.

(Keynes 1973c: 118)

The ambivalence in Keynes's analysis – the development of a formal structure, and then the making of observations that place its significance in doubt – already noted in his approach to investment, gives rise to different interpretations of his analysis. There is, for example, Hicks's IS-LM approach that concentrates on possible equilibrium positions, given stable functions. But if emphasis is placed on the importance of changeable expectations, expectations that cannot be explained by the model, then there are important limits to the scope for this type of formal analysis. It becomes necessary for economists to pay more attention to the historical, social, and institutional frameworks within which investment decisions are made and interest rates are determined.

---

[4] Vicarelli (1984: 138) points to uncertainty as this 'fundamental link striking at the two functions' very existence and their significance'.

5.3 THE CLASSICAL THEORY OF INTEREST

Keynes views the classical theory as holding that the rate of interest is determined by the demand and supply for current saving. This demand is investment demand, 'the demand for [the command over?] investible resources and saving represents the supply, whilst the rate of interest is the "price" of [the command over?] investible resources at which the two are equated' (Keynes 1936: 175). The independent functions in this theory are the investment demand schedule, which shows this demand to be inversely related to the rate of interest, and the supply schedule of saving, which shows this supply to be positively related to the rate of interest.[5] But these two schedules cannot determine the rate of interest, because in this specification they are not independent. The supply of saving also depends on income, which in turn is a function of investment. Shifts in the investment demand schedule will cause shifts in the saving supply schedule. Keynes considers that this classical theory is incomplete on its own grounds, because there are two variables to be determined, the rate of interest and the level of income, and only the single equation that shows investment equal to saving. (It can be saved from this charge of incompleteness if there were forces that always acted to maintain the level of income at some fixed value, such as the full employment value, in spite of disturbances like those emanating from the investment function. Keynes's analysis denies the existence of such forces. There is no reason to expect that the rate of interest, which is determined largely independently of the current investment and saving flows, will have the value required to bring about full employment.) It is to his liquidity preference function that he turns in order to complete this system: 'If, however, we introduce the state of liquidity preference and the quantity of money and these between them tell us that the rate of interest is [a particular value], then the whole position becomes determinate' (181). This statement could have been better phrased, since it appears to imply that the demand for money depends only on the rate of interest and not on the level of income as well, but the conclusion would be unaffected by the recognition of this dependence. There would be two independent

---

[5] It had been recognised, as Keynes noted, by economists in the 'classical' tradition, e.g. Marshall and Cassel, that a higher rate of interest might not lead to higher saving. A change in the rate of interest has an income as well as a substitution effect, and it is only the latter that leads without exception to a change in saving in the same direction as the change in the rate of interest. The former may act to lower saving when the rate of interest is higher.

equations to determine the two unknowns, since the supply of money is assumed to be an exogenous variable.

The fundamental objection to the classical theory of interest that arises from the analysis in *The General Theory* is that the former mistakenly looks for the determinants of the rate of interest in the current *flows* of investment and saving. But its determinants are the *stock* of money in existence, and the terms at which the public is prepared to hold this stock (or alternatively, the stock of securities and the terms at which the public is prepared to hold this stock). There is only one rate of interest, in the highly-developed capital markets assumed by Keynes, for securities of the same length of maturity (and lender's risk). The stock of old securities and the mass of money existing at each point in time so far exceed the new securities issued and the current flow of saving, that this rate is determined in the markets for the former. Securities prices (for both old and new securities) are dominated by the terms at which old securities can continue to be held. The interest rate that can be earned by current saving, or that which must be paid by those issuing new securities to finance investment, is thus dependent on these flows only indirectly, through their effects on the level of income or long-term expectations, and thus on the demand for money.

Keynes did not express this fundamental difference between the two theories of interest in a particularly revealing way. 'The mistake [in the classical theory] originates from regarding interest as the reward for waiting as such, instead of as the reward for not hoarding' (182). The problem with this statement is that interest can also be seen as the reward for saving that is not hoarded.[6] The market rate of interest can be an inducement for an act of saving (i.e. waiting) with the saving invested in bonds. 'Hoarding' is not a good expression for the demand for money that is often held only temporarily, as far as individual motives are concerned. Thus 'the reward for not-hoarding' does not help to convey the sense of the interest rate as the price that induces those who own wealth to be content to hold the existing stock of securities, with the remaining portion of financial wealth being held in money.

Keynes often places difficulties in the way of his readers because he did not make clear the assumptions on which his statements depend.

---

[6] Viner, in his review of *The General Theory*, adopted this position: 'The rate of interest is the return for saving without liquidity' (Viner 1936: 157). Robertson (1937: 431) put this in terms of the satisfaction of two margins: 'The fact that the rate of interest measures the marginal convenience of holding idle money need not prevent it from measuring *also* the marginal inconvenience of abstaining from consumption'.

For example, in emphasising that an act of saving does not result in an equal act of investment because the latter is a function of prospective yield, a yield that is not increased by this act of saving, he points to money and debts as ways of holding wealth that are alternatives to the ownership of real capital assets. The yields of each of these ways of holding wealth are being continuously reassessed, with the current rate of interest as the starting point for the calculation of the minimum prospective yield of real capital assets that is required to ensure their production. Keynes then states clearly and succinctly his theory of the determination of the rate of interest: 'the current rate of interest depends, as we have seen, not on the strength of the desire to hold wealth, but on the strengths of the desires to hold it in liquid and in illiquid forms respectively, coupled with the amount of the supply of wealth in the one form relatively to the supply of it in the other' (213). What follows, however, is a challenge that raises more questions than it answers, because it implies, contrary to Keynes's own theory, that an increase in the propensity to save will leave the level of income unchanged.

'If the reader still finds himself perplexed, let him ask himself why, the quantity of money being unchanged, a fresh act of saving should diminish the sum which it is desired to keep in liquid form at the existing rate of interest'. According to his theory the rate of interest will be decreased by this 'fresh act of saving' only if the desire for liquidity is decreased. But what does he mean by 'a fresh act of saving', and what other changes take place that allow saving to be higher? If it is an actual increase in saving that is due to an increase in the propensity to save, with no increase in intended investment, then it must be matched by an equal increase in investment, an increase that will be the result initially of unintended increases in inventories of unsold goods. This will not, however, be the end of the story, as firms adjust production to the lower demand for their goods. With a lower income, the transactions demand for money will also be lower, and thus there will be a diminution in 'the sum which it is desired to keep in liquid form at the existing rate of interest'. This answer, drawn from his own theory, does not appear to be the one Keynes expects the reader to give. The wording of the challenge implies that there will be no decrease in the demand for liquidity, and thus with the supply of money unchanged there would be no change in the rate of interest. But this will only be the case if the 'fresh act of saving' is accompanied by a fresh act of intended investment, so that the new short-period equilibrium situation has the same income and employment as the old. The only immediate change is in the mix of production of consumption and capital goods. This would also be the outcome that can be deduced from the classical theory of interest for these assumptions. The independent shifts in the propensities to save and to invest cancel out their individual effects on the rate of interest and output.

5.4 THE 'SAFE' RATE OF INTEREST

Keynes's theory of interest cannot be properly understood without reference to the setting of his model in historical time. The expectations and concerns about a future that cannot be known, which are the bases for the precautionary and speculative motives, are very much affected by the details of past experience. The liquidity preference function – the position of the L-curve in figure 5.1 above – is thus influenced by recent history. Keynes expresses this in terms of views about 'safe' or 'conventional' levels of the rate of interest, views that are dependent on past experience. In explaining the speculative motive for holding money, he writes that 'what matters is not the *absolute* level of r but the degree of its divergence from what is considered a fairly *safe* level of r' (201). This level is then used to explain why the monetary authority might experience difficulty in bringing about substantial reductions in the long-term rate of interest, in contrast to its ability to control the short-term rate. 'But the long-term rate may be more recalcitrant when once it has fallen to a level which, on the basis of past experience and present expectations of *future* monetary policy, is considered "unsafe" by representative opinion' (203).

It is this view of a 'fairly safe' or 'conventional' level for the value of the rate of interest that provides an 'anchor' for the liquidity preference function. 'It might be more accurate, perhaps, to say that the rate of interest is a highly conventional, rather than a highly psychological phenomenon. For its actual value is largely governed by the prevailing view as to what its value is expected to be. *Any* level of interest which is accepted with sufficient conviction as *likely* to be durable *will* be durable; subject, of course, in a changing society to fluctuations for all kinds of reasons round the expected normal'.

Keynes did not go on, as might have been expected, to discuss the factors determining the 'safe' or 'conventional' level of the rate of interest. The value for this level remained purely subjective in his analysis, and thus it was very susceptible to the changing winds of opinion. Keynes explained why Wicksell's 'natural' rate of interest, or the version of it that appears in his own *Treatise*, could not serve as the anchor for the liquidity preference function. Different positions of short-period equilibrium are generally characterised by differences in the rate of interest, as well as in employment. Given the consumption function and the marginal efficiency of capital, a particular rate of interest can be said to be the 'natural' rate of interest for the corresponding equilibrium level of employment. But each rate of interest could also be considered under these conditions a 'natural' rate for its associated levels of investment and employment: 'for every rate of interest there is a level of employment for which that rate is the "natural" rate, in the sense that the system will be in equilibrium with that rate of interest and that level of employment' (242). If one of these 'natural' rates of interest is associated with the level of employment that is the full employment level, then Keynes suggests that it could be called the 'neutral' rate of interest. But since his analysis leads to the conclusion that the full employment position is only one of many possible positions of equilibrium, there is no reason why expectations would, in general, be focused on the 'neutral' rate as the 'safe' rate of interest.[7]

Keynes, in correctly emphasising that the long-term rate of interest is determined by the stock demand and supply for securities, neglected the extent to which the long-term expectations that are important determinants of this demand can be affected by current and projected flows. If, given the propensity to save, and expected income levels, the resulting saving flows are seen to be smaller than the expected rates of planned investment (as indicated, for example, by national surveys) at specified interest rates, then expectations of rising rates of interest will be reflected in higher current rates. Current rates of interest are affected because these long-term expectations will influence the terms at which the public is prepared to hold the existing stock of securities. It is in this way that the factors of productivity and thrift, which Robertson (e.g. 1936: 178) kept emphasising as determinants of the rate of interest, can enter into Keynes's analysis. The yields expected from the ownership of capital goods, their net productivity, are important determinants of the demand for loans, while forecasts of saving in the economy over time, in relation to the expected demands for loans will influence the terms at which wealth owners are prepared to hold long-term debts. Harrod (1948: 67) saw this as a way in which there could be some reconciliation between the approaches of Keynes and Robertson: 'I

---

[7] Harrod (1969: 183) stresses the importance of Keynes's neutral rate of interest, but he does not endow it with any of the 'anchoring' properties attributed here to the 'safe' or 'conventional' rate of interest.

do not think that Keynes compels us to suppose that the market in brooding upon future prices, and on the uncertainties thereof, pays no regard whatever to Professor Robertson's productivity and thrift.'

5.5 THE RATE OF INTEREST AND EMPLOYMENT

With the explanation of the factors determining the rate of investment, Keynes completes the formal model for the determination of employment in *The General Theory*. The level of investment was taken as given in the set of equations used to illustrate his theory of effective demand in chapter 3 above, but it can now be shown as one of the unknowns, with its value being determined by the marginal efficiency of capital and the rate of interest. Keynes kept emphasising that this value for the level of investment, given the propensity to consume, may not be sufficient to result in a short-period equilibrium with full employment. Changes in the economy, with the passage of time, result in a series of short-period equilibrium positions, but there was no reason to expect that the factors determining the level of employment would change in such a way as to bring about full employment. The rate of interest, determined by the demand and supply conditions for money, may not take the value that, given the marginal efficiency of capital, is consistent with the full employment level of investment. It might not even be possible to use monetary policy to bring about changes in the rate of interest that result in higher investment and employment, because of possible adverse effects on long-term expectations. The level of investment is likely to fluctuate as a direct result of the variability of these expectations, and there is nothing in the operations of a capitalist economy to anchor these fluctuations in investment to values that are consistent with full employment.

It is now possible to display Keynes's formal model in a set of equations that depict a situation of short-period equilibrium. The associated employment could, of course, differ from the full employment level. The set of equations to be presented here is an expanded version of the set used in chapter 3 to illustrate Keynes's initial presentation of his theory of effective demand. The first three of the equations in chapter 3 are repeated here, but it is now possible to give separate treatment to the determinants of effective demand. With the equations representing a situation of short-period equilibrium, short-term expectations of proceeds are born out by realised results. The expectation of proceeds Z, in equation (3.6) can thus be replaced by Y_w, the gross national product (the sum of wages and gross profits) measured in wage-units. This equation embodies, as we have seen,

the short-period technical relations of production, since it is concep-
tually based on the marginal cost curves of individual firms. Instead
of the single equation for total aggregate demand, we now have
separate equations for its two components, consumption (C_w) and
investment (I_w), each measured in wage-units. The national income
identity – gross national product is equal to gross national expenditure (the sum of consumption and investment expenditures) – is here
also given an equilibrium interpretation. This is possible, because the
realised gross national product is assumed to be equal to the
expectations of proceeds that gave rise to the level of employment
shown in the equations, while the values for both consumption and
investment expenditures are 'desired' values that are given by their
respective functions. The set of equations is then completed by
showing the equality between the demand for money and its supply,
which is taken to be determined exogenously. The equations are:

$$N_s = S\,(w/P_w) \quad (3.3); \quad w/P_w = H\,(N) \quad (3.4); \quad N \leq N_s;\; \bar{w} = w \;\;(3.5);$$
$$Y_w = g\,(N) \qquad (5.1); \quad C_w = C(Y_w) \qquad (5.2); \quad I_w = I(r) \qquad (5.3);$$
$$Y_w = C_w + I_w \quad (5.4); \quad Y = wY_w \qquad (5.5); \quad M = L\,(r,\,Y) \;\;(5.6);$$
$$M = \bar{M} \qquad\qquad (5.7).$$

There are 10 equations in this set to determine the 10 unknowns
(N_s, N, w, P_w, Y_w, C_w, I_w, r, Y, M). There is, in Keynes's theory, no
reason to expect that the level of employment (N) in the equilibrium
situation depicted would be equal to the amount of labour that
workers would want to supply (N_s) at the equilibrium real-wage rate.
Investment and consumption expenditures may not be sufficient to
bring about full employment. These equations are used to represent a
situation of short-period equilibrium. They cannot be readily manipulated to indicate how a change in one variable, e.g. the money-wage
rate, will affect the level of employment, because it cannot be assumed
that such a change will necessarily leave the forms of the functions in
the equations unchanged. For example, adverse changes in long-term
expectations, and thus in investment, might result from some of the
consequences of falling money-wage rates. The distinct possibility of
unemployment equilibrium, because of the unreliability and volatility
of investment is the 'central message' of the General Theory.

5.6 THE ESSENTIAL PROPERTIES OF INTEREST AND MONEY

In his formal model Keynes took for granted that investment in
physical assets had to pass the 'test' of the rate of interest on money.
The rates of return expected from the ownership of these assets had to

be at least equal to this rate of interest. Knowledge of the operations of capitalist economies and the ways in which investment decisions were made by firms, as well as the pervasiveness of the money rate of interest, provided the support for this implicit assumption. Keynes, in chapter 17 of *The General Theory*, paused to consider why money and its rate of interest should have this crucial role when an 'own-rate of interest' can be discerned for each commodity. This matter was an 'aside' as far as the General Theory was concerned, albeit an important aside for those trying to make clear the special role of money in the economy. Details of Keynes's treatment have been the subject of criticism (e.g. Lerner (1952)),[8] but only a relatively brief examination of the points raised by Keynes in this chapter will be presented.

Keynes went outside the analytical boundaries of his model in this chapter by considering what might happen when conditions are stable over an interval of time that is long enough for the production of capital assets in that interval to have a substantial effect on their total supply.[9] Some of the short-period equilibrium situations he referred to are mired in stationary conditions in which the properties of money lead to its becoming a 'bottomless sink for purchasing power'. There is, however, an implicit assumption of uncertainty over future conditions, because money is also being held as a store of wealth. As Keynes (1937a: 116) wrote: 'our desire to hold money as a store of wealth is a barometer of the degree of our distrust of our own calculations and conventions concerning the future'. The liquidity premium for money relative to other financial assets is thus dependent on the features of historical time. The relative stickiness of money-wage rates in the face of short-period variations in output is also a requirement for this liquidity premium.

An 'own-rate of interest' for a commodity, expressed in terms of itself, can be defined for any commodity that can be borrowed for an interval of time. This rate of interest is simply the difference between the amount that has to be repaid and the amount borrowed, divided by the amount borrowed. (The own-rate of interest of money, expressed in terms of money, is what has been referred to above simply as the rate of interest.) For example, in a situation where

---

[8] Robinson (1965: 138) noted that '[W]hen Keynes was writing ... chapter [17], he admitted that he was groping for ideas that were new to him, and I do not think that he ever quite succeeded in seizing them'.

[9] Potestio (1986) has emphasised the difference in the explanation of unemployment equilibrium to be found in chapter 17 from that in chapters 1–15 and 18–21.

wheat is expected to be in shorter supply next year, it might be possible to borrow 100 bushels of wheat this year, with only 98 bushels having to be repaid next year. The own-rate of interest for wheat, measured in terms of itself, is thus minus 2 per cent per year. Keynes first illustrated own-rates of interest for market equilibrium[10] situations in which arbitrage[11] in spot and forward markets had resulted in prices that equated all own-rates of interest expressed in the same commodity (Conard 1959: 129n). With an own-rate of interest for wheat measured in terms of itself of minus 2 per cent, the money-rate of interest in terms of wheat can also be shown to be minus 2 per cent under these equilibrium conditions.

In Keynes's example that illustrated the above property, the spot price of 100 units of wheat was £100 while the forward price one year hence was £107, and the money-rate of interest was 5 per cent. The £100 in the first year, which can purchase 100 units of wheat is equivalent to £105 in the second year, but this amount can only purchase about 98 ($= \frac{105}{107} \cdot 100$) units of wheat.[12] The rate of interest for money, when it is expressed in terms of wheat, is thus minus 2 per cent per year. From the same data it is possible to show that the own-rate of interest of wheat, measured in terms of money, is 5 per cent per year. The 100 units of wheat in the first year, which can

purchase £100 spot, is equivalent to 98 (or more precisely $\frac{105}{107} \cdot 100$) units of wheat in the second year. This amount of wheat can purchase £105, and thus the own-rate of interest of wheat in terms of money is 5 per cent.

For each numeraire there will, in general, be a different own-rate of interest, as in the above example of wheat and money. With so many possible interest rates to choose from, why accord so much prominence to the rate of interest for money, expressed in terms of itself? Keynes (1936: 223–4) argued

---

[10] The term 'market equilibrium' is used in its Marshallian sense, to indicate a situation in which market prices have adjusted to given quantities of the commodities. The relevant period is too short to allow any changes in the rates at which the various commodities are being produced.

[11] In these examples we abstract from transactions costs in spot and forward markets.

[12] Keynes used approximate numbers in his illustration. A forward price for 100 units of slightly more than £107 would be needed to give a value of 98 units for the amount of wheat that can be purchased on the forward market for £105.

that it is the *greatest* of these rates of interest ... which rules the roost (because it is the greatest of these rates that the marginal efficiency of a capital-asset must attain if it is to be newly produced); and ... there are reasons why it is the money-rate of interest which is often the greatest (because ... certain forces, which operate to reduce the own-rates of interest of other assets, do not operate in the case of money).

Before proceeding to the consideration of these 'certain forces', Keynes introduced another way of looking at own-rates of interest. In a market equilibrium, the benefit derived from holding one additional unit of a commodity[13] must be equal to its own-rate of interest.

Keynes argues that this rate of return from holding any asset (including money) depends on three attributes. They are: (i) Their yield or output, q, when they are used to help produce goods or to provide services to consumers; (ii) The wastage or carrying cost, c, involved in holding this asset for some period of time; (iii) The security afforded by ownership of that asset because it can provide immediate command over other goods, as indicated by its liquidity premium, l. All three returns are measured in terms of the particular asset, and thus the total return expected from the holding of a unit of that asset over some period (e.g. a year) 'is equal to its yield *minus* its carrying cost *plus* its liquidity-premium, i.e. to $q - c + l$. That is to say, $q - c + l$ is the own-rate of interest of any commodity, where q, c and l are measured in terms of itself as the standard' (226).[14]

For physical assets, generally, the yields should normally exceed the carrying costs, while the liquidity premiums are negligible. Money, on the other hand, has a zero yield,[15] a negligible carrying cost, but a significant liquidity premium. It is this difference in the relative values for carrying cost and liquidity premium that Keynes sees as 'an essential difference between money and all (or most) other assets' (227). In order to compare expected returns from the owner-ship of various assets, it is necessary to adopt some standard unit of account, such as money. For example, with money as the unit of account, the expected money return from ownership of, say, a house for a year is $a_1 + q_1$, where a_1 is its expected appreciation in terms of

---

[13] Lerner (1952: 172) calls this the 'marginal efficiency of holding' the asset. This differs from the marginal efficiency of capital of the asset, because it is calculated on the basis of the demand price for the asset, while the marginal efficiency of capital uses its cost of production.

[14] Keynes (1973: 76), in correspondence with Hicks, wrote that this, rather than the definition in terms of spot and future contracts is 'the accurate definition of the rate of interest'.

[15] Keynes was writing at a time when no interest was paid on checking accounts.

money over that year, and q_1 is its yield in terms of itself, with its carrying cost and liquidity premium taken to be negligible. This expected return can be compared with that obtained from holding money, l_2, with money's yield and carrying cost being negligible. In a stock equilibrium situation, $a_1 + q_1$ must be equal to l_2, for owners of wealth who can switch from holding one asset to holding another.

This requirement for stock equilibrium should be distinguished from the flow equilibrium condition that the demand price of an asset be equal to its supply (or production) price, since a situation of stock equilibrium does not imply that there is also flow equilibrium. For example, consider an initial position in which there is both stock and flow equilibrium for a capital good. This is then disturbed by an increase in the expected future price for this asset, all else, including q_1 and l_2, unchanged. Restoration of stock equilibrium requires an increase in the current price (which is the same as the demand price) of the asset, since the supply of the asset is fixed. This increase lowers its expected appreciation in terms of money, a_1. Although this increase in the current price restores stock equilibrium, it disturbs the flow equilibrium by causing a positive gap between demand and normal supply prices that leads to increased production of this good.[16] An alternative way of recording this gap is to note (see above, section 4.4) that the marginal efficiency of capital of this asset is greater than the rate of interest. Keynes then goes outside the short-period framework of his analysis to consider the special case where accumulation over time, with stable long-term expectations, has resulted in stationary conditions.

Now those assets of which the normal supply-price is less than the demand-price will be newly produced; and these will be those assets of which the marginal efficiency would be greater (on the basis of their normal supply-price) than the rate of interest ... As the stock of the assets which begin by having a marginal efficiency at least equal to the rate of interest, is increased,

---

[16] This example shows how changes in expectations of future conditions could change, almost immediately, the current prices of durable goods for which there are organised markets. These changes in prices could be significant and persist for substantial intervals of time, for goods that take a considerable time to produce and that do not have close substitutes. Townshend (1937) has emphasised the radical implications for the classical theory of value of Keynes's approach. The former explains prices on the basis of conditions at the margin of production, while the latter shows that current prices for many durable goods depend on the conditions for stock equilibrium. (One difference in terminology should be noted. Townshend refers to the increase in expected future prices for durable goods – he uses residential housing as his example – as increasing the liquidity premiums for these goods. It is more in keeping with Keynes's usage to reserve this term for money, and to handle the consequences of the changes in expectations through their initial effects on a.)

their marginal efficiency (for reasons, sufficiently obvious, already given) tends to fall. Thus a point will come at which it no longer pays to produce them, *unless the rate of interest falls* pari passu. When there is *no* asset of which the marginal efficiency reaches the rate of interest, the future production of capital-assets will come to a standstill. (228)

The reason for diminishing marginal efficiency of capital in this case is not the rising short-period supply price of the capital good which is used in Keynes's short-period analysis but diminishing returns to this good as its supply increases over time, relative to the supplies of other capital goods and labour. The conjectures here about stationary conditions thus go outside the usual boundaries of his model. The occurrence of these stationary conditions can be explained in terms of the decreases in the current (or demand) prices for capital goods that are required for stock equilibrium. With a combination of declining prospective yields for capital goods as the stocks of these goods increase, and a constant liquidity preference for money, the maintenance of stock equilibrium, which holds at each point in time through the revaluation of assets, requires a rising value for the *a* terms. Under these conditions of declining prospective yields for capital goods, the increases in the *a* terms cannot be due to increases in the expected future prices for these goods. Thus, they imply declining current prices for these goods. When these prices fall to equality with their normal supply prices at zero net output, stationary conditions prevail. This scenario assumes that money continues to have a positive, roughly unchanged, own-rate of interest, even though other rates are falling. Keynes argued that these assumptions are reasonable because of two characteristics of money.

The first characteristic which tends towards the above conclusion is the fact that money has, both in the long and in the short period, a zero, or at any rate a very small, elasticity of production, so far as the power of private enterprise is concerned, as distinct from the monetary authority; elasticity of production meaning, in this context, the response of the quantity of labour applied to producing it to a rise in the quantity of labour which a unit of it will command. (230)

The second *differentia* of money is that it has an elasticity of substitution equal, or nearly equal, to zero; which means that as the exchange value of money rises there is no tendency to substitute some other factor for it. (231)[17]

Keynes infers from this second characteristic that 'money is a bottomless sink for purchasing power, when the demand for it

---

[17] Davidson (1978) has emphasised the importance of these two properties of money.

increases, since there is no value for it at which demand is diverted . . . so as to slop over into a demand for other things'.

Keynes recognises that even with the quantity of money given, its value in terms of wage-units, or in purchasing power over goods in general, could be increased substantially if money-wage rates and prices fell. The effectiveness of a fall in the money-wage rate requires that it also fall relative to its expected future value. But Keynes believed that money-wage rates tended to be sticky, in terms of money, especially under downward pressures, so that changes in these rates were unlikely to disturb the equilibrium established by the given money supply. Even with a sizeable increase in the proportion of the community's wealth represented by the stock of money, Keynes expected money to maintain a liquidity premium that could impede investment and result in involuntary unemployment. The reason given for this is the low carrying costs of money that 'cause the rate of interest to be insensitive, particularly below a certain figure, even to a substantial increase in the quantity of money in proportion to other forms of wealth' (233).

The two characteristics of money that Keynes gave as the source of its special properties are not independent of the dividing line used to separate money from other financial assets. They also depend on the assumption about the relative stability of money-wage rates, and thus of prices in general. There is a definitional problem in deciding which financial assets fall in the 'money' category that Keynes noted before he assumed that only bank deposits are money (167n). But the existence of other financial instruments, and their proliferation due to financial innovations at times of high rates of interest and credit constraints, would seem to indicate that the private sector can, in effect, produce money. This would be the case during inflationary periods when monetary authorities are trying to restrict the money supply. When there is a considerable amount of excess productive capacity and unemployment, the monetary authorities are quite eager to accommodate any increased demand for money. Keynes's statement of the second characteristic of money presumably refers to an absence of substitutability of physical assets for money, because of the high substitutability between money and many types of financial assets. But even in this case a rigid position is untenable, as Kahn recognised when he gently took Keynes to task on this point. 'It is strange that . . . Keynes contemplated no liquid forms of wealth other than cash and fixed-interest securities. There is an appreciable elasticity of substitution between money and equities; and also between money and houses, and between money and commodities which are dealt with in organised produce markets' (Kahn 1984: 140). Here too, under inflationary conditions with a rapidly increasing money supply, money would lose its role as a store of wealth, and thus its liquidity premium, even though it continued to act as a unit of account and a medium of exchange.[18]

The liquidity premium attached to money thus derives in large part from the fact that contracts are fixed in terms of money, which in turn is a practice that is reasonable if money-wage costs are expected to be relatively stable over the lives of the contracts: 'the expectations of a relative stickiness of wages in terms of money is a corollary of the excess of liquidity-premium over carrying-costs being greater for money than for any other asset' (Keynes 1936: 238). Keynes warned against tying money-wage rates to the prices of wage goods. In his model a change in employment, as we have seen, is associated with a change in real-wage rates in the opposite direction. Employment and prices, with money-wage rates and productive capacity given, are positively related as they both respond to changes in effective demand. The attempt to index money-wage rates would then mean that 'every small fluctuation in the propensity to consume and the inducement to invest would cause money-prices to rush violently between zero and infinity. That money-wages should be more stable than real wages is a condition of the system possessing inherent stability' (239).[19]

5.7 FINANCE

Keynes wrote three short articles (Keynes 1937b, 1937c and 1938) in response to criticisms of his theory of interest,[20] and to counter what he saw as attempts to re-introduce, in disguised form, the notion that the rate of interest is determined by the demand and supply of saving. They contain a minor amendment to his model, the recognition of the increased demand for money when investment decisions are increased. The banking system is assumed to accommodate this demand – he calls it a demand for 'finance' – by increasing the money

---

[18] This was noted by Keynes (1936: 241 n.1) when he wrote: 'Money itself rapidly loses the attribute of "liquidity" if its future supply is expected to undergo sharp changes.'

[19] Lerner (1952: 192) sees the statement of the importance of the stability of money wage costs, with its implications for supply prices as 'the essential lesson of the chapter. The usefulness of money depends ultimately on a certain degree of stability in its purchasing power'.

[20] The publications he refers to are Ohlin (1937a), Hicks (1936), Robertson (1936), and Hawtrey (1937).

supply, and thus the demand for money is given a role in determining this supply.[21] These articles are important because they make explicit the role of the financial system in making investment independent of saving. This independence of investment was assumed in *The General Theory* – it was a vital element, the causal factor in his model – but Keynes did not indicate (as he had in the *Treatise*, e.g. Keynes 1930b: 96) the crucial role of the financial system in this regard. The extension of credit by banks made possible an increase in investment that, through increases in employment and output, resulted in an equal increase in desired saving. These articles continued, however, to reveal confusion about the nature of the investment-saving equality, and Keynes did not succeed in showing that investment is independent of the propensity to save under all circumstances.

A good example of the confusing statements about the investment-saving equality that entangled Keynes is the following: 'The novelty in my treatment of saving and investment consists, not in my maintaining their necessary aggregate equality, but in the proposition that it is, not the rate of interest, but the level of incomes which (in conjunction with certain other factors) ensures this equality' (Keynes 1937b: 211). If the expression 'necessary aggregate equality' is taken literally, then neither the level of incomes, nor any other variable can be considered as adjusting to ensure this equality. If, however, this statement is referring only to situations of short-period equilibrium, with 'necessary aggregate equality' referring to the behavioural equality that is a necessary condition for that equilibrium, then income can be seen as the equilibrating variable. This latter interpretation is consistent with the approach taken here, and that considers the formal analysis in *The General Theory* as focusing on situations of short-period equilibrium.[22] Keynes's subsequent statement on this matter, however, seems to refer to the definitional equality. 'Aggregate saving and aggregate investment, in the senses

---

[21] Robertson (1937: 432) welcomed the introduction of 'finance' for this reason. He had drawn attention to the inadequacies of the treatment of the money supply in his review of *The General Theory* (Robertson 1936, 181n).

[22] E. S. Shaw, in correspondence with Keynes that arose out of these finance articles, had suggested a reconciliation of the liquidity preference and loanable funds theories of interest, with the former being concerned with an instantaneous situation where flows are irrelevant, and the latter dealing with flows (Keynes 1979: 277). Keynes replied: 'I am not concerned with instantaneous snapshots, but with short-period equilibrium, assuming a sufficient interval for momentary decisions to take effect' (280). But Keynes ignores this requirement for the passage of time, that is the need for 'a sufficient interval', in drawing equilibrium consequences for finance from the *ex post* equality of saving and investment (Keynes 1937c: 222).

in which I have defined them, are necessarily equal in the same way in which the aggregate purchases of anything on the market are equal to the aggregate sales' (211–12). It is this definitional view of the investment-saving equality, that is then sometimes treated as though it had equilibrium properties, which was the source of erroneous statements.

Ohlin, in his rejoinder to Keynes, moved towards the latter's theory of the determination of the rate of interest by explicitly recognising the importance of the stock demand and supply of financial assets and money in determining the rate of interest. 'The situation every day must fulfill the condition that at existing prices of claims and assets people prefer to hold the existing quantities of cash, claims and assets rather than exchange part of some of them for a little more of the others'[23] (Ohlin 1937b: 427). But Ohlin also sees current flows ('the willingness and ability of people to save and invest') as affecting the rate of interest.

Keynes did not accept as valid the restated version of Ohlin's theory of interest because of the role given to the supply of saving, but he saw merit in the latter's emphasis on the role of *ex ante* investment. 'He [Ohlin] has compelled me to attend to an important link in the causal chain which I had previously overlooked, and has enabled me to make an important improvement in my analysis' (Keynes 1937c: 216). This led to a clear distinction between investment decisions and investment, whose absence in *The General Theory* was noted in section 4.4, above. 'Now, *ex ante* investment is an important, genuine phenomenon, in as much as decisions have to be taken and credit or "finance" provided well in advance of the actual process of investment'.[24] Keynes attached a footnote to 'finance' that defined this term 'to mean the credit required in the interval between planning and execution'. Although finance thus seems to be restricted to a short-term role during the period of construction of the investment project, conditions in the long-term bond market are also important. 'The entrepreneur when he decides to invest has to be satisfied on two

---

[23] Ohlin adds to the sentence just quoted: 'But cash holds no special place, as it does in Mr. Keynes's theory'. Whether this theory is stated in terms of equilibrium in the bond or money market is irrelevant. With short-period equilibrium in the commodity markets, equilibrium in the money market implies equilibrium in the bond market, and vice versa.

[24] With the statement that investment decisions are taken 'well in advance of the actual process of investment', Keynes opens the way for the recognition that current investment expenditures are largely determined by economic conditions and decisions taken in the preceding short periods. It is this point, as we saw in section 4.5, that Keynes denied in his correspondence with Kalecki.

points: firstly, that he can obtain sufficient short-term finance during the period of producing the investment; and secondly, that he can eventually fund his short-term obligations by a long-term issue on satisfactory conditions. Occasionally, he may be in a position to use his own resources or to make his long-term issue at once; but ... it is convenient to regard the twofold process as the characteristic one' (217). The terms at which these funds can be made available are explained by his theory of interest: 'the rate of interest relevant to *ex ante* investment is the rate of interest determined by the *current* stock of money and the *current* state of liquidity preferences at the date when the finance required by the investment decisions has to be arranged' (218). The only change that Keynes sees as required is the explicit recognition of the demand for liquidity because of investment decisions. The banking system is looked to as the source of supply to meet this demand, and the independence of investment from saving is said to be preserved:

> the transition from a lower to a higher scale of activity involves an increased demand for liquid resources which cannot be met without a rise in the rate of interest, unless the banks are ready to lend more cash or the rest of the public to release more cash at the existing rate of interest ... This means that, in general, the banks hold the key position in the transition from a lower to a higher scale of activity ... The investment market can become congested through shortage of cash. It can never become congested through shortage of saving. This is the most fundamental of my conclusions within this field.
>
> (222)

In trying to demonstrate this independence of investment from saving Keynes made use of the notion of a 'revolving fund of liquid finance', but the inconsistencies in his treatment of the investment-saving equality raise questions about the validity of this demonstration.

5.8 A REVOLVING FUND OF LIQUID FINANCE

A revolving fund of finance first appears in Keynes (1937b: 209) when 'investment is proceeding at a steady rate ... one entrepreneur having his finance replenished for the purpose of a projected investment as another exhausts his on paying for his completed investment'. The underlying mechanism was not explained by Keynes, but it requires the special characteristics of a situation in which investment has been proceeding at a steady rate, so that at each point in time there is short-period equilibrium with desired (or equilibrium) saving, and not only *ex post* saving, equal to the rate of investment.

This equilibrium saving is assumed to be used, directly or indirectly, to purchase the long-term bonds of the firms who have completed their investment projects, and who use the proceeds to repay the short-term loans they obtained to cover the construction period of these projects. The banks can then extend short-term loans of equal value to firms embarking on new projects without changing their overall liquidity position. It is only when investment decisions are increasing that there is an additional demand for money, and the banking system has to decide on the terms at which it 'is ready to become more ... unliquid' (Keynes 1937c: 219).

When Keynes referred again to the revolving fund, it was in connection with any short-period situation, and not only one that was part of a sequence in which investment had been proceeding at a steady rate. But he implicitly assumed that the same conclusions held for both situations. 'As soon as it ['finance'] is "used" in the sense of being expended, the lack of liquidity is automatically made good and the readiness to become temporarily unliquid is available to be used over again.' Keynes apparently bases this statement on the *ex post* equality between saving and investment: 'there will always be *exactly* enough *ex post* saving to take up the *ex post* investment and so release the finance which the latter had been previously employing' (222). This *ex post* equality is, however, not sufficient for his purposes. It is only equilibrium saving, saving that is in the desired relation to income, that is potentially available for the purchase of long-term bonds that will enable firms that have completed investment projects to repay bank loans. This would allow banks to extend new loans to those making investment decisions, without changing their overall liquidity position.[25] It takes time for an equilibrium position to be re-established after an increase in investment (the multiplier process is not completed instantaneously), and thus 'the lack of liquidity' is *not* 'automatically made good' as soon as finance is 'used'.

Robertson (1938: 315) pointed out the inconsistency in Keynes's position. The banking system's lack of liquidity is not automatically made good by the spending of a bank loan. All that this does is to change the ownership of bank deposits. It is the repayment of bank loans with its cancellation of bank deposits, that is required for the restoration of bank liquidity.

Keynes left matters in a muddle by intermingling statements about finance for working capital with those for fixed capital, and by his

---

[25] Banks may not have any particular reason to want their initial liquidity position restored before they extend new loans. They grow and prosper by becoming less liquid, by increasing their loans, as long as interest is always earned on these loans.

apparent failure to understand Robertson's question on the liquidity
position of the banks. His statement that 'consumption is . . . effective
in liquidating the short-term finance' refers to funds borrowed to
permit the production of consumption goods. With these goods sold,
firms are in a position to repay their bank loans. They would only do
so if they decided to reduce working capital.[26] In what he said was an
answer to Robertson (1938). Keynes wrote that for an investing
entrepreneur 'the demand for cash, due to the requirements of
"finance", is automatically at an end as soon as the finance is
expended' (Keynes 1938, 230). Although this assertion is correct, it
does not deal with Robertson's question about the automatic restoration of the *banks'* liquidity position once the finance is expended; it
simply changes the question.

In spite of this attempted evasion of Robertson's criticism,
Keynes's short comment contains implicit recognition of its validity.
Keynes divides the active demand for cash 'into two parts: the
demand due to the time lag between the inception and the execution
of the entrepreneurs' decisions, and the part due to the time lags
between the receipt and the disposal of income by the public and also
between the receipt by entrepreneurs of their sale proceeds and the
payment by them of wages, etc.' From this he infers that even if the
first demand is at an end, the second would still be present until 'the
circulation [or multiplier][27] period is complete', at which time 'the
banks cannot keep the previous amount of cash outstanding at the
same rate of interest, unless a new activity is coming along to replace
the old activity or there is an increase in the inactive demand.' That
is, their initial liquidity position is restored, as long as there is no new
demand for loans, once the multiplier effects of the increase in
investment have occurred.

Keynes did not, on reflection (in a 1938 letter to Shaw), consider
the introduction of finance into his theory to have been an important
addition, because he considered that he had previously allowed for
the influence of changes in activity on the demand for money: 'the
finance required by the planning of activity was one of the ways, by

---

26 Shaw took issue with Keynes on this point of the effectiveness of consumption in
    'liquidating' finance. 'If the entrepreneur uses the proceeds of his sales of consump-
    tion goods for repaying bank loans, he cannot also use them for maintaining his
    stocks or keeping up with replacement requirements . . . . The decision to consume
    is not the crucial fact, but rather the decision to disinvest' (Keynes 1979: 279).
27 This 'circulation' period is the interval during which there is a demand for money
    because of time lags in the income-expenditure relation, and it is thus equal to the
    time required for the multiplier process to be completed.

no means negligible, in which changes in the level of activity affected the demand for liquid resources, a factor which had always played a prominent part in my theory. Substantially my theory is exactly what it was when I first published my book' (Keynes 1979: 281). This statement seems to indicate that he had reverted to the view that an explicit statement was not required to cover the role of the financial system in making investment independent of saving. It could be left implicit, as something obvious to any careful observer of the operations of a capitalist economy.

5.9 THE TERM STRUCTURE OF INTEREST RATES

Implicit in the treatment by Keynes of the financing of investment decisions, is the assumption of a stable term structure of interest rates. He recognised, as we saw above, the importance to those making these decisions of the availability of short-term finance and expectations of reasonable long-term rates (Keynes 1973c: 217). But it is only the shortage of cash supplied by banks (in the form of short-term loans) that is seen as a potential source of congestion in the investment market. Kaldor (1939) examined the conditions under which long-term rates would be unchanged as investment is increased and maintained at a higher level. 'Speculators' (Kaldor's term), or intermediaries, are assumed to facilitate the financing of this investment (in the interval before desired saving can increase in response to the increase in investment), by borrowing from the banks and lending by purchasing the bonds of investing entrepreneurs. Kaldor assumes that the increase in desired saving that follows investment is used, directly or indirectly, to purchase the long-term securities of investing firms. The size of the speculative commitment required to facilitate a permanent increase in the rate of investment depends, given the amount of the increase, on the value for the propensity to save. Once the multiplier process is completed, and desired saving has caught up with the new level of investment, the speculative commitment stops growing. Kaldor concludes that if 'the total required increase in the size of speculative stocks is not too large relatively to the resources of the market (i.e. provided it does not impair the degree of price-stabilising influence) there will be no pressure on the price of securities (i.e. no tendency for the rate of interest to rise) either in the long run, or in the short run' (Kaldor 1939: 50). This means that the validity of Keynes's statement that only a shortage of cash, and not a shortage of saving, can result in a congested investment market requires that this price-stabilising influence be very large. If it is not, then long-term interest rates could rise, thus discouraging investment.

Kaldor wrote that for a closed economy 'the degree of price-stabilising influence, though not perhaps infinite, is very much larger in the case of long-term bonds than for any other commodity; and this means that the Keynesian theory, though a "special case", gives, nevertheless, a fair approximation to reality' (52). This judgement reflects economic conditions at the time of writing of Kaldor's article. With considerable unemployment, idle productive capacity, and no inflationary fears, the expectation of stable long-term rates makes feasible the use of short-term loans to purchase long-term bonds. In different circumstances, concern about adverse changes in future long-term interest rates could significantly limit the size of speculative commitments that could be undertaken without a significant increase in current long-term rates, even though short-term loans are readily available (Asimakopulos 1983: 231–2). Kaldor's analysis of an open economy, where the increase in imports means that domestic saving will not increase by the amount of the investment, even in short-period equilibrium, also shows that long-term interest rates will increase. 'In the situation contemplated there is no shortage of cash, and no pressure on the short-term rate of interest. The long-term rate rises *relatively* to the short-term rate simply because, owing to a shortage of savings, speculators are required to expand continuously the size of their commitments: and there are limits to the extent to which this is possible' (Kaldor 1939: 51).

Keynes's theory of interest is dependent on the long-term expectations that determine the position and shape of the liquidity preference function. He did not recognise that these long-term expectations could be affected by comparisons of projected rates of investment and projected savings (based on the economy's propensity to save) in future periods. If it appears that investment would be greater than normal saving, concern over future interest rates could bring about immediate increases in long-term rates that act as a damper on investment plans. Thus, the independence of investment from saving – a key element in Keynes's theory – does not hold under all circumstances.

Entrepreneurs might choose to finance investment in fixed capital by means of short-term bank loans that they keep renewing, even after their investment projects have been completed, if long-term interest rates are high. In making this choice they would be adding uncertainty over the eventual interest cost of investment to the uncertainty over its prospective yield. This behaviour has been profitable for some, but for others it has led to serious problems, and even to bankruptcy, when interest rates increased sharply. When the urge to expand is strong, entrepreneurs often add interest rate risks to the risks that are inherent in their investment projects. Robinson, in setting out the determinants of her model of accumulation, decided that finance 'is best treated, along with the "animal spirits" of the firms, as an element in the propensity to accumulate of the economy' (Robinson 1962: 43). The uncertainty that pervades the attitudes to liquidity and investment makes it difficult to keep the two separate. One of the themes running through the General Theory, even though it goes counter to the analytical framework that Keynes often refers to, is that investment and the rate of interest are determined by elements that cannot be represented adequately by means of stable functions.

5.10 CONCLUSION

Keynes sees the presence of money, and its use as a store of wealth, as one of the ways in which uncertainty and changing expectations of an unknown future can affect current economic activity. Money is held – demanded – because it is required for transactions purposes, but it is also demanded for precautionary and speculative reasons. Uncertainty about when money would be required to satisfy contractual obligations or to meet some other need, together with uncertainty over the price of other assets at that time, give rise to the precautionary motive. The speculative motive for holding money is based on the belief that the market's estimate of future long-term interest rates – as reflected in current rates – is mistaken, and that these rates will increase. Individuals holding these views will move a portion of their wealth from bonds to money, in order to avoid capital losses that would outweigh the interest income from bonds over the interval being considered.

The total demand for money – a stock demand at a point in time that arises from the three motives listed above – is represented by a demand schedule that is based on what Keynes calls a liquidity preference function. If income and expectations are given, then this schedule can be represented by a negatively-sloped demand curve for money, with the rate of interest as the independent variable. The total supply of money is determined, in the model of *The General Theory*, by the monetary authority, and the rate of interest is given by the point of intersection of the vertical line showing this supply of money, and the demand curve for money. Thus, the rate of interest at each point in time takes the value required to equate the demand for money to the existing supply. Those who hold money are content to have that portion of their wealth represented by the money supply kept in this form. (Alternatively, the prices of bonds take the values required to induce individuals to hold the existing supply of bonds.) Interest rates (bond prices) are sensitive to the state of long-term expectations, and they can change immediately when these expectations change.

Keynes maintained that saving, and the propensity to save, had no role in the determination of the rate of interest. Thus, the unemployment that would be caused by an increase in the propensity to save would not be offset by a significant fall in the rate of interest that could stimulate investment. The long-term expectations that determine the position and shape of the liquidity preference function were taken to be exogenous, and assumed not to be affected by anything to do with current or projected investment and saving flows.

Stock equilibrium for owners of wealth requires that the expected returns from holding different types of assets be equalised. Keynes stated that these returns are due to three attributes of individual assets. These are: their yield or output of services; their carrying costs; and the security they provide in making possible immediate command over goods. The return from holding money is derived from its immediate command over goods, from its liquidity premium, while yields are important for physical assets. Keynes argued that an essential difference between money and physical assets is that the yields from the latter decline continuously with increases in the amounts of these assets, while money's liquidity premium remains positive even when it accounts for a substantial proportion of the community's total wealth. This is why the rate of interest – money's own-rate of interest – can bring accumulation to an end by absorbing purchasing power. Keynes points to two characteristics of money that allow it to have this role: a very small elasticity of production; and a very small elasticity of substitution. It is by no means clear that the values for these two elasticities are as negligible as Keynes had claimed.

Keynes's writings on finance show his continuing efforts to deny a role to saving and investment in the determination of the rate of interest. They also indicate continued confusion about the two types of investment-saving equality, the definitional and the behavioural. With banks responding to demands for short-term loans to facilitate investment decisions, the public was accorded a role in determining the money supply. An important element of endogeneity in the determination of the money supply was thus introduced. Keynes's attempt to maintain the independence of investment from saving met with problems, because it could be shown that in some circumstances, concern over the adequacy of normal saving, relative to investment intentions, could affect long-term expectations and thus lead to high long-term interest rates that could act to discourage current investment decisions.

6

EQUILIBRIUM, CHANGE AND TIME

6.1 INTRODUCTION

The formal model to be found in *The General Theory* has been presented in the preceding chapters. This model was set in a particular interval of historical time, Marshall's short period, that Keynes adopted along with many other Marshallian tools of analysis. Keynes emphasised the historical time framework in which his analysis is placed by making a clear distinction between past, present, and future conditions. This analysis focused on current short-period equilibrium situations, in particular, on the factors determining the short-period equilibrium level of employment. This concentration on equilibrium values – even though they are only short-period and not long-period equilibrium values – partly takes his analysis out of historical time. Essential aspects of time are frozen in any equilibrium analysis, with even the values for variables that could change appreciably being kept constant in order to derive the equilibrium values of the variables of interest, given the assumed values for the independent variables. Any 'movement' towards these equilibrium values (such as the movement deduced from the analysis of the stability of the equilibrium position given by the intersection of the aggregate demand and supply functions) is a movement not through historical time but through analytical time, because the values for the parameters that determine the positions of these functions are assumed to be unchanged. This did not prevent Keynes from implicitly identifying actual values with these short-period equilibrium values. This is one instance where a reader should be aware of implicit assumptions.

In spite of the limitations of short-period equilibrium analysis, it served as a useful starting point for Keynes. It was, as emphasised above, set in an actual interval of historical time that allowed him to bring into his analysis factors that he considered to be very important in the real world. His use of these equilibrium values allowed for a direct comparison with the results of classical theory (or at least his version of it), since this theory dealt only with equilibrium values. Keynes's critique of classical theory thus had two aspects. This theory's equilibrium results were special – he proposed a more general set of equilibrium results that included them – and it did not pay attention to the complications introduced by historical time. Keynes's vision and interest went much beyond the short period of his formal model, and at many places in *The General Theory* there is reference to changes occurring over time. He treated these changes as the result of changes in the values of the factors determining short-period equilibrium positions, changes that can occur 'without much warning, and sometimes substantially' (Keynes 1936: 249). His model could only be a starting point or guide for the consideration of movements in employment over time, whose further analysis depends on 'our practical intuition'.

The reconciliation between the short-period equilibrium focus of the formal analysis in *The General Theory*, and Keynes's statement that '[T]his book ... has evolved into what is primarily a study of the forces which determine changes in the scale of output and employment as a whole' (vii), thus involves the introduction of changing values for the determinants of this equilibrium. Both the marginal efficiency of capital and the liquidity preference function are liable to sudden changes because they are, as we have seen, so much influenced by changing views of future conditions. Throughout *The General Theory* there are statements that make it appear unlikely that these functions would be unchanged long enough to permit actual values to coincide with the short-period equilibrium values. The one place where Keynes tries to analyse in some detail the interdependence between changes occurring in the economy and the determinants of equilibrium is in his consideration of the effects of changing money-wage rates. This analysis indicates possible outcomes rather than definitive results. But it is dynamic in that it attempts to trace through time the possible consequences of a change in a particular variable that could affect the environment in which it is taking place.

The various statements to be found in *The General Theory* about long-term problems, such as the tendency for full-employment saving to outstrip the likely levels of investment (e.g. 220), are not based on any formal analysis of changes that are likely to take place over time. There is no attempt to link a sequence of short periods and to trace the changes from one to the other that lead to growth and to cyclical movements. Keynes's chapter on the trade cycle is used to illustrate how his theory can explain some of the features of cyclical movements, but it is not intended to be more than a preliminary consideration of the trade cycle. Similarly, after Keynes provides a summary of his General Theory, there is a brief consideration of the changes over time in employment, output and prices that could be expected on the basis of this theory. Long-period equilibrium does not play any role in any of these considerations, even though this term appears a few times in *The General Theory*. It, unlike short-period equilibrium, does not serve as a centre of attraction for actual values in his theory.

Keynes's use of short-period equilibrium for the economy can be seen as an extension to the economy of Marshall's short-period equilibrium analysis for a particular industry. But it does not lead, as did Marshall's, to a consideration of long-period equilibrium. There is no place in Keynes's vision of the operation of actual economies for movements to anything approximating long-period equilibrium situations. These economies are subject to a variety of shocks the nature and timing of which can only be determined after the event. The stable conditions for long intervals of time, which are required to give credence to long-period equilibrium analysis, were so remote from Keynes's view of the world that he had no patience with this type of analysis. In abstaining from long-period equilibrium analysis, Keynes was observing the limitations imposed by historical time. Long-period equilibrium, in the latter context, can only be a very special case that is explored only for purposes of illustration and completeness. It cannot be the focus of the analysis.

6.2 INDEPENDENT VARIABLES AND CHANGES

Keynes's General Theory of Employment can be re-stated using equations, as was done in section 5.5 above, as long as it is recognised that the functional forms of these equations may themselves change in response to changes in the dependent variables. It thus may not be possible to determine the effects of changes in the value for one of the independent variables by comparing the values for the dependent variables obtained by inserting the new and old values for this independent variable into functions having the *same* values for the parameters. This means that these equations should only be used to provide a general framework for showing the interrelations between the variables of interest. Misleading conclusions could be obtained for the effects of changes in the values for independent variables, such as, the money supply and the money-wage rate, if these equations are taken out of the specific, historical context in which Keynes's analysis is embedded. This context affects the responses of the dependent variables to the changes in the independent variables. These changes, by altering expectations, may trigger shifts in the propensities and attitudes that determine the precise forms of the basic equations of the model.[1]

Keynes pointed out both the importance of formal economic analysis 'without which . . . we shall be lost in the wood' (297), and its limitations: 'The object of our analysis is, not to provide a machine, or method of blind manipulation, which will furnish an infallible answer, but to provide ourselves with an organised and orderly method of thinking out particular problems.' The conclusions arrived at can only be 'provisional' because it is necessary to allow for the probable interactions among the 'independent' factors of the analysis. He thus distinguished his approach from the methods of mathematical analysis that provide definitive conclusions by assuming strict independence between the factors involved. This independence does not exist in the real-world historical context in which Keynes tried to place his theory.

The formal analysis in *The General Theory* is concerned with the factors determining the level of employment in a particular short period in a non-stationary economy. For example, Keynes notes that '[w]e take as given the existing skill and quantity of available labour, the existing quality and quantity of available equipment, the existing technique . . . This does not mean that we assume these factors to be constant' (245). The changes that occur in the values of these 'given' factors over the interval of time occupied by his short period are small relative to their initial values, and thus it is legitimate to ignore these changes in looking at the variables that mainly determine the level of employment in such an interval. Keynes treats as 'independent variables' the consumption function, the liquidity preference function, the expectations of prospective yields from capital goods, the money-wage rate, and the quantity of money in the economy. The difference between these independent variables and his 'given factors' is that changes in the former are assumed to have a dominant influence (within the short-period time frame of the analysis) on the dependent variables, while the changes in the latter are so slow that they 'have only a small and negligible short-term influence' (247).

[1] This respect for the historical context of the analysis is the major difference between Keynes's General Theory and the purely equilibrium models, such as Patinkin's (1965), that examine some of the same questions. The latter are ahistorical, and uncertainty over future conditions is suppressed in order to get determinate results (cf. Asimakopulos: 1973).

There is no guarantee, given the values of the independent variables, that the resulting effective demand will be sufficient to provide full employment. When a change occurs in one of the variables that Keynes labels 'independent', repercussions could spread beyond the dependent variables to the other 'independent' variables. 'Hence the extreme complexity of the actual course of events' (249). Keynes sees his analysis – the 'schematism' that can be sketched in a system of equations – as making the examination of any actual problem 'more manageable; and our practical intuition (which can take account of a more detailed complex of facts that can be treated on general principles) will be offered a less intractable material upon which to work'.

6.3 CHANGES IN MONEY-WAGE RATES

The key dependent variables in *The General Theory*, the volume of employment and the amount of national income, are measured in wage-units. In developing his model, Keynes assumed that the money-wage rate is constant, even though he recognised that when employment is increasing, money-wage rates also tend to increase (e.g. 249). When two alternative situations in a particular short period with different levels of employment are compared using the model, their price levels will be found to differ for two reasons. There is the difference due to higher marginal costs (measured in terms of wage-units) in the situation with higher employment and output, to which is added the difference in money-wage rates. The translation of a given amount expressed in wage-units to money values at different sets of money-wage rates, involves only mechanical calculations, but the question of the consequences of a *change* in the money-wage rate from one level to another cannot be handled mechanically.

If the reduction in money-wage rates leaves the consumption function, the marginal efficiency of capital, and the rate of interest unchanged then the level of employment will also be unchanged. This result can be deduced from a subset of the system of equations set out in section 5.5. They are: $Y_w = g(N)$ (5.1); $C_w = C(Y_w)$ (5.2); $I_w = I(r)$ (5.3); $Y_w = C_w + I_w$ (5.4). With the rate of interest being unchanged, by assumption, at its initial value even after the decrease in the money-wage rate, there are 4 unknowns (Y_w, N, C_w, I_w) in these 4 equations. If the forms of these functions are also assumed to be unchanged, then these equations show that under these assumptions effective demand measured in wage-units (Y_w) and thus employment (N), will be unchanged by the reduction in money-wage rates. A favourable impact of employment will only occur if the reduction in money wages produces suitable changes in the determinants of the equilibrium position. The examination by Keynes of the effects of falling money-wage rates, in response to unemployment, thus involves him in a dynamic analysis that attempts to trace the possible changes in other factors that are set off by declining money-wage rates.

It is only through its effects on the determinants of the short-period equilibrium position that a reduction in money-wage rates can increase the level of employment. Keynes considers first the possible effects of falling money-wage rates on the economy's propensity to consume. The lower prices that accompany lower wage rates (although prices might not fall to the same extent, because other costs might not be reduced) redistribute income in favour of rentiers, who have a significant proportion of income that is fixed in money terms. Keynes felt that with rentiers richer, on average, than workers, this change is likely to reduce the average propensity to consume in the economy, but he is cautious in his conclusions. 'What the net result will be on a balance of considerations, we can only guess. Probably it is more likely to be adverse than favourable' (262). There is certainly no support here for the view that falling money-wage rates would tend to increase employment.

The marginal efficiency of capital would be shifted upward, if the current reduction in money-wage rates is considered to be a reduction relative to future rates, because this would increase the prospective yield of current investment. But the opposite effect would occur if the current fall in money-wage rates led to the expectations of further cuts in the future, as entrepreneurs wait for more favourable conditions before investing. The circumstances in which wage reductions take place, since they influence these expectations, might thus be important in determining whether decreases in money-wage rates lead to an increase in investment. Higher investment might also result from the fall in the rate of interest that could be a consequence of lower wage rates. With prices also lower, the transactions' demand for money would be decreased, and if the supply of money is unchanged, the increased amount available for speculative purposes will put downward pressure on the rate of interest. Here too, the surrounding circumstances could be very important, because the long-term expectations that determine the position of the liquidity preference function could be affected by concerns set in motion by falling wage rates, and the interest rate may not fall. Entrepreneurs, and thus investment, could also be adversely affected by the increase in the real burden of their debts due to falling prices. Falling prices, if they are extensive, could lead to bankruptcies that cause serious disruptions in the functioning of the economic and financial systems.

Keynes concludes that, for a closed system, favourable effects on the marginal efficiency of capital would only occur if the wage reductions were seen as being temporary, with a reversal expected shortly. A sharp, once-and-for-all, reduction of wages across the board would tend to lead to the view that these wages would likely increase in the future, and thus such a reduction could help promote investment and employment. But in decentralised capitalist economies this type of change cannot occur, and the piecemeal reductions produced by collective bargaining, fiercely resisted in each case, are unlikely to lead to the changes in expectations that would foster an increase in investment. In fact, they could very well further weaken the incentive to invest, as gradual reductions in wages that spread from one sector to the other lead to the expectations of further reductions. This leads Keynes to conclude that the pattern of falling wage rates in a real-world context will not provide a boost to the marginal efficiency of capital, and 'that with the actual practices and institutions of the contemporary world it is more expedient to aim at a rigid money-wage policy than at a flexible policy responding by easy stages to changes in the amount of unemployment' (265–6). As for the favourable effects of falling wages and prices on the rate of interest, Keynes feels that they are similar to those that would accompany an increasing money supply, with money-wage rates unchanged.

Just as a moderate increase in the quantity of money may exert an inadequate influence over the long-term rate of interest, whilst an immoderate increase may offset its other advantages by its disturbing effect on confidence; so a moderate reduction in money-wage may prove inadequate, whilst an immoderate reduction might shatter confidence even if it were practicable.

There is, therefore, no ground for the belief that a flexible wage policy is capable of maintaining a state of continuous full employment; – any more than for the belief that an open-market monetary policy is capable, unaided, of achieving this result. The economic system cannot be made self-adjusting along these lines.   (266–7)

In spite of these similarities between the two policies, Keynes prefers a flexible money policy, because it is accompanied by fewer undesirable redistributive effects that impinge on weaker groups in the society. He makes one of his asides about changes over a long period of time at this point, after noting that with money-wage rates rigid the stability of prices in the short period is tied to stable output and employment. In the long period, the changes in technology and equipment that lower marginal costs in terms of wage-units mean that a rigid wage policy would result in falling prices. Keynes would prefer a policy that allows money-wage rates to increase over time in such circumstances because it would keep the burden of entrepreneurial debt from increasing and would have a favourable effect on the marginal efficiency of capital. But his analysis is concerned with short-period situations, and detailed consideration of the merits of different wage policies in the long period 'would lead me beyond the scope of my present purpose' (271).

Keynes recognised that in an open economy a reduction in its money-wage rates could provide it with a competitive advantage at given exchange rates vis-à-vis foreign countries, if these countries' money costs remain unchanged. Demand for its goods will be higher, and this improvement in the trade balance could lead to higher investment. But this gain may be limited by fluctuations in exchange rates, or by the imposition of tariffs and quotas. He did not consider the possible gains from a reduction in money-wage rates relative to foreign wage rates sufficiently great to change the conclusion he reached for a closed economy, given the possible repercussions on various trading arrangements and on exchange rates: 'the money-wage level as a whole should be maintained as stable as possible, at any rate in the short period' (270).

Keynes's negative conclusion on the usefulness of falling money-wage rates as a cure for unemployment is not definitive. It is based on a balance of considerations, none of which can be made precise, and the assessment of which requires judgement and experience. This is the nature of economic analysis when it attempts to deal with changes occurring over historical time in actual economies. Keynes, in a 1936 letter, made this very clear when he tried to encourage Shove to continue in his attempt to re-work the classical analysis of the firm and industry by stressing the role of expectations, even though he could not 'make it precise'. 'But you ought not to feel inhibited by a difficulty in making the solution precise. It may be that a part of the error in the classical analysis is due to that attempt. As soon as one is dealing with the influence of expectations and of transitory experience, one is, in the nature of things, outside the realm of the formally exact' (Keynes 1973c: 2). Keynes believed that it was necessary to work outside this realm if policy proposals relevant to an actual, changing world are to be devised.

6.4 EQUILIBRIUM IN A CHANGING ENVIRONMENT

Keynes boldly identifies his short-period equilibrium results with actual values at a point in time by claiming to have shown in the chapters that set out his General Theory 'what determines the volume of employment at any time' (313). The context of statements like the one just quoted makes clear that by 'at any time' he means in any short period, an actual interval of time during which it is reasonable to abstract from the changes in productive capacity, technology and skills that are continually taking place in a dynamic economy. But in using equilibrium values to represent actual values in such situations, Keynes is going beyond the limits of the comparative static analysis on which his formal theory is based. In considering the changing economy he wants to analyse, it is necessary to take into account the time required for actual values to move towards short-period equilibrium values that are themselves changing through time. This problem was pointed out in earlier chapters in connection with Keynes's implicit assumption that the multiplier process set in motion by a change in investment is completed within the short period.

Keynes's defence of his approach, the importance of isolating the 'fundamental forces which determine ... the equilibrium position' (Keynes 1973c: 182), is sufficient if equilibrium positions exert such a strong attraction on actual values that the latter are always very close to the former. But this may not always be the case, and short-period equilibrium analysis – whose potential usefulness is not being denied here – should be supplemented by consideration of the time required for actual values to adjust to changes in equilibrium values.

There are two sections in *The General Theory* where Keynes indicates how his analysis, even though it is limited to situations of short-period equilibrium, can be used to explain the pattern of changes in output and employment that occur over time. The first is found in chapter 18, just after his summary of the General Theory, and the second (to be treated in the next section) is in his notes on the trade cycle.

Taking as his starting point the position that his theory can explain the experiences of actual economies, Keynes deduces the special characteristics of his independent variables, which affect the movements and average values of output, employment and prices, that would tend to reproduce these experiences. He observes that

it is an outstanding characteristic of the economic system in which we live that, whilst it is subject to severe fluctuations in respect of output and employment, it is not violently unstable. Indeed it seems capable of remaining in a chronic condition of sub-normal activity for a considerable period without any marked tendency either towards recovery or towards complete collapse. Moreover, the evidence indicates that full, or even approximately full, employment is of rare and short-lived occurrence. Fluctuations may start briskly but seem to wear themselves out before they have proceeded to great extremes, and an intermediate situation which is neither desperate nor satisfactory is our normal lot ... The same thing is true of prices, which, in response to an initiating cause of disturbance, seem to be able to find a level at which they can remain, for the time being, moderately stable. (Keynes 1936: 249–50)

This relative stability of the economic system is taken to indicate that the multiplier effects of changes in investment are not very large, and thus the short-period marginal propensity to consume must be relatively small. Similarly, moderate changes in the prospective yields of investment in capital goods, or in the rate of interest, will not result in substantial changes in investment. The relative stability of prices implies that the increasing short-period costs incurred when output is increased are not very large in relation to the increase in output, and thus the fall in real-wage rates that is associated with higher employment is not so drastic as to result in large changes in money-wage rates.[2] Keynes also adds the observation that fluctuations in investment will tend to reverse themselves due to the effects on the marginal efficiency of capital of above, or below, average rates of investment that are 'continued for a period which, measured in years, is not very large' (251). With this extension of the analysis to cover intervals of time longer than the short period, the changes in the available capital equipment that result from changes in investment are added to the determinants of investment decisions.

Keynes's defence of the restrictions he places on his independent variables to make his theory's 'predictions' correspond to outcomes observed for actual economies, draws on experience rather than on *a priori* considerations. The importance of established levels of consumption (and programmes of government relief) are given as reasons why consumption expenditures will not be very responsive to short-period changes in income. Increasing short-period supply prices of capital goods are used to justify the presumption that there will only be a moderate change in investment in response to an

---

[2] The inverse relation between employment and real-wage rates that Keynes deduced from his theory, and which he uses in this consideration of the relative stability of prices, has not been confirmed by empirical studies. See above, section 3.3.

increase in prospective yields or to a fall in the rate of interest.[3] It is recognised that this restraint will not be operating initially if the favourable changes in expectations occur at a time when there is considerable idle capacity in the investment-goods sector. The limited response of money-wage rates to the decline in real-wage rates that is experienced in his model when employment is increased, is explained by the importance of relative money-wage rates in the bargaining process. Even though it is recognised that wages will be under increased upward pressure as employment increases 'workers will not seek a much greater money-wage when employment improves or allow a very great reduction rather than suffer any unemployment at all' (253). Keynes thus draws on observations of changes in actual economies to flesh out the theoretical framework of his analysis. He concludes that his independent variables are then

adequate to explain the outstanding features of our actual experience; – namely, that we oscillate, avoiding the gravest extremes of fluctuation in employment and in prices in both directions, round an intermediate position appreciably below full employment and appreciably above the minimum employment a decline below which would endanger life.

But we must not conclude that the mean position thus determined by 'natural' tendencies, namely, by those tendencies which are likely to persist, failing measures expressly designed to correct them, is therefore, established by laws of necessity. The unimpeded rule of the above conditions is a fact of observation concerning the world as it is or has been, and not a necessary principle which cannot be changed.   (254)

Keynes is drawing conclusions here about the average values for employment and output over a sequence of short periods, even though his analysis is concerned with the factors determining their values in a particular short period. He recognises that investment and employment will be high during a boom, but the volatile factors determining investment cannot be expected to maintain, on average, over a sequence of short periods a value sufficient to provide full employment. He looks to economic policies, and in particular to a greater role for government investment (e.g., 220), as the means by

---

[3] Keynes here adopts a condition that 'sets a limit to the instability resulting from rapid changes in the prospective yield of capital-assets due to sharp fluctuations in business psychology or to epoch-making inventions – though more, perhaps, in the upward than in the downward direction' (252). There is no hint of such a limit in other statements that point to investment as, e.g., the 'factor which is most prone to sudden and wide fluctuation' (Keynes 1973c: 121). But he consistently points to the absence of a reliable mechanism to ensure an amount of investment sufficient to provide full employment.

which a more satisfactory average level of employment will be achieved.

6.5 THE TRADE CYCLE

Keynes briefly outlined how his General Theory can be used to explain the important features of the trade cycle. In doing so, he provides an indication of the ways in which his formal analysis, which is limited to a particular short period, can shed light on changes that occur over a sequence of short periods. This extension of the analysis is not mechanical, with the values in future periods being determined by the application of some mathematical formula to values in earlier periods. The long-term expectations that affect the determination of investment and the liquidity preference function cannot be accurately modelled from past data.[4] Individual decisions and actions in these spheres are not based on mathematical expectations that can be derived from probability distributions of the consequences of these actions.[5] Rational choice from alternatives that have future consequences cannot be reduced to a choice between meaningful numerical outcomes.

Generally speaking, in making a decision we have before us a large number of alternatives, none of which is demonstrably more 'rational' than the others, in the sense that we can arrange in order of merit the sum aggregate of the benefits obtainable from the complete consequences of each. To avoid being in the position of Buridan's ass, we fall back, therefore, and necessarily do so,

[4] In his comments on the proofs of Tinbergen's (1939) League of Nations study on the statistical testing of business cycle theories, referred to in chapter 4, n14 above, Keynes expressed his reservations on the use of past data for this purpose by posing two questions. 'Is it assumed that the future is a determinate function of *past statistics*? What place is left for expectation and the state of confidence relating to the future?' (Keynes 1973c: 287) Keynes can thus be seen as denying what Samuelson (1968) has called the 'ergodic hypothesis'. Samuelson considered this to be an 'assumption implicit and explicit in the classical mind. It was a belief in unique long-run equilibrium independent of intial conditions . . . we theorists hoped not to introduce *hysteresis* phenomena . . . [that take] the subject out of the realm of science into the realm of genuine history' (11–12). See also, Davidson (1982–3).

[5] Townshend (1937b: 325) in a review of Hawtrey (1937a), summarised his understanding of Keynes's treatment of investment and the liquidity preference function, as follows: 'The prospect of future returns (whether from enterprise or from the realisation of accumulated assets) is not expressible as a *mathematical* expectation. This, at least, is what I conceive Mr. Keynes to mean'. Townshend, before writing this review wrote to Keynes in order to get confirmation that the basic problem Keynes saw with classical theory was its assumption that risk exists without uncertainty (Keynes 1979: 257). Keynes replied 'that you have put your finger on the spot in saying that they are trying to describe a world in which risk exists without uncertainty' (258).

on motives of another kind, which are not 'rational' in the sense of being concerned with the evaluation of consequences, but are decided by habit, instinct, preference, desire, will, etc.   (Keynes 1979: 294)

Keynes sees the details of any actual trade cycle as being 'highly complex and that every element in our analysis will be required for its complete explanation' (Keynes 1936: 313). But it is mainly to the fluctuations in the marginal efficiency of capital that he turns for an explanation of the cyclical nature of changes. 'The Trade Cycle is best regarded, I think, as being occasioned by a cyclical change in the marginal efficiency of capital, though complicated and often aggravated by associated changes in the other significant short-period variables of the economic system.' In his sketch of a theory of the cycle he tries to provide reasons for its regularity and for the appearance of a 'crisis', the sudden replacement of an upward movement by a sharp downward tendency. The crisis was considered to be an essential part of the unfolding of the cycles, and any explanation of cycles must cover this characteristic if it is to be adequate.

He begins his analysis of the cycle at the later stages of the boom, just before the onset of the crisis. Optimistic expectations are still strong enough to override the evidence of increasing productive capacity, and rising costs of production for capital goods, as well as the rising interest rates that are generally found as the boom develops. These expectations are fed by speculation in stock exchanges that drive up the prices of equities, which come to bear little relation to reasonable estimates of the future yields from ownership of capital goods. The speculative excesses eventually lead to the crisis as some catalyst, often minor in itself, causes market sentiment to shift, and precipitates a downward movement in financial values that feeds on itself.

It is of the nature of organised investment markets, under the influence of purchasers largely ignorant of what they are buying and of speculators who are more concerned with forecasting the next shift of market sentiment than with a reasonable estimate of the future yield of capital – assets, that, when disillusion falls upon an over-optimistic and over-bought market, it should fall with sudden and even catastrophic force.   (315–6)

The concerns occasioned by this collapse in equity prices (to which Keynes ties the marginal efficiency of capital, and thus investment, as we saw in section 4.4 above) act on the liquidity preference function and there is a sharp rise in the rate of interest. But in any case, the sharp decline in the marginal efficiency of capital is so overwhelming that investment could not be maintained even if the rate of interest were reduced.

The recovery depends on the revival of the marginal efficiency of capital – on the return of confidence – which only occurs after the passage of time that is required to allow for the elimination of excess productive capacity and excess stocks of commodities. This interval of time that is required for the absorption and disappearance of the excesses produced by the boom, provides Keynes with his explanation for the length, and regularity, of the downward movement in output. The reduction in demand for working capital during this phase gives a further push to declining output and employment. He also believed that the collapse of equity prices had an adverse effect on the propensity to consume of those who invested in equities, especially if they did so with borrowed funds. When these negative influences are finally dissipated, the increased demand for working capital as short-term expectations improve, gives a boost to effective demand that has a favourable effect on long-term expectations. The resulting increase in investment expenditures begins to feed on itself, and the recovery is speeded up and then moves into the early stages of the boom.

Keynes saw the trade cycle as an inevitable outcome of *laissez-faire* capitalism: 'In conditions of *laissez-faire* the avoidance of wide fluctuations in employment may, therefore, prove impossible without a far-reaching change in the psychology of investment markets such as there is no reason to expect. I conclude that the duty of ordering the current volume of investment cannot safely be left in private hands' (320). He also favoured policies that would increase the propensity to consume as a method for maintaining a high level of employment. 'Whilst aiming at a socially controlled rate of investment with a view to a progressive decline in the marginal efficiency of capital, I should support at the same time all sorts of policies for increasing the propensity to consume' (325).

Keynes merely sketched the outlines of an approach to the trade cycle based on his General Theory, and our interpretation of that theory indicates that he could not go much further than his suggestive comments and observations. He was prepared, and possibly too willing, to accept short-period equilibrium values as good proxies for actual values, but he was not prepared to assume that the investment function would be unchanged over a sequence of short periods.

It is interesting to contrast his approach in this regard with that of Kalecki. There are important similarities in their analyses of short-period situations; investment was independent of the propensity to save, and fluctuations in its value over time gave rise to cycles. But Kalecki (1935, 1937), unlike Keynes, tried to develop a mathematically-determinate theory of the cycle that drew on the double-sided relationship between profits and investment, and the change in the capital stock. Current investment is a determinant of current profits, while current profits through their influence on the expectations of the profitability of investment, are determinants of current investment decisions, and thus of future investment expenditures. The larger the capital stock, other things given, the lower the value for investment decisions. Keynes, in correspondence with Kalecki that touched on the differences in their approaches to the determination of investment, objected to the special assumptions, to the 'precision', that Kalecki needed to get a determinate solution for his business cycle equations: 'I feel that you are making too much of a discontinuity between your periods. I quite agree, however, that the amount of unexecuted decisions which the entrepreneurs are ready, so to speak, to have at risk, is an important element in holding up the pace of investment and cannot be neglected. It is only the precision of your conclusion which I was criticising' (Keynes 1983, 798).

6.6 LONG-PERIOD EQUILIBRIUM IN *THE GENERAL THEORY*

The General Theory draws heavily on a restricted form of equilibrium where, given the inherited productive capacity, the firms' rates of output are appropriate for the demand conditions facing them. The searching by firms for these appropriate rates of output is assumed to be reasonably successful within the short period, so that the actual rates of output can be represented by the short-period equilibrium rates. Both consumption and investment expenditures are also assumed to have adjusted to actual conditions within the short period. But no use is made of the more general form of equilibrium that assumes the inherited productive capacity is the one that would be just right for current demand conditions. This full equilibrium appears only peripherally in *The General Theory* because it cannot have a significant role in a theory that embodies Keynes's vision of the volatile nature of capitalist economies. In such economies, the investment decisions that are always based on incomplete and uncertain knowledge of future conditions, will generally not give rise to just the amount of productive capacity required in any future short period. Long-period equilibrium values can be deduced for the conditions ruling in any particular short period, but they are changing over time in a non-stationary economy and they do not serve as poles of attraction for current values or for investment decisions. Keynes's distrust of long-period equilibrium analysis as a guide to current affairs is reflected in the well-known aphorism in his 1923 *Tract on Monetary Reform*, '*In the long run* we are all dead' (Keynes 1971: 65). Because of the volatility of actual economies 'economists set themselves too easy, too useless a task if in tempestuous seasons they can only tell us that when the storm is long past the ocean is flat again.'

Reference is sometimes made to long-period equilibrium in *The General Theory* in order to clarify the meaning of the short-period concepts in that theory. It is used in this way to show the difference between long-period and short-period supply prices. The former includes supplementary, interest and risk costs, as well as prime costs 'so that in long-period equilibrium the excess of the marginal prime cost over the average prime cost is equal to the sum of the supplementary, risk and interest costs' (Keynes 1936: 68). Long-period equilibrium is also implicit in Keynes's definition of long-period employment that was examined in section 3.8 above. This is the steady level (or steady rate of change) of employment that is determined by an unchanging state of expectation that has been held for so long that all current employment is in line with this expectation. Actual conditions must turn out to be in line with expectations, that is, each point in time is characterised by long-period equilibrium, in order for these expectations to remain unchanged over time. Keynes's experience was of a different world, and his brief examination of long-period employment was in the nature of an aside. It played no role in his theory.

Long-period equilibrium also appears in some of Keynes's comments on classical theory. In discussing Ricardo's theory of the rate of interest, Keynes points out the implicit assumption in that theory that 'there is only one possible level of employment in long-period equilibrium' (191). According to his own theory where there may not be full employment, 'even in the long period', it is possible to conceive of 'a number of positions of long-period equilibrium corresponding to different conceivable interest policies on the part of the monetary authority'. Each of these positions corresponds to a different rate of interest that, with given and unchanging long-term expectations, determines a constant level of employment. But these are very special cases in his model, while in Ricardo's theory 'there is in fact only one possible rate of accumulation of capital and, consequently, only one possible value for the marginal efficiency of capital. Ricardo offers us the supreme intellectual achievement, unattainable by weaker spirits, of adopting a hypothetical world remote from experience as though it were the world of experience and then living in it consistently' (192).

The few references in *The General Theory* to events 'in the long period' are all outside the main framework of his analysis. They are used to indicate some of the possible implications of the analysis, or to point out the greater range of choice among policy variables in a larger time frame. An example of the latter is his comment on the stability of prices, referred to in section 6.3 above, a stability that in short-period situations with constant money-wage rates is tied to the avoidance of fluctuations in output. But in the long period the increase in labour productivity due to improved equipment and techniques makes it possible to achieve stable prices even though money-wage rates and output are slowly increasing. Keynes commented on the eventual consequences of the achievement of a rate of investment sufficient to provide full employment in the capitalist economies of his day. He thought that it would 'be comparatively easy to make capital-goods so abundant that the marginal efficiency of capital is zero' (211). Reflections along these lines lie well outside his formal theory, and in this case the result is a fantasy of a capitalist world in which there would be a way 'of gradually getting rid of many of the objectionable features of capitalism ... the rentier would disappear'.

6.7 CONCLUSION

Keynes assumed that actual values could be represented by the short-period equilibrium values for employment and output that were explained by his General Theory. Because of the unreliability of the factors determining investment, these values could be less than those for full-employment situations. There is a specific, historical context for Keynes's model, with the consumption function, the marginal efficiency of capital, the liquidity preference function, the money supply and the money-wage rate all being given. Keynes's method of dealing with the consequences of the changes over time that occur in the values of these variables is indicated by his examination of the effects of changing money-wage rates and by his notes on the trade cycle. He recognises that allowance must be made for the interactions among the independent variables of his analysis. Changes in one variable can lead to changes in other variables, and the full effects of any intitial change depend on these interactions. The complexity of these interrelations means that the analysis of changes over time cannot be adequately handled by mathematical equations. Keynes goes beyond the short period when he combines his formal analysis with experience of the operations of actual economies that provide some indication of the nature and extent of likely changes in his independent variables. The time paths for employment and output that are deduced from this extension of this theory are 'illustrative' rather than 'determinate'. They show what would happen *if particular patterns of interaction occurred*. They provide the analyst with an indication of likely outcomes, but the actual time paths of the dependent variables depend on the circumstances surrounding the initiating changes.

There was no place in Keynes's analysis for long-period equilibrium. To each set of actual conditions in a particular short period, the corresponding long-period equilibrium values can be deduced, but they keep changing with changing conditions over time. Because they are changing, they do not exert a strong attraction on actual values, and they cannot be used to represent the latter. Keynes's indication of how his analysis could be extended to deal with some of the changes occurring over time thus did not refer to long-period equilibrium. The treatments of capital accumulation by Harrod and Robinson, to which we now turn, did not avoid the dangers of giving an important role to long-period equilibrium analysis.

7

HARROD AND DYNAMIC ECONOMICS*

7.1 INTRODUCTION

R. F. Harrod's attempt to move economic theory in a direction that would encompass dynamic models was based on ideas that pre-dated *The General Theory*. It stemmed from the view that a correct analysis of cyclical phenomena cannot take as the starting point a position of static equilibrium. These phenomena 'should be regarded as oscillations around a line of steady growth, (Harrod 1951: 261), and he tried to deal with them in this way in his 1936 book entitled *The Trade Cycle: An Essay*. This book's genesis was independent of *The General Theory*, and had as its central idea the interaction of J. M. Clark's accelerator with Kahn's 'multiplier' and it tried to show that the business cycle is one aspect of the growth process.[1] But Harrod had not yet arrived at his 'fundamental growth equation', which he was to use to generate his equilibrium path of steady advance. He recalled that this equation 'came to me in a flash on a particular day ... In the course of my "reflections" I suddenly saw it in a split second ... in July 1938' (Harrod 1973: 41). That Harrod then quickly wrote his basic paper on dynamic theory, which was published in March 1939, is evident from his 3 August, 1938 letter to Keynes that included the announcement: 'I have just finished writing my re-statement of the "dynamic" theory, which is, I think, a great improvement on my book' (Keynes 1973c: 301).

Harrod's dynamic theory is treated here as one of two major attempts to extend Keynes's short-period analysis to the consideration of accumulation over time, even though this theory's initial development was independent of *The General Theory*. With the publi-

---

* Some of the ideas in this chapter were first developed in Asimakopulos (1985, 1986).
[1] After pointing out the central role of these two elements, Harrod (1973, 41) noted that 'Keynes to the end refused to be interested in J. M. Clark's accelerator.' The reason for this refusal, according to the interpretation of Keynes's approach to economic theory given here, is to be found in the 'mechanical' nature of the accelerator, and in its implicit derivation of long-term expectations from the calculation of the rate of change of output.

cation of *The General Theory*, and even earlier, from the time in June 1935 when Keynes sent him the galley proofs, Harrod saw what he was trying to do in the light of what Keynes had accomplished. Keynes's terminology was utilised in his subsequent work where it was feasible, and Harrod's dynamic theory was 'Keynes-like' in spirit because investment was independent of the propensity to save. This independence was considered by Robinson to be the hallmark of Keynesian models, because they 'project into the long period the central thesis of the *General Theory*, that firms are free, within wide limits, to accumulate as they please, and that the rate of saving of the economy as a whole accommodates itself to the rate of investment that they decree' (Robinson 1962: 82–3). The only criticism that Harrod made of *The General Theory*, in the paper that he gave at the 1936 meeting of the Econometric Society in Oxford, concerned its static nature. *The General Theory* included dynamic elements, such as changing expectations about an unknown future, and it allowed for net saving to be positive, but it was only concerned with the level of output and employment. Harrod argued that saving entails growth, and that the resulting growth in income must be explicitly allowed for in working out equilibrium conditions. 'I envisage in the future two departments of economic principles. The first, the static theory, will be elaborated on the assumption that there is no growth and no saving ... In the second department, dynamic theory, growth and saving will be taken into account. Equilibrium theory will be concerned not merely with what size, but also with what rate of growth of certain magnitudes is consistent with the surrounding circumstances' (Harrod 1937: 86). In his subsequent writings, Harrod tried to develop this dynamic equilibrium theory. He saw this work as a necessary complement to Keynes's General Theory. With a central role in that theory being accorded to saving, 'the *General Theory* will not be fully satisfactory until it is brought into relation with Dynamics' (Harrod 1948: 10).

7.2 THE TRADE CYCLE

Harrod's 1936 book on *The Trade Cycle* was the first formal working out of his vision of the cycle as oscillations around a line of steady advance. His contention was 'that by a study of the interconnexions between the Multiplier and the Relation [the Acceleration Principle] the secret of the trade cycle may be revealed' (Harrod 1936: 70). Changes in investment are transformed into changes in output as a result of the multiplier, while these changes in output in turn, through the operation of the acceleration principle induce further changes in investment, which then feed into further changes in output, etc. For Harrod dynamic theory is concerned with rates of growth and thus the time lags that others see as an essential element in such a theory (e.g. Frisch 1933) are not at centre stage. The one time lag that enters explicitly into the theory arises from an inescapable feature of investment. Some interval of time must elapse after investment decisions are made, and expenditures undertaken, before the resulting investment goods are available for use: 'the fact that net investment is undertaken with a view to facilitating production in the future is clearly a central one; and the interval that elapses between placing an order for, or beginning to undertake the construction of, capital goods and their use in the productive process can hardly be neglected' (Harrod 1936: 88). These investment orders are seen as being based on 'recent experience' and on 'guess work' with regard to the future. In Harrod's working out of the theory, recent experience plays the dominant role in determining investment, presumably because he implicitly assumes that expectations of the future are largely determined by recent experience.

Harrod takes as the starting point of his analysis a situation of steady advance.

> A steady advance is defined as one in which the ratio of the increment of output to the previous level is constant ... the proportionate increase of net investment on the given day over net investment on the day preceding is equal to the proportionate addition to the stock of capital goods available for use on the given day. The experience of the given day will be the primary test as to whether the advance is likely to remain steady. (89)

The content of this experience depends on the values for what Harrod calls 'the three dynamic determinants'. They are : (i) the propensity to save of a representative income-receiver; (ii) the change in profit share resulting from the change in output; and (iii) the designed capital-output ratio for new capital goods in relation to that for pre-existing goods. These three elements are called 'dynamic' determinants because they are seen as determining the rate of growth of output at a particular point in time.[2]

---

[2] Harrod had previously listed four 'static' determinants that are related to the level of output at a particular point in time. These four determinants are '(i) The rates of pay at which prime factors of production can be secured. (ii) The efficiency of the prime factors. (iii) The elasticity of demand for commodities. (iv) The general price level' (50). The third of these static determinants, the elasticity of demand, is seen as relevant because Harrod, unlike Keynes, assumes imperfect competition in the markets for manufactured goods. That most of Harrod's *Trade Cycle* book had been

Harrod, before his examination of the cycle, considers the behaviour of his three dynamic determinants that would 'justify' the assumed rate of steady advance 'by the experience of the given day' (90). A rate of growth is said to be justified if demand grows at the rate required to utilise the new capital goods that become available at their designed rates of utilisation. The stock of capital goods is assumed to increase at the same rate as investment with a steady advance, and desired output also increases at the same rate if the multiplier value is unchanged. (Note that the full multiplier effects of the increase in net investment are assumed to be completed within the 'day', an interval of time that is short.) This increase would then be sufficient to utilise the new capital goods at their designed rates if there has been no change in the capital-output ratio. The steady rate of advance would thus be justified if '(i) ... representative income-receivers save the same proportion of their increment of income as they previously saved of the income of the day before. (ii) ... there is no shift to profit. (iii) ... the productive methods for which the new capital goods were designed are the same as those previously employed.'(90)[3] These requirements, as will be seen below, are very similar to those that he subsequently set out for his warranted rate of growth, but what is missing here is an equation for this rate of steady advance.

If any of the above three conditions is violated, then it is easy to show that capital goods would not be utilised at their designed rates. For example, a shift to profits, which increases the overall propensity to save of the economy means that the investment orders that gave rise to the new capital goods will not be 'fully justified'.[4] In this case 'the advance in consumption will not be fully proportional to the increase in capital goods available to provide for it' (91). Conversely, a situation where the new capital goods are of a more capitalistic design (as indicated by the ratio of the value of these goods to the

---

worked out before he even saw drafts of *The General Theory* is indicated by the absence of any reference to Keynes's determinants of equilibrium in the short period.

[3] Harrod notes in a footnote placed at the end of (i) that the use of a 'representative income-receiver' is resorted to in order to keep separate the possibility of a change in the proportion of profits in total income. 'Otherwise the first and second dynamic determinants might be lumped together as proportion of income saved' (90n). It is the latter approach that he followed in his subsequent writings, even though this made possible the misrepresentation of his work, the mistaken reading into it of the assumption that the propensity to save is independent of the proportion of profits.

[4] The shortfall of orders might result in lower-than-expected rates of utilisation of older equipment rather than of the new capital goods, but the conditions for a steady advance are violated in any case.

value of output they are designed to produce[5]) would mean that even with a constant value of the multiplier, the increase in demand would be greater than the output these goods were designed to produce. The entrepreneurial responses to these deviations from the desired rate of utilisation of capital goods are assumed to be such as to move the economy away from the line of steady advance. 'If the previous orders now maturing prove over-justified on the given day, then on the basis of the most recent experience the rate at which new orders for capital goods, and so of new net investment, is increased is likely to rise. Conversely, if the previous orders now maturing do not prove fully justified' (91–2). (These considerations are, of course, the basis for Harrod's instability principle in his later writings.) Cyclical movements are seen as occurring because the three dynamic determinants are considered likely to behave in a manner that is inconsistent with the assumed line of steady advance. Individuals are said to save a larger proportion of higher income, so that a path of steady advance in which per-capita incomes are increasing is likely to be disrupted by the consequent decrease in the value of the multiplier. The profit share might change if output is increasing at a steady rate as a result of increasing marginal costs and because of the diminishing elasticity of demand that Harrod sees as increasing profit margins. The third determinant might tend to counteract the restrictive influence on the rate of growth of the first two determinants if inventions 'increase the amount of capital required per unit of output' (93). Harrod is cautious about predicting that inventions will be of this character, and in any case there is no reason to expect that the changes in the values of the three determinants along a line of steady advance will be exactly offsetting. 'We cannot rely on the three determinants to maintain it [a steady advance] ... If there is any drop in the rate of advance, a recession must occur' (104). Harrod is depending here on the action of the acceleration principle to lead to a decrease in net investment, with the latter's effects being reinforced by the multiplier. Before continuing with Harrod's explanation of the cycle, we should note the limited role in this analysis of the line of steady advance, as opposed to the more extended role of his later warranted rate of growth.[6] The line of steady growth serves simply to place the

---

[5] The method used by Harrod to indicate the capital intensity of production is the one that he subsequently employed in defining the nature of technical progress. The values of capital per unit of output, using the same interest rates, are compared for the new and old techniques.

[6] The term 'warranted' is used by Harrod in this book *en passant* in referring to an advance that would be 'warranted by the normal increase in efficiency through inventions and improvements within the period' (105).

analysis of the cycle in the dynamic setting that he considers to be appropriate, while the warranted rate of growth, which is defined by an equation, takes on much more importance for Harrod.

We can pick up Harrod's explanation of the trade cycle with the start of a downturn due, say, to the restrictive influence of the first two determinants outweighing any expansionary effects from changes in the capital–output ratio. The failure of output to increase sufficiently means that the under-utilisation of capital equipment serves to drag down net investment, which then leads to a decline in consumption that quickly pushes net investment towards a zero value. The shift away from profit that occurs in the downswing tends to increase the marginal propensity to consume, and it thus acts as a restraining force on falling demand. The 'bottom' of the cycle occurs at an output at which the gross investment due to necessary replacements, and to the improvements of plant that still appear to be profitable, is sufficient to absorb desired saving ('what will be voluntarily saved' (101)). Revival is thus seen as coming from the mere passage of time because of the increases in investment expenditures for replacement purposes that eventually exceed amortisation allowances, and thus result in an increase in net investment. With this increase the multiplier effects can begin to induce further increases in investment.[7] The upward movement of the economy will eventually cease because of the restrictive forces due to the increase in the propensity to save of representative individuals, and due to the increase in the profit share that becomes noticeable in the later stages of the boom.

Harrod's summary of this 'central part' of his theory is as follows:

As soon as disappointment in the results of past investment occurs or is anticipated in consequence of the working of the three dynamic determinants, the rate of increase of investment slows down. This, in accordance with the Multiplier, entails a further slowing down in the rate of increase in consumption. This, in accordance with the Relation, entails an absolute fall in net investment. This, in accordance with the Multiplier, entails an absolute fall in income and consumption. This, in accordance with the Relation, entails that net investment is rapidly reduced to a very low level, if not to zero. (98)

He recognises that the recession might not be as rapid as is indicated by his theory because of the time lag between the placing of investment orders and their completion that might result in significant

---

[7] Harrod's assertion at this point is not very clear on the mechanics of the expansion. He simply writes that the rise of net investment 'gives scope for the three dynamic determinants to ordain a period of steady or cumulative advance' (101).

amounts of net investment (in spite of cancellations) even after the pace of new orders drops sharply. There could also be a different timing of changes in different industries that tends to create some evening-out of activity. Further, output in the agricultural sector where the producers are also the owners follows a different pattern.[8] These producers try to maintain output even in depressed times, and if dealers or middlemen who are in charge of marketing these crops allow stocks to accumulate during times of depression, then they are providing support for investment that 'retards the general recession' (99). These factors might be strong enough to prevent a downward fluctuation of net investment from leading to a full recession, even though they cannot always be counted on to do so.

7.3 TRANSITION TO THE 1939 'ESSAY'

The major difference in Harrod's later writings on dynamic theory, as compared with *The Trade Cycle* is the equation for the (entrepreneurial) equilibrium rate of growth. It was when he had worked it out that Harrod wrote to Keynes, in a letter dated 6 July 1938: 'I have now got my "dynamic" theory, I think, into a much better form than I had it in my book' (Keynes 1973c: 298). The correspondence with Keynes about the latter's reaction to *The Trade Cycle* (to be found in Keynes 1973c: 150–79), made clear the need to develop an equation that set out the conditions for a steady advance. Keynes did not always understand the points that Harrod was trying to make – at times Harrod would respond that Keynes's criticisms were based on a 'static' view of a 'dynamic' matter (e.g. 163) – but they helped him to see where he should try to make his ideas more precise.[9]

The fundamental difference between these two economists that could never be resolved was their approach to investment. Keynes was critical of the assumption of 'a constant value for the relation throughout the trade cycle' (151). Harrod, on the other hand, was

---

[8] The reason why they follow a different pattern, according to Harrod, is because the producers work with their own equipment; they are outside the social relations of capitalism. Their output is determined by individual preferences (the marginal utility of consumption and the marginal disutility of labour) and the terms at which they can change their produce for other goods. Harrod notes (34n) that the distinction he is making is separate from the one that might be made on the basis of the perfectly competitive markets that are found for agricultural products, as opposed to the existence of imperfect markets for manufactured goods.

[9] In the final letter he wrote in this exchange, Harrod began: 'Many thanks for your letter and interesting notes. So far as I am concerned the matter should not end here; I shall try to develop my ideas for a form suitable for publication in the light of your reaction' (174).

critical of Keynes's notes on the trade cycle in *The General Theory*, because they did not make use of a fully specified investment function. 'But your treatment of the trade cycle was merely fragmentary for lack of a theory as to what governs the volume of investment' (175). This difference was reflected in the difficulties that Keynes had with Harrod's concept of a warranted rate of growth, quite apart from the occasional misunderstanding of the terms being employed. (The draft that Keynes commented on has been lost so that it is not possible to see what changes Harrod made as a result of Keynes's comments.)

Keynes (1936: 48n) had shown with his footnote comment on long-period employment under conditions of a steady increase in wealth or population, that had been foreseen sufficiently far ahead, that he had no difficulty in visualising or defining a special equilibrium growth path. What he had a problem with was the attribution to such a growth path, characterised by long-period equilibrium at each point in time, of any 'reality' or substance in a modern capitalist economy. Keynes's attitude is indicated, for example, in a May 1936 letter to Henderson, where he wrote: 'I should, I think, be prepared to argue that, in a world ruled by uncertainty with an uncertain future linked to an actual present, a final position of equilibrium, such as one deals with in static economics, does not properly exist' (Keynes 1979: 222).[10] It is thus not surprising that Keynes's fundamental objection to Harrod's theory concerns the existence of a warranted rate of growth. In his final letter to Harrod on this topic, he wrote: 'In general there is *no* warranted rate, and special conditions are required for a warranted rate to be possible' (Keynes 1973c: 346). As we shall see in a later section of this chapter, Harrod came in time to share at least some of Keynes's skepticism about the existence of a warranted rate of growth.

7.4 DYNAMIC EQUILIBRIUM

Harrod's 'An Essay in Dynamic Theory' was presented as a 'tentative and preliminary attempt to give the outline of a "dynamic" theory' (Harrod 1939: 14). An essential element in this attempt was the definition of dynamic equilibrium that was to be the counterpart to equilibrium in static economics. Harrod's view of the domain of dynamic economics – the concern with rates of growth – ensured that

---

[10] Keynes had made it clear in an earlier passage of this letter than by 'static economics' he meant one that assumed 'static conditions where the future does not affect the present or where it of necessity always resembles the past' (221).

this dynamic equilibrium would be a rate of growth with special characteristics. He stated that the basis of his theory 'consists in a marriage of the "acceleration principle" and the "multiplier" theory', but these elements are implicit in Harrod's development of his theory, because he does not embody them in an equation that makes use of the time lags usually assumed in theories that combine these elements.[11] Harrod wants attention to be focused on what he considers to be the fundamental difference between dynamic and static theory – the former's concern with rates of growth in the values of the variables, and the latter's with the values for these variables. The acceleration principle is reflected in his theory by the assumption that investment in a subsequent time period is affected by the relation between the change in output over the present and the concurrent change in productive capacity. Saving in each period is assumed to be in the desired relation to income, that is, it is determined by the economy's propensity to save (given the distribution of income)[12] and the level of income in the period. The full multiplier effects of investment in the period have thus been implicitly assumed to be completed within the period.[13]

Harrod re-stated his dynamic theory in a set of lectures that were delivered at the University of London in 1947, and then they were published in 1948 under the title *Towards a Dynamic Economics*.[14] There were some changes in notation from that used in the 'Essay', and there was room for a more extended treatment of some topics (for example, technical progress), as well as an extended consideration of matters briefly touched on in the article (for example, the foreign balance), but the core of the dynamic theory was unchanged. It was only after the passage of time, and the many comments on his theory, that Harrod reconsidered the generality of his theory – a reconsider-

[11] Time lags are used, for example, by Samuelson (1939).

[12] Harrod was mistakenly interpreted, and not only by textbook writers, to have assumed that the proportion of income saved is independent of the distribution of income between wages and profits. For example, Robinson (1970) based her interpretation of Harrod's model on this assumption. Harrod (1970: 737) denied, with justification, ever having made such an assumption.

[13] In his affirmation of the existence of the multiplier effects in his equation for the warranted rate of growth, Harrod (1959: 454) mistakenly asserts that the desired saving ratio in that equation 'is the reciprocal of the multiplier.' This would only be the case, of course, if his average propensity to save was always equal to the marginal propensity to save, a condition that he does not impose on his basic equation.

[14] Harrod saw his work as returning to the concern with dynamic theory of classical economists, such as Ricardo. Harrod (1948: 20) noted that he had discarded two factors that figure prominently in earlier dynamic theories: the Malthusian approach to population size; and the law of diminishing returns from the land.

ation that received its final expression in a 1973 book with the title *Economic Dynamics*. In the presentation of his theory in this chapter, the notation found in that book will be employed.

Harrod's dynamic theory makes use of three main categories of rate of growth. They are the actual, the warranted, and the natural rates of growth. There are also two sub-categories of the warranted rate: the 'normal' warranted rate that is relevant to situations in which there are normal rates of utilisation of productive capacity; and the 'special' warranted rates, each of which assumes a particular degree of under- or over-utilisation of capacity. The switch from the General Theory's 'static' focus on the level of output, to the dynamic consideration of the rate of growth of output, can be formally accomplished very simply. Saving must be equal to investment in each period of time, and these periods are short,[15] with a form of Keynes's short-period equilibrium, as shown by equation (7.1), holding in each period.

$$I = S \tag{7.1}$$

Unlike these terms in Keynes's theory, I and S now represent *net* investment and saving.[16] Saving is assumed to be in the desired relation to income, and thus

$$S = s_d Y \tag{7.2}$$

where s_d is the desired saving ratio in the economy, given the distribution of income in the period. Investment in equation (7.1) is simply the investment that happens to take place in the period, and it need not be equal to the investment that was planned for the period. If equation (7.2) is substituted in equation (7.1) and the left-hand side of the resulting equation is multiplied by $\Delta Y/\Delta Y$, with the terms being rearranged, we obtain $(\Delta Y/Y)(I/\Delta Y) = s_d$, or

$$GC = s_d \tag{7.3}$$

---

[15] In defining the rate of growth, Harrod takes as the numerator the difference in average output in two adjacent periods, and notes 'we suppose the period to be short' (1939: 16). He subsequently gave six months as a calendar estimate of the possible length of his short period, with growth measured 'per six months' (26). This length is within the range of Keynes's short period.

[16] The use by Harrod of net values for investment (saving) sets his theory in a long-period equilibrium mould, since meaningful estimates of depreciation can only be made in such situations. With his focus on changes in productive capacity, and on rates of growth of output, the use of net investment obviously appears to be more appropriate to Harrod than the use of gross investment. Keynes used gross investment because the short-period situations being examined could very well be ones where entrepreneurial investment expectations are not being borne out by events, and estimates of depreciation are not reliable.

G is the rate of growth of output (the difference in average output in this period as compared to average output in the preceding period, divided by output in the present period),[17] and C is the capital coefficient that is observed in the period. It is equal to the ratio of investment in fixed and working capital, and work in progress, to the increase in output in the period. Equation (7.3) is a 'dynamic' equation, and it can be used to show that the *actual* rate of growth of output, G, is equal to the ratio of the desired saving rate to the capital coefficient.[18]

Equation (7.3) becomes Harrod's fundamental equation for dynamic equilibrium when the value for the capital coefficient in that equation is equal to the value for the *required* capital coefficient (C_r). The value of C_r 'depends on the state of technology and the nature of the goods constituting the increment of output. It may be expected to vary as income grows and in different phases of the trade cycle; it may be somewhat dependent on the rate of interest' (17). It is important to note that Harrod does not make use of a capital–output ratio in his theory, he only employs the ratio of net investment to the current increase in output. C_r is the marginal requirement for new capital. The investment that occurs in this period can be said to have been 'justified' by the growth in output that occurred over the period if C turns out to equal C_r. This rate of growth or output is called the 'warranted' rate (G_w), and equation (7.3) can be rewritten for this case as

$$G_w = s_d/C_r \qquad\qquad (7.4)$$

The value for C_r, other things being given, depends on the length of the period over which output is measured. For example, a new plant that cost \$1,000,000 to put in working order and which produces an annual output, under normal rates of utilisation, that sells for \$200,000, has a value for C_r of 5. If the period over which output from this plant was measured was six months, then the value for C_r would be 10. With a value for s_d of 0.10, then G_w would be 0.02 per annum, or 0.01 per six months.

Harrod sees equation (7.4) as providing more than just the definition of dynamic equilibrium at a point in time; it also indicates

---

[17] Harrod initially used the preceding period's output in the denominator but he realised, following Alexander's (1958) comment, that he had to use the current period's output if s_d is to be the desired saving ratio of current income.

[18] Its 'dynamic' nature would be unchanged if the actual saving ratio in the period, represented by s, was not in the desired ratio to income. The equation for the actual rate of growth could then be written as GC = s, or G = s/C.

the investment response of entrepreneurs to their finding that the period's net investment had been justified. He assumes that 'it will put them into a frame of mind which will cause them to give such orders as will maintain the same rate of growth' (Harrod 1939: 16). One of the problems with this use of total values in the economy to infer individual actions is that a given total value will comprise a wide range of different experiences for individual producers. Harrod recognises that even with the achievement of a warranted rate of growth for the economy some entrepreneurs may feel that they have invested too much or too litte. The effects of these individual dissatisfactions are assumed to cancel out: 'but the ups and downs should balance out and, in the aggregate, progress in the current period should be equal to progress in the last preceding period' (Harrod 1948: 82). This was an assumption that Harrod came to realise, as we shall see below, could not be justified in the type of world he wanted to analyse.

Of the many possible warranted rates of growth defined by equation (7.4), Harrod centres his analysis on the 'normal' warranted rate which allows for steady advance with productive capacity being fully utilised. ('We will call the initial warranted rate, as pertaining in a steady advance, the "normal" warranted rate, and others special warranted rates' (Harrod 1973: 36).) Harrod's examination of equation (7.4) is primarily concerned with this normal warranted rate. In considering it, he admits that a particular period's increase in output is not sufficient to justify all the net investment occurring in that period, because capital equipment is long-lived and its provision 'is connected with long-range planning' (Harrod 1939: 20). This problem is dealt with by subtracting the portion of investment that is tied to long-range planning from total investment. The latter is thus seen as being composed of two parts: a portion K that is based on long-term planning; and a portion $I-K$, whose justification is to be found in current changes in output. Equation (7.1) can be rewritten as

$$I - K = S - K \qquad (7.1')$$

This equation can be transformed into a dynamic equation by substituting $s_d Y$ for S. Multiplying both sides by $\Delta Y/\Delta Y$, and rearranging terms, we obtain:

$$GC = s_d - k \qquad (7.3')$$

where C is now equal to $(I-K)/\Delta Y$, and k is equal to K/Y. If the net investment that is related to current requirements turns out to be equal to what is required in the light of the actual increase in output, $C = C_r$, and $G = G_w$, where

$$G_w = (s_d - k)/C_r \qquad (7.4')$$

It is thus possible in this formal manner to allow for long-range investment planning within Harrod's theoretical framework. His analysis can be seen as focusing on that part of investment that is particularly related to current output. Even here 'there must be some lag between the increased provision of equipment (and stocks?) and the increased flow of output which they are designed to support' (20), but Harrod feels free to neglect this point because he considers it to be more relevant to studies that deal specifically with time lags. In addition, with his attention focused on a steady advance, the difference between the increase in output over successive pairs of periods will be negligible. 'In other words, it matters not whether we regard the increment of capital as required to support the increment of total output in the same period or in the one immediately succeeding it.'

This derivation of Harrod's fundamental equation for dynamic equilibrium has made clear that C_r, is not an *ex ante* concept, even though Harrod (1939: 19) initially refers to it in this way. When doing so, he noted that the term was being used in a special sense to relate current investment to current output.[19] *Ex ante* investment, as that term is commonly understood, refers to planned investment, which is related to the expected increase in demand. Harrod's 'justified' investment, in contrast, depends on the actual increase in output. The difference between these two concepts was emphasised by Harrod in a book based on his lecture notes, which was published when he retired from teaching. 'C_r is emphatically not an *ex ante* concept. Entrepreneurs may have planned to have something quite different from what they *now* find it convenient to have, since when they made their plans it could not be foreseen what the demand for their products would be' (Harrod 1969: 165n). If *ex ante* and *ex post* investment in a period differ because of differences between expected and actual demand, which are absorbed in inventory adjustments, then a simple relation between *ex ante* and justified investment can be deduced (Harrod 1951: 270). When *ex ante* investment is greater than *ex post* investment, because demand was greater than expected, then

---

[19] Keynes (1973c: 322) had objected to Harrod's usage of *ex ante* in this way. Harrod responded that 'with regard to *ex ante* ... I don't think the usage is sufficiently established for anyone to be able to say I mustn't use it the way I have' (337). He subsequently changed his mind on this point, as noted in the text below.

Harrod's justified investment would be greater than *ex ante* investment. In the opposite case, when *ex ante* investment is smaller than *ex post* investment, Harrod's justified investment would be even smaller than *ex ante* investment.

The category of dynamic equilibrium, the warranted rates of growth, that Harrod places at the center of his analysis, refers to entrepreneurial equilibrium in the sense that it is the entrepreneurs (or producers) who, on balance, consider that the increase in output in the period justified the investment they made in that period. This is a limited concept of equilibrium even for entrepreneurs (since it is only in the case of the normal warranted rate that there is normal utilisation of productive capacity), and its achievement is consistent with the existence of involuntary unemployment. Another equilibrium concept, the natural rate of growth, is related to full employment. 'This is the maximum rate of growth allowed by the increase of population, accumulation of capital, technological improvement and the work/leisure preference schedule, supposing that there is always full employment in some sense' (30).[20] Harrod also refers here to what he calls the 'proper' warranted rate, 'that warranted rate which would obtain in conditions of full employment'. This rate could differ from the 'normal' warranted rate, because the distribution of income appropriate to each, and thus the desired saving ratios, differ. There is no tendency in Harrod's model for the warranted and natural rates to coincide, since their determinants differ. Harrod's consideration of the trade cycle makes use, as we shall see below, of possible differences between the warranted and natural rates of growth.

7.5 THE LINE OF STEADY ADVANCE

Harrod postulated the existence of a line of steady advance, of '[A] unique warranted line of growth [that] is determined jointly by the propensity to save and the quantity of capital required by technological and other considerations per unit increment of total output. Only if producers keep to this line will they find that on balance their production in each period has been neither excessive nor deficient' (Harrod 1939: 23). This line of output that is traced by the normal warranted rate of growth is said to be 'a moving equilibrium, in the sense that it represents the one level of output at which producers will

---

[20] In his 'Second Essay on Dynamic Theory' (Harrod 1960), which he saw as a 'companion piece' to the 1939 'Essay', Harrod concentrated on the saving required for the achievement of a natural rate of growth.

feel in the upshot that they have done the right thing, and which will induce them to continue in the same line of advance' (22).

There are three issues connected with this postulate. They are: (i) the existence of a unique value for the normal warranted rate which underlies this steady growth path; (ii) the conditions that will cause producers to feel 'in the upshot that they have done the right thing'; and (iii) the basis for the assertion that the achievement of the normal warranted rate in one period 'will induce them to continue in the same line of advance.' Each of these points will be dealt with in turn.

With regard to the first issue, an examination of equation (7.4) makes clear that a unique and constant value for G_w requires that both s_d and C_r should have unique and constant values over time (the case where complementary variations in s_d and C_r maintain G_w constant is so special that it merits no attention). The desired saving ratio would be constant over time, if attitudes toward saving and the distribution of income between profits and wages were unchanged. This constancy of s_d would be fostered if the rate of interest (and rate of profits) were constant and technical progress was consistent with an unchanging distribution of income under these conditions. This type of technical progress – which is defined as neutral technical progress by Harrod – will maintain the value of C_r unchanged when the value for the rate of interest is constant. Constancy of the rate of interest (and the rate of profits[21]) over time is thus a necessary condition for the value of the warranted rate of growth to be constant. A unique value for this growth rate also requires that only one possible rate of profits be consistent with maintenance of a moving equilibrium. In postulating a 'unique warranted line of growth', Harrod was implicitly assuming that there is only one possible value for the equilibrium rate of profits in a particular economy. In this he differed from the position of others who developed Keynesian theories of growth, such as Kaldor (1957) and Robinson (1956), who assumed that the equilibrium rate of profits adapted itself to the requirements of dynamic equilibrium. Harrod entertained the possibility that there could be more than one value for the equilibrium rate of profits in his response to Robinson's (1970) comment on his theory. He objected, with cause, to her statement that he ignored the differences in the propensities to save out of wages and profits, but he agreed 'that, if there is more than one possible equilibrium profit share in a dynamic equilibrium, consistent with other dynamic determinants, there must be more than one equilibrium growth rate' (Harrod 1970: 738).

---

[21] In Harrod's model the equilibrium rate of profits is made up of the rate of interest plus an additional amount for the earnings of management.

The distribution of income was not a topic that received much attention in Harrod's writings on dynamic economics. The equilibrium distribution was taken as given, rather than explained by Harrod's model, and he admitted that he had not gone deeply into the question of income distribution. What little he has said on this topic is consistent with Marshall's theory of distribution in long-period equilibrium, which is built up from a normal rate of profit that comprises the rate of interest and gross earnings of management (Marshall 1920: 313). For example, Harrod (1970: 738) wrote:

> There is in the broad field of enterprise a minimum acceptable rate of return on capital – with a minority of entrepreneurs undercutting that – with which is associated a certain rate of mark-up of prices over costs. The influence of those whose monopoly position is so secure that they can safely indulge in substantially higher mark-ups can be exaggerated.

This approach is also reflected in a later statement: 'firms often have some standard rate of profit, which includes interest, that they add to the input costs' (Harrod 1973: 44). He also follows Marshall in viewing interest as 'the reward for waiting' (47).[22] Differences in the rate of interest might lead to different equilibrium rates of profit – 'sustained low interest will presumably in the long run reduce the normal rate of profit' (111) – and thus to more than one value for the warranted growth path. This recognition represents some movement away from the initial bold statement of 'uniqueness' for the value of the warranted growth rate, but it should not be exaggerated. 'I would not deny that a multiplicity of equilibrium profit shares and profit rates is a possibility; but it seems to me unlikely' (Harrod 1970: 738).

The constancy of the value for C_r, as well as s_d, is tied to a single value for the equilibrium rate of interest, because it is contingent on the choice of techniques and the nature of technical progress. Harrod (1948: 23) defines neutral technical progress 'as one which, at a constant rate of interest, does not disturb the value of the capital coefficient; it does not alter the length of the production process'.[23] If the rate of interest is constant over time, and technical progress is neutral, then the value of C_r will also be constant.

---

[22] Harrod (1948: 70) had recognised that a reward was necessary for parting with liquidity. 'It must be agreed ... that two activities are necessary before capital can be provided, namely (1) waiting and (2) parting with liquidity ... If a reward for waiting is necessary in order that there shall be waiting, those who want to enjoy the benefit of it will have to pay that reward, the liquidity preference question apart.'

[23] Capital-using technical progress, in contrast, would increase C_r under these conditions, while capital-saving technical progress would reduce its value. Technical progress that is neutral or capital-using, must obviously be labour-saving in order to qualify as technical progress.

Neutral technical progress, according to Harrod's definition, means that labour productivity is increasing at the same rate in all stages of production.[24] If the rate of profits is unchanged while this type of technical progress is occurring, then real-wage rates would be increasing at the rate of technical progress. For example, assume that 1,000 workers in the investment sector were producing, in a year, a plant whose selling price was $50 million, and that it provided employment for 500 workers when it was operated at a normal capacity rate of utilisation. Assume further that the resulting annual rate of output had a sales value of $10 million. From this information we can calculate a value of 5 for the C_r of this plant. Neutral technical progress would be said to have occurred if the 1,000 investment sector workers now produce a plant (which employs the same number of consumption-sector workers), but which has a larger productive capacity that now sells (at the same prices) for, say, $11 million, an increase of 10 per cent. The productivity of workers in the investment sector is determined by the productive capacity they produce for the consumption sector. In the case of our example, it can readily be calculated that the productivity of workers in each sector has increased by the same amount, 10 per cent. With this being neutral technical progress the value of the plant must be $55 million, with the value for C_r remaining at 5. If money-wage rates also increase by 10 per cent, and the rate of profits is constant, then the distribution of income between profits and wages will also be constant. Both total wages and total profits increase by 10 per cent.

Technical progress might be 'embodied' or 'disembodied'. In the former case it is the result of the development and production of new equipment that raises labour productivity, while in the latter it is a result of organisational changes that allow workers to increase output from a given plant. Both sources of technical progress could give rise to neutral technical progress, because the productivity of workers in the investment sector depends on the productive capacity of the equipment they produce, and thus their productivity in increased, even though they continue to produce the same equipment in the same way, when it is used in a new and more efficient manner.

Harrod's neutral technical progress is obviously a special occurrence, and he observed that 'it must not be taken to be implied that a

---

[24] With capital-using technical progress, the percentage increase in labour productivity in the consumption sector is greater than the percentage increase in the investment sector, while the reverse is the case for capital-saving technical progress (cf. Asimakopulos and Weldon 1963).

neutral invention as defined is the most likely kind of invention' (Harrod 1948: 28). He qualified this, however, with the statement that 'it is not my impression that in recent years inventions have been predominantly of a character tending to raise the capital coefficient', implying that the assumption of neutrality might not be wide of the mark. It is the type of technical progress that is consistent with his line of steady advance, and he was prepared to assume 'that on average all the various inventions and improvements accruing in a unit period are neutral, those requiring more capital per unit of output balancing the effect of those which require less' (83). But more than neutrality of technical progress is required if the economy is to follow a path of moving equilibrium. This technical progress must also be occurring at a steady rate so 'that the tempo of change is recognised by entrepreneurs, [and] they will fix their depreciation allowances accordingly' (84). Unexpected bursts of innovation could lead to losses that disrupt equilibrium.

The requirements for the existence of a unique warranted rate of growth, a line of steady advance, Harrod's moving equilibrium, are thus very stringent indeed. Harrod's approach to it, even initially, was ambivalent. He wanted the concept of a dynamic equilibrium as the centre-piece of his analysis, and he made special assumptions in an attempt to give it substance, but reality kept intruding. 'There is, in the real world, no steady advance. Inventions come irregularly and we have the perplexities of the trade cycle. And the future is necessarily involved in great uncertainty' (59). At a later stage, as we shall see below, this recognition (recall Keynes's statement, quoted in section 7.3, that there is no warranted rate of growth) led to the dissolution of his vision of a line of steady advance.

The second of the issues connected with the postulate of a moving equilibrium concerns the 'feelings' of producers at each point in time (that is, short period) on this path. Entrepreneurs must feel, on balance, that their investment decisions have been justified by the increase in output that has occurred since the preceding short period. Firms must thus, in some sense, be in long-period equilibrium at each point in time along this steady growth path. Harrod, with his attention on the requirements for an equilibrium advance, thought that perhaps their productive capacity at each point in time should be a bit less than what would normally be required for current output, so that it would act as a goad to producers. If they had precisely the capital required 'they might lapse into a stationary condition' (86). In other statements, Harrod treated the warranted growth path as

though it were characterised by long-period equilibrium for producers.[25] This ambiguity in Harrod's references to the warranted
growth path, which leaves open the question of 'whether the firms are
supposed to be content with the stocks of productive capital that they
are operating or with the rate at which it is growing' (Robinson 1962:
49n) is the reason Robinson gave for using the *desired* rate of
accumulation for entrepreneurs' equilibrium in her model of
accumulation, rather than Harrod's warranted rate.

A serious, and in the end an unresolved, problem for Harrod was
his inability to justify his postulate that the achievement of the
warranted rate of growth in one period would lead entrepreneurs to
make decisions that would result in the same rate of growth being
repeated over the next period. It was Alexander (1950) who pointed
out that Harrod simply asserts that the same percentage rate of
growth will be maintained under these conditions. Harrod conceded,
in response to Alexander, that 'my particular definition of a warranted advance depends on an assumption, which is rather special and
may be unjustified' (Harrod 1951: 271). In trying to give a satisfactory explanation of how an economy, in a world that had been
defined by Keynes, would end up following an equilibrium or war-
ranted-growth path, Harrod was faced with an impossible task.[26] (As
he observed: 'In Dynamics, we must not, any more than in Statics,
think away uncertainty' (Harrod 1948: 65).) Investment decisions
are made by a very large number of entrepreneurs producing
different types of goods, and in a world characterised by uncertainty
it would be a fluke if these individual decisions added up to the
investment corresponding to that required by a warranted growth
path. It would be even more remarkable if they continued to do so.
There was recognition in some of his comments of the very special

[25] For example, Davidson (1978: 45n) reports that in

> a conversation (31 January 1969) Harrod indicated that the warranted rate of
> growth occurs when entrepreneurs correctly foresee the point of effective demand
> each period *and* the supply price includes a normal return on standard volume.
> Consequently if the economy is on a warranted growth path it must mean that
> although at any point of time the existing stock of capital is optimal for this
> period's demand, the 'animal spirits' of entrepreneurs will suggest demand next
> period will be greater and therefore additional capital will be needed.

[26] It is important to realize that this equilibrium growth path has a 'real' existence in
Harrod's theory, and the ability of entrepreneurial investment decisions to keep the
economy on this path, under ideal conditions is part of that theory. Kregel (1980:
104–5) refers to two ways of considering the warranted growth path: 'as a purely
"notional" or reference concept'; or as an '*actually* prevailing equilibrium'. He
considers Harrod's *Trade Cycle* to have used the former approach, with the 'Essay'
and *Towards a Dynamic Economics* using the latter.

nature of the warranted growth. For example, he wrote: 'G is a quantity determined from time to time by trial and error, by the collective trials and errors of vast numbers of people. It would be great luck if their collective appraisals caused them to hit precisely upon the value G_w' (86). In spite of this recognition, he implicitly assumed the existence of a 'state of mind' that will keep the economy growing at this warranted rate.[27]

It was noted above that the achievement of the warranted growth rate in the economy reflects some 'average' experience. While some producers find that their investment is more than justified by experience, others are disappointed by the increase in demand for their output. Harrod stated that 'the ups and downs should balance out and, in the aggregate, progress in the current period should be equal to progress in the last preceding period' (82). When this bold assertion was challenged by Alexander, Harrod tried to make use of

the concept of a *representative* entrepreneur. He is taken to be representative in those attitudes of courage and restraint, of optimism and pessimism, etc., which together govern a man's reaction to the current out-turn of business. He may be defined more precisely as one whose orders in response to a given out-turn are such that the sum of the excesses of all entrepreneurs in the economy who would order more in a precisely similar situation over what he would order is equal to the sum of the shortfalls of all those who would order less. The formula that correctly describes the state of mind of this representative entrepreneur may be applied to the macro-economy.

(Harrod 1951: 272–3)

This device is, however, illegitimate in the type of world assumed by Harrod.

The investment and employment that occur in a capitalist economy are the results of the decisions of a very large number of entrepreneurs; these decisions are made on the basis of the entrepreneurs' individual circumstances, energy, and visions of the future, and they cannot be replaced by the decisions of a non-existent 'representative entrepreneur'. It may be of some interest to examine what the consequences would be if these many individual decisions *just happened* (one of a very large number of possible situations) to result in an equilibrium advance, and it may even happen that an actual economy may exhibit fairly steady growth over some stretch of time. There is, however, no justification for using such an equilibrium path, as does Harrod, as the basis for the discussion of the

---

[27] He subsequently admitted that 'in advancing the view … [of] a sustainable steady growth rate, I implicitly introduced an assumption about how entrepreneurs would behave' (Harrod 1964: 903).

trade cycle in actual economies. This use implies that in the absence of accidental disturbances or external impediments, entrepreneurial decisions would lead the economy to proceed along a warranted growth path.

There was a change in Harrod's position in his last book on economic dynamics. He repeated his view that dynamic equilibrium for producers encompasses both their ('average') contentment with the way matters have been proceeding *and* their making of decisions that cause them to carry on in the same way. The problem raised by Alexander is introduced, as is the concept of a representative entrepreneur, but no attempt is made to justify its use, or to defend the earlier assumption that this entrepreneur's decisions, once G_w is achieved, will be such as to maintain the same rate of growth. There are interrogatory, rather than positive, statements concerning this entrepreneur's behaviour. 'Will he, all having turned out well, continue in his previous growth rate? Or will he stay put at the same absolute level of orders?' (Harrod 1973: 19). The only thing that Harrod is prepared to 'stand firm on [is] the proposition that the second equation $[G_w = s_d/C_r]$ simply gives a definition of what we may call the "warranted" growth rate' (20). With this failure to support the assumption that entrepreneurs will, if they chance on it, follow an equilibrium path of steady advance, such a path can no longer play the role of the moving equilibrium for the economy. A path with a non-constant growth rate may, instead, indicate the moving equilibrium of the economy. Which kind of path it will be depends on the entrepreneurial response to the achievement of G_w,[28] a response that is no longer stipulated. 'Whether we regard G_w, or not, as an "equilibrium" value – that depending on questions relating to the actual "behavioural parameter" of entrepreneurs – a constant value of G_w has no more claim to be an equilibrium position in a dynamic system than a growing or declining value of it' (31). Harrod thus, in effect, admits that he has failed in his attempt to develop a rationale for the line of steady advance, which was a key element in his dynamic theory.[29]

---

[28] Harrod (1973: 19) also states this in terms of the behaviour of his fictitious representative entrepreneur. 'The idea that G_w is an equilibrium rate of expansion implies a certain behavioural parameter in the representative entrepreneur.'

[29] With the line of steady advance having lost its position as the path of moving equilibrium, there is no longer the need to assume constant values for s_d and C_r. Technical progress need not be neutral, and s_d could vary with changes in the level of incomes and the rate of interest. It is always possible to define G_w at a point in time, given the appropriate values for s_d and C_r at that point in time.

7.6 THE INSTABILITY PRINCIPLE

Harrod's excitement with the development of his notion of dynamic equilibrium was increased by the recognition that the considerations which led to this equilibrium ensure that it is unstable. This is an important difference from static analysis where the equilibrium positions are generally assumed to be stable. Let us examine Harrod's argument for the instability of dynamic equilibrium by considering an upward departure from the warranted rate of growth, so that G becomes greater than G_w. An examination of equations (7.3) and (7.4) for these growth rates shows that as a consequence C must be smaller than C_r. The investment that has taken place is less than what is required by the increase in output, and *entrepreneurs are assumed to respond by increasing investment orders*, thus further raising the rate of growth of output. 'G, instead of returning to G_w, will move further from it in an upward direction, and the farther it diverges, the greater the stimulus to expansion will be' (Harrod 1939: 22).[30] For a downward departure from the warranted growth rate, C would be greater than C_r, the investment that has taken place is excessive in relation to the increase in output and entrepreneurs are assumed to cut back on their investment orders, causing total demand and output to grow at a still lower rate. '... if G falls below G_w, there will be a redundance of capital goods, and a depressing influence will be exerted; this will cause a further divergence and a still stronger depressing influence; and so on.'

The second major proposition of Harrod's dynamic theory (the first proposition states that existence of a 'unique warranted line of growth') refers to the instability of the equilibrium line of growth. 'On either side of this line is a "field" in which centrifugal forces operate, the magnitude of which varies directly as the distance of any point in it from the warranted line. Departure from the warranted line sets up an inducement to depart farther from it. The moving equilibrium of advance is thus a highly unstable one' (23). His demonstration of the inherent instability of the warranted line of advance depends on the assumption that investment decisions react to the difference between C and C_r, and that the values for s_d and C_r are independent of the value for G. He showed that very substantial

[30] Harrod (1939: 21) observed that the instability principle would still operate if the difference between G and G_w results in a difference between s_d and the actual saving ratio (s) instead of to a difference between C and C_r. For example, if $G > G_w$, then it is possible to have $s > s_d$, while $C = C_r$. Those who thus find themselves with 'excess' saving will increase consumption expenditures, and as a result give a further boost to G.

changes in s_d would be required to invalidate the instability principle. His demonstration of this point can be paraphrased as follows:

Let x be the amount by which output in the present period has increased, an increase that is greater than that which would have occurred if the warranted rate of growth had been maintained. Let s_m stand for the fraction of x that is saved (it can be called a 'marginal saving ratio' since it is applied only at the margin, to the increase in income). With an upward departure of G from G_w, Harrod's instability principle is set in motion if the investment that would have been justified by this increase in output (i.e. $C_r x$) is greater than the extra saving (and thus investment) that took place because of this increase in output (i.e. $s_m x$). Decisions to further increase the rate of growth will thus be taken if $s_m x < C_r x$ or $s_m < C_r$. From equation (7.4), we see that C_r is equal to s_d/G_w, and thus the condition for the operation of the instability principle can be rewritten as, $s_m < s_d/G_w$. The interval of time over which G_w is measured must be given before the significance of this condition can be evaluated. Harrod estimates that the time for reaction to be produced, to a positive or negative stimulus arising from a difference between actual and justified investment, is six months (26). He thus measures G_w as growth per six months. For purposes of illustration, he assumes that the warranted growth rate is 1.25 per cent per six months (e.g., $s_d = 0.10$, and $C_r = 8$), and thus the operation of the instability principle is assured if $s_m < s_d/0.025$, or $s_m < 80 s_d$. The fraction of the increased output that must be saved in order to obviate the instability principle is 80 times the desired saving ratio! 'Thus for any normal warranted rate of growth and level of saving, the instability principle seems quite secure' (26). When a substantial proportion of investment is of a long-term nature, with its justification independent of the current rate of growth, then the required value for s to prevent the instability principle from operating is not as extreme. From equation (7.4′), we see that $C_r = (s_d - k)/G_w$, and the above condition becomes $s_m < (s_d - k)/G_w$. The greater the fraction of total income devoted to financing long-term projects, that is, the higher the value of k relative to s_d, the more likely it is that the marginal fraction of income saved would be large enough to prevent the instability principle from coming into operation. Harrod did not believe that even in this case such an occurrence was generally likely, but it 'might well arise in certain phases of the trade cycle, especially when capital capacity was redundant and saving low. In that case a stable equilibrium of advance might for a time be achieved.' (28).

Harrod continued to place emphasis on the response of entrepreneurs to differences between actual and justified investment as a guide to entrepreneurial behaviour in *Towards a Dynamic Economics*. There is the same vision of 'centrifugal forces' at work around the line of steady advance.

> If the aggregated result of trial and error by numerous producers gives a value for G which is different from G_w, there will not be any tendency to adapt production towards G_w, but, on the contrary, a tendency to adapt production still farther away from it, whether on the higher or lower side.
>
> (Harrod 1948: 87)

It was these strong statements that led Solow (1956) to coin the term 'knife-edge' for the unstable balance of Harrod's equilibrium.

There was a subtle qualification to Harrod's instability principle that was not noticed, but to which he returned later, as we shall see below. It related to the reaction time (six months) required for entrepreneurs to respond to investment deficiencies or excesses. He noted that for a downward departure from the warranted path of output to bring the centrifugal forces into operation, this departure should be 'of sufficient importance to outlive one reaction time' (Harrod 1939: 29). This statement is not further explained, but presumably it is designed to exclude those minor departures from the warranted growth path, *during* the six month period over which G_w is measured, that are cancelled out within this interval. If, however, such a downward departure is reflected in the actual six-month growth rate then the 'downward lapse will then continue until the warranted rate, determined by the values of the right-hand side of the equation itself moves down' (29). Harrod saw the cyclical changes in the warranted rate as being dominated by the changes in s_d, which drag down its value during depression as the profit share falls, and raise it during boom periods by an inflation of prices and profits. The stage is then set for a recovery from a depression when the warranted rate is reduced in this way to a level as low as the actual rate. Conversely, the expansion comes to an end, according to this scenario, when the warranted rate catches up with an actual growth rate that is constrained by increasing problems due to limitations of productive capacity. It is also in this connection that Harrod brings in the natural rate of growth, because it sets an upward limit to the actual rate of growth over time. If the 'proper' warranted rate, the rate that pertains to a situation of full employment is greater than the natural rate, then 'there will be a chronic tendency to depression' (30), as the actual rate tends to be kept below this warranted rate. Conversely, there will be 'a recurrent tendency to develop boom conditions' (Harrod 1948: 88) if G_w exceeds G_n. It is in this connection that Harrod refers to 'the heart of the contrast between Keynesian economics and classical economics. Saving *is* a virtue and beneficial so long as G_w is below G_n. While it is disastrous to have G_w above G_n, it is not good to have it too far below, for in that case, although we may have plenty of booms and a frequent tendency to approach full employment, the high employment will be of an inflationary and thereby unhealthy character. In these circumstances saving is a virtue since, by raising G_w, it enables us to have good employment without inflation. But if G_w is above G_n saving is a force making for depression' (88–9).

Harrod's analysis of the trade cycle is very limited, and he acknowledged that: 'It is far from my purpose to give a finished theory of the trade cycle' (89). But he believed that his instability principle must be part of a full treatment of the cycle. 'Lags, psychological, monetary and other factors no doubt play their part. I should suggest that no theory can be complete which neglects the fundamental causes of instability expressed in the equations which have been set out.'

Harrod responded initially to criticisms of his instability principle by making minor concessions that slightly modified the dependence of changes in investment on the difference between justified and actual investment. For example, he recognised, in response to Baumol's (1951) criticism that entrepreneurs may not increase their rate of orders when they experience a shortage of capital, if they consider 'the current tempo of advance as abnormal and not capable of being sustained indefinitely' (Harrod 1959: 464). He thus added a third reason to the two previously given for the possible termination of a boom before the full employment ceiling is reached. The earlier ones were: (i) a sufficient rise in the value of s_d over time, allowing G_w to catch up with G; and (ii) the slowdown in G due to the appearance of bottlenecks in the supply of specific types of capital equipment. In addition, entrepreneurs' scepticism about the economy's ability to grow at a rate in excess of the natural rate 'could serve to bring the boom to an end before full employment is reached' (463). He also added a disclaimer about the operation of the instability principle when there is a large difference between the actual and warranted rates. 'While I hold that the instability theorem is safe, in the sense that the warranted rate of growth is surrounded by centrifugal forces and that a chance divergence from the warranted rate will be accentuated, I do not claim to have made any thorough-going analysis of the regions lying farther afield from the warranted rate' (460).

Harrod's attitude to the field of operation of the 'centrifugal forces' appeared to have undergone a greater change in his reply to Robinson's (1970) comment on this theory. Harrod took the opportunity to state that the 'knife-edge' was an inappropriate term to use in describing the instability of his dynamic equilibrium, and that it would be better described as a 'shallow dome'.[31] The type of displacement required to get a cumulative movement in the case of a 'shallow dome' could be larger than in the case of a 'knife-edge', since there would be more scope for 'friction' to restrain such movement. He concluded that 'it needs empirical study, rather than theory, to evaluate the amount of friction' (Harrod 1970: 740). Harrod tried to reconcile this position with his earlier stance by referring to his six-month estimate for the reaction time for 'an undue accretion or depletion of capital goods to exert its influence upon the flow of goods' (Harrod 1939: 26). This response ignores his earlier clear and unequivocal statements that the dynamic equilibrium was a 'highly unstable one' which led to the 'knife-edge' designation.

In his last book on this topic, Harrod's approach reflects his position in the 1970 comment:

> It would be almost a miracle if the aggregate of decisions resulted in an acutal growth rate equal to the "warranted" growth rate. There are likely to be some deviations all the time. But if they are of moderate dimensions, I would not suppose that they would bring the instability principle into operation. That is why I so much object to the knife-edge idea. It requires a fairly large deviation, such as might be caused by a revision of assessments across the board in some important industry, like the motor car industry, to produce a deviation sufficient to bring the instability into play.
>
> (Harrod 1973: 33)[32]

With this requirement for a 'fairly large deviation' to set it off, Harrod was prepared to defend the instability principle and its

---

31 In both the article mentioned and in an earlier one entitled 'Harrod's Knife-Edge' (Robinson 1965: 52–65), Robinson used the term 'knife-edge' to denote the unique value for the 'normal' warranted rate. In his response, Harrod followed Solow's usage in taking the term to refer to the degree of instability of equilibrium, and it is clearly in this connection that he wrote 'I hope that we shall hear no more of the 'Harrod knife-edge' (Harrod 1970: 741).

32 Compare the tone of this position with the statement of a similar situation 25 years earlier. 'G is a quantity determined from time to time by trial and error, by the collective trials and errors of vast numbers of people. It would be great luck if their collective appraisals caused them to hit precisely upon the value G_w. But if they do not do so their experience will tend to drive them farther and farther from it' (Harrod 1948: 86).

significance. 'I am confident that the theory that the "warranted" equilibrium growth rate of *laissez-faire* capitalism, without management or interference, is unstable, stands firm; and that is the fundamental explanation of the business cycle' (45). But this 'confidence' in the instability principle is unsupported by the 'empirical study' he thought necessary 'to evaluate the amount of friction' in the economic system. Harrod's dynamic system, which is expressed solely in terms of rates of change, is not broad enough to provide a framework for such a study. He failed to do more than assert that the instability of the warranted growth path 'is the fundamental explanation of the business cycle'. There was no satisfactory justification, as we saw, for placing the warranted rate of growth at the centre of an analysis of capitalist economies, while the assumption that changes in investment are determined by the comparison of two types of rates of growth of output is not sufficiently robust to explain the behaviour of investment over time.

7.7 CONCLUSION

Harrod boldly set out to develop the framework of dynamic theory in his 'Essay on Dynamic Theory'. This attempt was consistent with his earlier insight that the trade cycle should be explained as oscillations around a line of steady advance. Harrod's quest was also spurred on by *The General Theory* which, according to his terminology, was static because it concentrated on a particular short period and dealt with the levels of output and employment, rather than with their rates of change. He thus saw that Keynes's analysis was incomplete because it contained an important dynamic element, positive net saving (investment). The short periods, in which Keynes's analysis was based, were not linked into a sequence that takes into account the changes in productive capacity resulting from the investment whose demand-creating effects were emphasised. Harrod automatically linked adjacent short periods with his analysis of rates of change of output.

Harrod's reflections on his earlier writings on the trade cycle, and Keynes's comments on these writings, led to the intuitive revelation of his fundamental equation. This provided him with the central element of his theory, the normal warranted rate of growth, a dynamic (entrepreneurial) equilibrium. Built into this concept is the assertion that if this equilibrium rate is achieved, then entrepreneurs will take actions that are consistent with the economy continuing to grow at the same rate. Harrod's fundamental equation thus is concerned with a moving equilibrium. This same line of reasoning led Harrod to the instability principle, to the postulate that any deviation from the warranted growth path would become accentuated over time. He claimed that this principle provided a fundamental explanation of the trade cycle.

Crucial aspects of dynamic theory relating to the possible use of an equilibrium growth path in such a theory and to the explanation of the trade cycle were dealt with in Harrod's theory. Their treatment, however, depended on special assumptions that could not be justified for the type of economy whose workings the theory was supposed to illuminate. He wanted to deal with Keynes's world 'in which our previous expectations are liable to disappointment and expectations concerning the future affect what we do today' (Keynes 1936: 293–4). In such a world, as Keynes had noted, the analysis of a moving equilibrium could only be a 'simplified propaedeutic'[33] (293), a preliminary exercise, since essential features of the real world are assumed away. This equilibrium would be relevant only to an economy 'subject to change, but where all things are foreseen from the beginning.' Keynes's reservation about Harrod's dynamic theory, mentioned above, his statement that 'in general there is *no* warranted rate, and special conditions are required for a warranted rate to be possible' (Keynes 1973: 346) could not be shown by Harrod to be groundless. In spite of this, Harrod's work on dynamic theory is a useful pioneering analysis. It is in this light that Keynes saw it. He wrote, in a 15 June 1939 letter to Pigou: 'In the final result, I do not find myself in agreement, but I do think that he has got hold of a very interesting point which, subject to the necessary qualifications, is of real importance' (320).

---

[33] *Propaedeutic* – 'preparatory instruction basic to further study of an art or science' (*The Collins Concise Dictionary of the English Language*, 2nd edn., 1988).

8

ROBINSON ON THE ACCUMULATION OF CAPITAL

8.1 INTRODUCTION

Both as a member of the 'Circus' and as a commentator on drafts of *The General Theory*, Joan Robinson was very much involved in Keynes's transition from the *Treatise* to *The General Theory*. Not only was she an important expositor of the General Theory, but she also tried to extend its scope. Robinson fully understood that Keynes's formal analysis was limited to short-period equilibrium,[1] and she recognised how it enabled him to arrive at an understanding of the factors determining the level of employment at any point in time. With this limitation, however, there was the inevitable question for anyone raised in the Marshallian tradition like Robinson about how the analysis could be extended to deal with the long period.

Robinson's first attempt at making this extension was undertaken even before *The General Theory* was published. She wrote to Keynes, in a letter dated 19 June 1935, that 'I have been working out this long-period stuff' (Keynes 1973b: 648), a reference to her paper 'The Long-Period Theory of Employment' in Robinson (1947), most of which was first published in *Zeitschrift für Nationalökonomie* in 1936. This paper was very much a beginning exercise, and it was restricted to the comparison of positions of stationary (long-period) equilibrium that differed because of differences in the rate of interest, or in the degree of thriftiness, or in technology. Robinson adopted, in this case, the Marshallian conception of equilibrium as a position of rest towards which the system is tending at any moment, a position that

---

[1] 'Keynes' General Theory of Employment is an application to output as a whole of the analysis developed by Marshall of the short-period equilibrium of a particular industry' (Robinson 1952: 3). This view was reflected earlier in a comment that Robinson wrote to Keynes when she saw a reference to long-period equilibrium in the proofs of what became chapter 16 of *The General Theory*. 'You have stopped [sic] rather suddenly in this section out of the short-period with fixed equipment to which the rest of the book belongs' (Keynes 1973b: 647), and in response Keynes deleted this reference to long-period equilibrium.

she later vehemently abandoned.[2] This use of static (long-period) equilibrium was, in any case, very much at variance with what became her view of the theoretical significance of Keynes's General Theory. She kept emphasising the importance of its treatment of time, with an analysis set in 'the present, here and now, when the past cannot be changed and the future cannot be known' (Robinson 1971: ix) that departed radically from the stationary states for which long-period equilibrium was relevant. An extension of the General Theory to deal with the behaviour of economies over time, would thus have to avoid reliance on these stationary states.

Robinson's subsequent attempts to extend the General Theory to the long period were influenced by Harrod, and they dealt with dynamic, growing economies. In these analyses, a moving long-period equilibrium was often quite prominent even though it did not accord with her general methodological position, or with her interpretation of the General Theory. In a preliminary treatment of an economy growing over time in her paper 'The Generalisation of the General Theory' (Robinson 1952), she was very careful not to attach undue importance to steady growth. This growth path was taken 'as a standard of reference, in order to classify the various types of disturbances to which actual economies may be subject' (30). Robinson also refrained from describing this steady growth as an 'equilibrium' situation, because 'it has not the property of restoring itself in the face of a chance shock' (26). This caution in handling long-period equilibrium situations was not always observed in her two subsequent major writings on this topic, *The Accumulation of Capital*, and 'A Model of Accumulation'. Even though equilibrium growth paths were described as special cases in these writings, assumptions were made to endow them with stability. As a result, they were probably given more importance in her treatment of accumulation than she intended.

This prominence of equilibrium growth paths, which we also met in Harrod's dynamic economics, is not in line with Keynes's vision of the development of capitalist economies, and for this reason, Robinson's extension of the General Theory to the long period was flawed. But her work on accumulation also makes reference to other possible growth situations, to some of which she gave colourful names, and this work also contains discussion of cyclical influences that are more in line with Keynes's approach. If sufficient weight is given to these

[2] 'Long-period equilibrium is not at some date in the future; it is an imaginary state of affairs in which there are no incompatibilities in the existing situation, here and now' (Robinson 1965: 101).

situations, then Robinson's analysis of accumulation can be taken as indicating the rate of possible growth outcomes for an economy, with the actual outcomes being very much dependent on particular historical and institutional circumstances.

For Robinson, the distinguishing characteristic of 'Keynesian' models, including hers, is that they 'are designed to project into the long period the central thesis of the *General Theory*, that firms are free, within wide limits, to accumulate as they please and that the rate of saving of the economy as a whole accommodates itself to the rate of investment that they decree' (Robinson 1962: 82–3). This accommodation takes place in Robinson's writings through changes in output and in the distribution of income. Differences in the degree of thriftiness, or in Keynes's 'animal spirits', would be reflected in differences in the distribution of income as well as in the equilibrium rate of growth. This possible variability of income distribution in equilibrium, which is built into her analysis, is an important difference between her theory and that of Harrod.

The starting point for the presentation of Robinson's theory of accumulation in this chapter will be her 'Model of Accumulation', because it begins with the short-period equilibrium relations. These relations, with their emphasis on the distribution of income as an equilibrating factor, make clear that she adopted Kalecki's approach to the theory of effective demand in trying to extend Keynes's General Theory to deal with the behaviour of an economy over time. Another advantage of concentrating on the 'Model' – which Robinson 'regarded as an introduction ... to my *Accumulation of Capital*' (Robinson 1962: v) is that it avoids Robinson's detailed analysis of accumulation with given technology to be found in the *Accumulation*, an analysis that she later repudiated (Robinson 1975: 33–4).

8.2 THE DETERMINANTS OF THE SYSTEM

Robinson made frequent reference to the influence of Harrod's dynamic theory on her own work on the accumulation of capital, but one of the criticisms[3] she made of Harrod's theory was that its expression solely in terms of rates of growth did not give sufficient emphasis to initial conditions (Robinson 1965: 55). The initial stock

[3] Robinson's interpretation of Harrod's theory was not always correct. In particular, Robinson kept referring to an assumption, which she attributed to Harrod, that the proportion of income saved is given and independent of the distribution of income between wages and profits. Even after Harrod (1970: 737), in response to her comments, pointed out that his theory made no such assumption, Robinson (1975: 33) kept attributing it to him.

of capital goods, and the state of expectations formed by past experience, are thus part of the determinants of the system in her discussion of short-period equilibrium. The inclusion of these elements makes possible a period by period analysis, with the events in each period affecting productive capacity and expectations in subsequent periods. Robinson, however, mainly proceeds by focusing on rates of accumulation in a manner that does not differ very much from Harrod's. In doing so, she requires a value for capital, a value that Harrod avoided by concentrating on the equilibrium rate of growth of output.

Robinson set up a model of a capitalist economy, with no government or international trade. Production is controlled and organised by independent firms that produce investment and consumption goods. Investment goods are produced by firms in the investment sector, and consumption goods by those in the consumption sector. Investment goods are purchased by firms in both sectors, while consumption goods are purchased by households. The model abstracts from the scarcity of natural resources, with all output being produced by some combination of labour and man-made equipment.[4] Both the size and quality of the labour force change over time, and investment in education, training and research can have a significant impact on the productivity of labour. Changes in the productivity of labour may not be independent of the scarcity of labour, as firms try to grow by maintaining, or even increasing, their market shares when faced with labour constraints.[5] There is no natural rate of growth in her model that is independent of the competitive spirit of entrepreneurs. The rate of technical progress cannot be taken as exogenous, and this is one way in which her model differs from that of Harrod.

The difficulty in trying to explain the determination of investment over time is recognised by Robinson. 'To attempt to account for what makes the propensity to accumulate high or low we must look into historical, political and psychological characteristics of an economy' (Robinson 1962: 37). The model must thus be left open to allow for these characteristics, and a variety of scenarios have to be explored to give some idea of the wide range and nature of possible outcomes.

---

[4] Robinson (1962: 74–6) briefly notes some of the complications that must be introduced into the analysis when the existence of resource-based goods is recognised.

[5] Robinson (1963: 410) refers to the inclusion in her model of the assumption that the excess demand for labour speeds up the rate of technical progress because of the response of firms to such situations, as 'the most interesting and important Marxian idea incorporated in my model'.

Given these characteristics of an economy, however, Robinson introduces into her model the assumption that the rate of accumulation is positively related to the expected rate of profits. The finance that makes it possible for firms to invest is obtained from retained earnings, from bank loans, and from the sale of bonds and equities. There may be a difference between the desire of firms to accumulate, and their ability to obtain finance for this purpose. Robinson thus treats finance 'along with the "animal spirits" of firms, as an element in the propensity to accumulate of the economy' (43). It thus affects the placement of the curve that in her analysis relates the rate of accumulation to the expected rate of profit. The more readily available is finance, or the stronger the animal spirits, the greater the planned rate of accumulation for any expected rate of profit. The rate of interest and monetary policy are given minor roles to play by Robinson, except when there is a sharp rise in prices that results in severe credit constraints, which are assumed to curtail investment by significant amounts. Under non-inflationary conditions, the banking system is assumed to allow its total lending, and thus the money supply, to increase in response to the increased demand for investment finance, at a constant rate of interest.

Saving in this model is undertaken by firms when they retain a portion of net profits, and by the households of capitalists. These households include both those of capitalist entrepreneurs who control firms and organise production, and those of rentiers who derive all their income from the holding of bonds and shares of firms. Capitalist households are assumed to save some proportion of their incomes. The proportion of gross profits retained by firms depends on the way depreciation is calculated, the terms at which bond finance had been raised, and on the firms' policies with respect to dividends. The proportion of the economy's total income saved in any period depends on the above factors and on the share of profits in total income. One of the determinants of this share is, as we shall see below, the level of investment in the period being considered.

Competitive conditions in goods markets enter into Robinson's model with the statement of how money prices are established. If these prices are assumed to take whatever values are required, given demand conditions, to sell normal capacity output, markets may be said to be competitive in the short-period sense. Alternatively, 'normal' or 'target' prices, that are arrived at by adding to costs a mark-up that incorporates a normal or a target rate of return when plant is operated at normal or target rates of utilisation, may be assumed to hold even in the face of short-period variations in demand. This would be the case when markets for manufactured goods are oligopolistic. Even though Robinson was usually critical of the assumption of competitive conditions (in the short-period sense) for manufacturing industries, she made use of it in setting out her model of accumulation.

The level of money-wage rates is an important determinant of the price level in her model, as in Keynes's, because of its effects on the costs of production. She assumes that it is exogenously given except in two kinds of situations. Money-wage rates are assumed to increase when there is an excess demand for labour at existing wages, or when the rate of investment and rentiers' consumption is so high given available productive capacity, that prices are sharply increasing. This increase in prices depresses real-wage rates below what workers are willing to accept, and 'an irresistible demand for higher money wages makes itself felt' (42). In such a situation the 'inflation barrier' (Robinson 1956: 48) is said to have been reached, and the monetary authorities are assumed to respond by imposing credit restraints that restrict investment. The inflation barrier thus imposes a limit on the ability of firms to accumulate as they please in this 'Keynesian' model. The level of real-wage rates at which the inflation barrier is established depends very much on the levels of real-wage rates achieved in the past, the degree of organisation of workers, and on class relations between workers and employers, in general. This is one of the important areas where historical and social factors affect the analysis, because sharp class antagonisms that keep bringing the inflation barrier into play, would impede accumulation and growth.

These determinants of the system, and the initial conditions, interact to determine output, prices and real-wage rates. The model is said to be in a state of internal equilibrium, when the stock of capital goods in existence is just the amount required to accommodate the rate of accumulation firms desire, and this rate does not bring the inflation barrier into operation. The resulting current rate of profit (with the capital stock being valued at normal prices) is equal to what was expected when the investment decisions that resulted in that capital stock were made. This is obviously a very special case, and Robinson tries to provide a general basis for her model by beginning with an initial situation that is not necessarily characterised by internal equilibrium. Once the short-period equilibrium results are obtained, however, she makes special assumptions that lead back to situations of internal equilibrium.

8.3 SHORT-PERIOD EQUILIBRIUM

Two sectors of production, one for consumption goods and the other for investment goods, are recognised in Robinson's model. The consumption sector produces a fixed basket of goods that is assumed to be unchanged over time, while the investment sector produces equipment for itself as well as for the consumption sector. The type of goods this sector produces may change over time with technical progress. Robinson follows Kalecki in assuming that in any particular short period the rate of gross investment, as well as productive capacity available in each sector, are given. This rate is determined by decisions taken in previous periods, as long as its value is not such that with rentiers' consumption expenditures it would bring the inflation barrier into operation. When the inflation barrier is breached, the rate of investment is no longer pre-determined for the particular short period. (Its value depends on the current actions of the monetary authorities.) In all other cases, employment in the investment sector depends on the nature of productive capacity available in that sector, and on the exogenously-given amount of gross investment in wage-units ($I_w = I/_w$, where w is the money-wage rate). Employment in the consumption sector in short-period equilibrium would be such as to produce the goods that can be purchased out of the total wage bill,[6] and the consumption goods demanded by rentiers. Rentiers' consumption expenditures are assumed to be a lagged function of their incomes, with these incomes being 'determined by the profits of the recent past' (Robinson 1962: 46). These two lags will be combined here, and rentiers' consumption will be shown as a proportion of profits in the previous period. The value for this proportion depends on the rentiers' average propensity to consume (represented by $(1-s_r)$), and the proportion β of total profits in the previous period that is distributed as interest and dividends. Wages are assumed to be spent in the period in which they are earned, and thus total consumption expenditures (C) in the current period can be written as $W + (1-s_r) \beta \pi_{-1}$, where W is the total wage bill, and π_{-1} is the level of profits in the previous period.

In setting out the short-period equilibrium of her model, Robinson assumes that the markets for consumer goods (but *not* for investment goods) are competitive in the short-period sense. As a result, prices take on whatever values are required to sell normal capacity output

---

[6] In Robinson's simple model with no government expenditures or unemployment allowances, it is assumed that the 'workers as a whole live from the earnings of those who are employed' (Robinson 1962: 37).

of the consumption sector, given the money demand for these goods. The effect of this assumption is to set the employment in the consumption sector at a level determined by the nature of the inherited productive capacity in that sector. Total employment (and thus the total wage bill W) in the current short period can thus be taken to be pre-determined, since employment in the investment sector is determined by investment decisions taken in earlier periods.

The equations that describe a situation of short-period equilibrium can be written in money values (with the money-wage rate being given) as:

$$I = \bar{I}; \quad I \leq I \text{ max} \tag{8.1}$$

$$Y = W + \pi + D = C + I \tag{8.2}$$

$$S = Y - C = W + \pi + D - W - (1 - s_r) \, \beta \, \pi_{-1}, \text{ or}$$

$$S = \pi + D - (1 - s_r) \, \beta \, \pi_{-1} \tag{8.3}$$

$$S = I \tag{8.4}$$

$$\pi + D = \bar{I} + (1 - s_r) \, \beta \, \pi_{-1} \tag{8.5}$$

Equation (8.1), states that investment in the period is equal to a given value ($\bar{I}$), which is determined by decisions taken in previous periods, subject to a maximum value (I max) determined by available productive capacity in the investment sector. The necessary equality between gross national product (the sum of factor incomes) and gross national expenditure is expressed in equation (8.2). The expression for saving (S), when it is in the desired, or equilibrium, relation to income, is shown by equation (8.3) when use is made of the relation for consumption presented above. Saving must be equal to investment, as indicated by equation (8.4). This becomes an expression of short-period equilibrium when, as in this case, saving is in the desired relation to income, and investment is equal to what is planned for the period.

Equation (8.5) is derived from equations (8.1) to (8.4), and it shows that profits are determined, in this case of a closed economy with no government expenditures and no workers' saving, by capitalists' expenditures. The distribution of income is such as to result in desired saving that is equal to the investment for the period. A higher level of investment will lead to higher prices for consumer goods, as more investment sector workers spend their wages on the given output of consumer goods. A similar effect will result from higher capitalists' consumption. These higher prices mean that the real-wage rates in the given short-period situation are lower, and that the profit share is higher.[7] It is this inverse relation between capitalists' expenditures and real-wage rates in a given short-period situation that can give rise to an inflation barrier.

To complete the consideration of the particular short period, it is necessary to deal with the investment decisions taken in that period, which will be implemented in subsequent periods. These decisions depend on the long-term expectations of firms, which could be affected by the current level of profits, the degree of utilisation of investment-sector capacity, and the profit margins they have realised in the consumption sector. A higher level of profits in the current period would thus tend to have a favourable effect on long-term expectations of profits and, as a consequence, on current investment decisions. The financial returns from these decisions depend on future conditions that can only be guessed at. Keynes (1936: 152) had referred to the use in such circumstances of the assumption 'that the existing state of affairs will continue indefinitely, except in so far as we have specific reasons to expect a change.' The double-sided relationship between profits and investment, which figured promi-nently in Kalecki's theory of the business cycle, is based on this influence of current conditions on current long-term expectations.[8] Current investment expenditures (determined by decisions made in previous periods) have a positive effect on current profits, while these profits have a positive effect on current investment decisions, and thus on future investment expenditures. By bringing in a value for capital, Robinson makes this into a double-sided relationship between the rate of profit and the rate of accumulation. In doing so, however, she reduces the generality of her analysis, because a unique measure of the value of capital goods cannot be generally made, as she herself forcefully indicated.

The evaluation of a stock of capital goods is the most perplexing point in the whole of the analysis which we have undertaken. Indeed, in reality it is insoluble in principle, for the composition of output, the characteristics of

---

[7] When allowance is made for overhead labour in the model, as in Robinson (1969), then higher investment expenditures would result in a higher profit share even with prices and real-wage rates constant. These prices, and real-wage rates, could be constant in the face of short-term variations in demand when markets for consumer goods are oligopolistic. With the higher output resulting from higher investment demand, unit labour costs would be lower, thus leading to a higher profit share even with constant prices (cf. Asimakopulos 1970).

[8] Keynes's failure to allow for this double-sided relation in his argument for a downward-sloping marginal efficiency of capital schedule, was noted in section 4.4.

men employed and techniques in use are all different in any two positions, and in any one position the stock of capital goods in existence is not that which is appropriate to the conditions obtaining in that position, but is made up of fossils representing the phases of development through which the economy has been passing. The historic cost of existing equipment is out of gear with its value based on expected future earnings, and that value is clouded by the uncertainty that hangs over the future. Only the roughest kind of measurement can be made in actual cases.   (Robinson 1956: 117)

In spite of her emphasis on the special nature of any single value for an economy's given inheritance of capital goods, Robinson obtained such a value in her 'Model of Accumulation' by projecting current conditions into the indefinite (and uncertain) future. 'On the basis of prices and wages ruling today, firms calculate the rate of profit to be expected on investment' (Robinson 1962: 47). This rate of profit (r) is then used to obtain a value (K) for the existing stock of capital by 'capitalising' current net profits.

$$K \equiv \frac{\pi}{r} \qquad\qquad (8.6)$$

The rate of net investment in the period can then be expressed as a rate of accumulation (gk) on the basis of the value of capital defined in (8.6).

$$\frac{(I-D)}{K} \equiv gk \qquad\qquad (8.7)$$

In making these exact calculations, which are then used to define an entrepreneurial equilibrium rate of accumulation, Robinson has probably stretched beyond its limits Keynes's 'convention' about the use of the existing state of affairs in the formation of long-term expectations. The validity of these calculations can also be questioned on the basis of Robinson's comments in her *Accumulation of Capital* when she was dealing with the short period.

In reality, to find the expected rate of return which governs investment decisions is like the famous difficulty of looking in a dark room for a black cat that probably is not there, and to give a true account of realised returns is like the famous difficulty of the chameleon on a plaid rug.

(Robinson 1956: 192)

8.4 THE DESIRED RATE OF ACCUMULATION

Robinson's use of the double-sided relation between the rate of profit and the rate of accumulation allows her to derive the *desired* rate of accumulation. This is the rate of accumulation which results in a rate of profit that induces this particular rate of accumulation. It is her

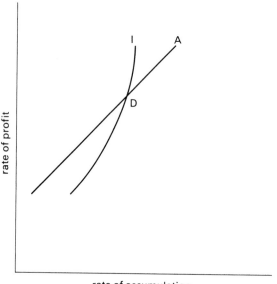

Figure 8.1

entrepreneurial equilibrium growth rate. Its determinants can be illustrated by figure 8.1, which is adapted from the diagram in Robinson (1962: 48).[9]

The line labelled A shows that the actual (which in this analysis is also the expected) rate of profit is an increasing function of the current rate of accumulation. It is obtained from equation (8.5) when use is made of the values for K and gk from equations (8.6) and (8.7). The positively-sloped curve I shows that the rate of accumulation firms want to undertake is positively related to their expected rate of profits. At point D, where the two curves intersect, the rate of accumulation is such as to generate a rate of profit the expectation of which would induce this rate of accumulation. 'This may be conveniently described as the *desired* rate of accumulation, in the sense that it is the rate which makes the firms satisfied with the situation in which they find themselves' (49).

---

[9] Figure 8.1 differs from Robinson's diagram in showing only one point of intersection between the I and A curves, and in having the extension of line A cut the ordinate at a positive value rather than at the origin. The single intersection shown represents a desired rate of accumulation, and it is the one on which Robinson concentrates. The A-line would, if extended, cut the ordinate when rentiers' consumption is a lagged function of profits, which is the assumption made by Robinson.

Robinson goes beyond the definition of this equilibrium rate of growth when she argues that point D represents a stable equilibrium. The attribution of stability to this point is based on the continuous application of the assumption that current conditions are projected into the future, which allowed her to arrive at a value of capital in a situation that was not characterised by internal equilibrium. This assumption means

that at every moment entrepreneurs expect the future rate of profit obtainable on investment to continue indefinitely at the level ruling at that moment; that they expect the rate of technical progress (which may be nil) to be steady; and that they fix amortisation allowances for long-lived plant accordingly. When something occurs which causes a change, we assume that expectations are immediately adjusted, and that no further change is expected. (Robinson 1956: 67)

If firms find themselves to the right of point D on line A, the actual (and expected) rate of profit is less than what they need to generate the corresponding rate of accumulation, and they plan a lower rate of accumulation that brings them back towards point D. If they are to the left of point D, then they will be induced to increase their rate of accumulation, which will again move them towards point D.

Robinson was critical of this type of stability analysis, because it does not allow for the disturbing influence of disappointed expectations. 'A world in which expectations are liable to be falsified cannot be described by the simple equations of the equilibrium path. The out-of-equilibrium position is off the page, not in the same era of logical time as the movement along the path' (Robinson 1962: 25). This stability analysis does not really belong in her model where long-period equilibrium positions are clearly special cases, and there is no reason to make their occurrence appear more likely by assuming stability. It is sufficient for her purposes to examine the consequences of being in different kinds of equilibrium situations in order to indicate some of the effects of differences in, for example, the degree of thriftiness, or in animal spirits, or in trade union behaviour, and this is what she subsequently does.[10]

The achievement of an equilibrium position, such as that indicated by point D in figure 8.1, at one point in time does not necessarily

---

[10] She moved directly to such an examination in a 1959 article on 'Accumulation and the Production Function' (reprinted in Robinson 1960: 132–44), without providing plausibility to an equilibrium growth path. 'But why try to make it seem plausible, when we know that in real life nothing like it ever happens? Let us take it simply as an exercise, and postulate that accumulation does take place in this way for no other reason than that is what we choose to postulate' (133).

mean that this position will be maintained in the succeeding period. The relation between the rate of accumulation and the rate of profits may be disturbed by the time lag between rentiers' consumption and profits, and by uneven rates of accumulation in the past that change the net accumulation that results from a given rate of gross accumulation. If these complications are ignored, situations of internal equilibrium where the desired rate of accumulation is being realised under conditions of tranquillity can be examined.[11]

Robinson distinguishes between the desired and possible rates of growth, a distinction that is comparable to that made by Harrod between the warranted and natural rates of growth. The desired rate of growth may be insufficient to result in full employment of labour, given the rate of growth of population and the growth in output per head. When this desired rate tends to exceed the rate of growth made possible by labour force growth, Robinson notes that the active animal spirits that give rise to this high desired rate might also succeed in raising the rate of technical progress sufficiently to bring the possible rate of growth into line with the desired rate. But if the desired rate is so high that the induced rate of innovations falls short of what is needed to bring the two rates together, then the actual rate of growth has to be restrained. Before turning to some of the growth situations examined by Robinson, it is useful to consider the effects of differences in the degree of thriftiness on the desired rate of accumulation.

The degree of thriftiness in the economy affects the position of the A-line in figure 8.1. A higher degree of thriftiness, a higher value for s_r, or a lower value for β, means that the realised rate of profit for any given rate of accumulation is lower, as can be deduced from equation (8.5). The A-line thus lies further to the right in the figure when the degree of thriftiness is higher. Its point of intersection with an unchanged I-curve, one that reflects a given state of animal spirits or attitude to accumulation, would show a lower desired rate of accumulation in this case. Thus when the actual rate of accumulation is limited only by the desired rate, the higher the degree of thriftiness the lower the rate of accumulation. Robinson saw this as 'the central paradox of the *General Theory* projected into long-period analysis' (60). Her treatment of this 'paradox' is cautious, and it recognises that the degree of thriftiness might not be independent of the

---

[11] Robinson (1956: 66) had argued that 'in order to separate long-run from short-run influences it is a useful device to imagine an economy developing in conditions of tranquillity, and to postulate that the expectations about the future, held at any moment, are in fact being fulfilled'.

propensity to accumulate. For example, a higher propensity to accumulate might lead to a lower distribution of profits to rentiers, and thus to a lower proportion of total profits being consumed, as firms try to finance more investment out of retained earnings. The rightward shift in the A-line in this case is due to a rightward shift in the I-curve, and these two shifts have opposite effects on the desired rate of accumulation.

In Robinson's Keynesian growth model, as in Harrod's, the entrepreneurial equilibrium rate of growth, where investment decisions turn out to be justified by demand conditions, has a prominent role. She noted the similarity of her desired rate of accumulation to Harrod's warranted rate of growth, and gave as a reason for using a different term Harrod's failure to remove 'the ambiguity as to whether the firms are supposed to be content with the stocks of productive capital that they are operating or with the rate at which it is growing' (49, n2). An examination of the effects of the degree of thriftiness on these two rates of growth makes clear another important difference. Robinson's desired rate of accumulation is based on the interaction of accumulation and distribution that is absent in Harrod's theory. Harrod's warranted rate of growth depends directly on the economy's propensity to save and on the nature of technology. A higher value for this propensity to save, other things being given, results in a higher rather than in a lower value for this equilibrium rate of growth. Keynes's paradox of saving is reflected in Harrod's theory in the actual rate of growth, which can be affected by the relation between the warranted and natural rates of growth. When G_w exceeds G_n, as we saw in section 7.6, there is a tendency for G to be eventually forced below G_w, giving rise to a slump because of the operation of the instability principle. It is in this connection, with a higher propensity to save tending to raise G_w above G_n, that Harrod (1948: 88–9) refers to the paradox of saving.

8.5 GOLDEN, AND NOT SO GOLDEN, GROWTH PATHS

Robinson considers a variety of growth situations by postulating different relations between the desired rate of growth, which reflects the state of animal spirits of firms and the economy's degree of thriftiness, and the rate of growth made possible by the growth of population and technical progress. The term a *golden age*[12] is used to describe a situation in which growth is occurring at a steady rate with

---

[12] This term is used to indicate 'that it represents a mythical state of affairs not likely to obtain in any actual economy' (Robinson 1956: 99).

full employment of labour. The desired and possible rates of growth are the same, and equal to the sum of the rates of growth of the labour force and output per worker. Technical progress is assumed to be neutral according to the Harrod definition of that term, with equal rates of growth of output per worker in each stage of production. With technical progress occurring at a steady rate, the amortisation allowances turn out to be sufficient to replace plants when they become obsolete. The techniques of production chosen at each round of gross investment are appropriate to the ruling rate of profit, and they provide for the highest real-wage rate, given this golden age rate of profit. The inverse relation between the level of investment and the real-wage rate that was observed in comparing short-period equilibrium situations with the same capital equipment and propensities to save, reappears as an inverse relation between the rate of accumulation and the real-wage rate, when golden-age economies using the same techniques of production and having the same degree of thriftiness are compared. The economy with a higher rate of accumulation would have the higher rate of profit and the lower real-wage rate. This conclusion depends on the assumption of equal technical development. In so far as technical progress is introduced by new investment, the economy with the higher rate of accumulation would, over time, be at a higher stage of technical development, and might be able to show both a higher rate of profit and a higher real-wage rate.

A situation where there is a steady rate of growth and unemployed labour is called a *limping golden age*. Employment would grow over time if output is increasing at a faster rate than is output per worker, and it would decrease over time if the reverse were the case. The relation between the rate of growth of employment and the rate of growth of the labour force would indicate whether the economy is moving towards full employment, or whether the ratio of non-employed to employed workers would be increasing. This latter case could give rise to what Robinson has called a *leaden age*. The growing ratio of non-employment in the labour force, in a situation with lethargic animal spirits and no technical progress, lowers the standard of living of workers (recall that the unemployed are supported by the employed). This fall in living standards could reach a level at which 'Malthusian misery checks the rate of growth of population' (Robinson 1962: 54). It is this pressure that brings the rate of growth of the labour force down to the low rate of accumulation in a leaden age.

A *restrained golden age* represents a very different situation, where the desired rate of accumulation, even with induced technical progress, would exceed the possible rate of accumulation. Robinson points to two ways in which the desired rate may be held in check. One is through financial constraints imposed by the monetary authorities to control rising prices that follow rising money-wage rates, as firms scramble to try to hire more labour than is available. The other way is by reciprocal restraint exercised by employers who realise that there is not enough labour to meet all their needs. As a result, they lower the rate of accumulation they are trying to achieve. Neither of these restraints can be expected to be operated with precision, and restrained growth would be marked by considerable short-period variability. For example, any chance relaxation of credit would lead to a higher rate of accumulation, and rising money-wage rates and prices, that in turn lead to sharper credit restrictions. To be effective in curbing wage and price increases, these credit restrictions must create and maintain some margin of unemployment. 'Thus, paradoxically, an excess demand for labour may be said to cause unemployment' (61). It is in this situation that Robinson sees that a higher degree of thriftiness might assist the rate of accumulation by obviating the need for restraint, because it could bring the desired rate down to the possible rate of accumulation.

The inverse relation between the rate of accumulation and the real-wage rate could result in another type of limit on the rate of accumulation, even though there is substantial unemployment. A *bastard golden age* is the term used by Robinson[13] to describe a situation where the rate of accumulation is held in check by financial constraints that are imposed even though there is no scarcity of labour. Workers are in a position to insist on a minimum real-wage rate, and to resist the lower real-wage rate that would result from a higher rate of accumulation by winning substantial money-wage increases. The resulting sharp rise in prices would breach the 'inflation barriers', and thus the rate of accumulation is restrained. This is another case where a higher degree of thriftiness would result in a higher rate of accumulation, because it allows for a higher level of real-wage rates for any given rate of accumulation. The inflation barrier would then only be reached at a higher rate of accumulation.[14]

[13] This term appears to have been coined by Kahn (1959) to represent all situations of steady growth with unemployment, and not only those in which accumulation is limited because of the 'inflation barrier'.

[14] Kahn (1959: 202) noted that in this case 'it is the real-wage rate which is independently determined and greater thriftiness means a higher rate of growth and a less rapid increase of unemployment'.

In all of the above growth situations, the initial conditions are compatible with steady growth, because 'the ratio of plant for producing plant to plant for producing commodities is such that it can maintain itself' (Robinson 1962: 56). Robinson used the term *platinum age*[15] to describe situations in which the initial conditions are not compatible with steady growth. A *galloping platinum age* is one where animal spirits are high and there is a large mass of non-employed labour, but there is a constraint on investment due to insufficient productive capacity in the investment sector. A large part of investment would be devoted to enlarging the investment sector, and thus the profit share along with the share of investment in total output would be growing over time, while the real-wage rate would be falling, unless technical progress is sufficiently rapid to boost the supply of wage goods. This 'gallop' with increasing rates of accumulation, could be brought to an end by the inflation barrier, by full employment of labour, or by achieving the appropriate ratio of plants in each sector for steady growth. Robinson also refers to a reverse situation, a *creeping platinum age* where initially the basic investment sector plant is greater than what is required for the physically possible rate of growth. It is assumed that the rate of interest is used to bring down the rate of accumulation, and thus the rate of profit, with labour being transferred from the investment to the consumption sector. Real-wage rates would be rising during this process. Robinson refers to possible changes in the degree of mechanisation in these platinum ages as the rate of profit changes. In the galloping platinum age, the rising rate of profit could result in less mechanised techniques being adopted, thus giving a further boost to employment. The reverse case would hold in the creeping platinum age as lower rates of profit induce the adoption of more mechanised techniques, which relax the pressure on the labour market.

This catalogue of possible growth situations is not meant to be exhaustive, nor are all the situations considered to be plausible. They do, however, indicate some of the logical relations between the rate of accumulation, the degree of thriftiness, and the real-wage rate, that can affect the relations between the desired and possible rates of accumulation. Any of these basic growth situations could also be marked by short-term instability.

15 This term was borrowed from Little (1957).

8.6 INSTABILITY

Robinson's examination of possible growth situations assumed conditions of tranquillity with no disturbances, or developments of incompatibilities as the growth process unfolds, that disrupt growth. The process of accumulation in any actual situation would be subject to these disturbances. For example, if the economy has been growing at a steady rate, with the desired (and actual) rate of accumulation not sufficient to provide full employment, chance events, such as a sudden bunching of innovations, could raise effective demand, profits and the rate of accumulation. This would be indicated in figure 8.1 by a temporary shift of the I-curve that shifts its intersection with the A-line to the right. The resulting higher level of profits means that if the expected rate of return on investment is calculated on the basis of current conditions, then a rate of accumulation higher than the initial steady-state rate will be implemented even if the I-curve has returned to its initial (pre-fortuitous bunching of innovations) positions. Over time, however, profit expectations will turn out to be disappointed as effective demand does not increase sufficiently, when the economy is to the right of point D in figure 8.1, to lead to normal utilisation of productive capacity at prices that incorporate normal rates of return. This leads to a fall in the rate of accumulation, a fall that Robinson states will take it below point D, because the burst of investment has disturbed the steady-state relation of plants between investment and consumption-goods sectors. This new position will only be temporary, with steady-state equilibrium being established again after 'some wobbles around the desired rate' (64), unless there are fresh disturbances.[16]

Fluctuations in the rate of accumulation give rise to less than proportionate fluctuations in output, because of a less then proportionate response of consumption demand. If market conditions in the consumption-goods sector are competitive in the short-period sense, then variations in prices and real-wage rates would keep plants operating at normal capacity rates, so that consumption sector output is largely invariant to short-term fluctuations in investment. With the more usual case of imperfect markets for manufactured goods, prices and real-wage rates would tend to be sticky in the face of short-term fluctuations in demand caused by changes in the rate of accumulation. This would result in changes in output and employ-

---

[16] Robinson (1962: 64n) notes the similarity of her treatment of instability here to Kalecki's trade-cycle model. One difference she points to is that she has fluctuations around a rate of accumulation rather than around a stock of capital.

ment in this sector, but the time lag in the relation between rentiers' consumption and profits would keep these changes from being proportionate to the change in investment. 'The lag in expenditure from profits combines with whatever effect there may be of changing prices (raising real-wage rates in a downswing and reducing them in an upswing) to make movements of overall output much less marked than of gross investment' (65).

The formation of expectations would also be affected by an environment in which fluctuations have been occurring, so that revisions of expectations in the face of changes in profits would only occur after these changes have reached some threshold level of change and persistence. With fluctuations being more severe in the investment sector, investment decisions might respond more slowly to changes in demand and profits in that sector than they do in the consumption sector. This difference in response could be one of the factors that results in 'a stock of capital goods whose age-composition and division between sectors are not appropriate to steady growth' (66). This, in itself, could generate cyclical movements around a desired rate of accumulation. Fluctuations could also result from the way in which restraints are placed on an economy in which the desired rate of accumulation exceeds the possible rate. For example, they could operate to decrease investment, which causes unemployment, with the restraints being subsequently eased to allow this labour to be absorbed, which then leads to the need for the re-imposition of constraints, etc.

The model would become inherently unstable if expectations were based on a projection, not of levels of current prices and profits, but of the recent rates of change in these levels. This means that the desired rate of accumulation corresponding to any rate of profit would be higher when it has been rising, and lower when it has been falling, than the desired rate based on the projection of the current rate of profit. With this type of expectations, the economy cannot settle down to a desired rate of accumulation, because expectations would change as soon as that rate is reached, and it would then be no longer desired. Upward movements would be brought to an end by physical bottlenecks that impede the supply of required goods and thus slow down the rate of accumulation, or by the scarcity of labour and the resulting financial constraints that are designed to control inflationary pressures. Once ended, these upward surges would give way to downward movements. These latter would cease when consumption expenditures, which are lagged functions of income, increase sufficiently in relation to current income to bring the fall in profits to an end. This would then set the stage for an expansionary period. When expectations are formed in this way, the economy would show the instability that is predicted by Harrod's Instability Principle.

Robinson believed that her analysis of long-run growth would still be cogent 'in a broad way' even under the conditions that give rise to inherent instability. This belief is based on the view that the features she found relevant in the analysis of possible growth situations would still be operative even when a stable desired rate of accumulation cannot be defined. When animal spirits are high, and the degree of thriftiness is low, the range of rates of growth experienced over a series of fluctuations would be higher, on average, than if the values for these parameters were reversed. The relationship between the propensity to accumulate and the physically possible rate of growth would indicate whether booms generally have to be restrained because of scarcity of labour, or whether unemployment persists from boom to boom. There may also be a tendency for the proportion of investment to consumption to grow or fall from boom to boom. 'Thus the characteristic features of restrained and limping golden ages or of platinum ages can be discerned under the restless surface of unstable growth' (69).

8.7 CONCLUSION

Robinson's extension of Keynes's General Theory to the long period is faithful to essential features of that theory. The rate of investment is, in many cases, independent of the propensity to save, with the level of saving accommodating itself to the level of investment determined by firms. An important part of this extension is Kalecki's theory of income distribution, and Kalecki's double-sided relation between investment and profits, which Robinson turns into a relation between the rate of accumulation and the rate of profits. It is the current rate of accumulation that is a determinant of the current rate of profits, while it is the latter that is a determinant of current investment decisions and thus of the future rate of accumulation. This double-sided relationship provides Robinson with the elements for her definition of the desired rate of accumulation. This is her entrepreneurial equilibrium growth rate, and it is analogous to Harrod's warranted rate of growth. An important difference between these two rates is that Robinson's makes direct use of the inducement to invest and the effect of the propensity to save, given investment, on the distribution of income. As a consequence, Keynes's paradox of saving appears in Robinson's theory as an inverse relation between the degree of thriftiness and the desired rate of accumulation. The warranted rate of growth is directly related to the economy's propensity to save, and thus the paradox of saving is not reflected in Harrod's entrepreneurial equilibrium rate of growth. Where it appears is in the relation between the warranted and natural rates of growth. A higher degree of thriftiness tends to make the warranted rate greater than the natural rate, and thus it increases the likelihood of the actual rate being forced below the warranted rate. The instability principle would then come into play, moving the economy into a recessionary period.

Robinson's theory does not contain anything comparable to Harrod's instability principle. In defining the desired rate of accumulation she assumed that expectations were formed in such a way – the projection of the current level of profits into the future – that the desired rate of accumulation was stable. There was recognition, however, that expectations might be formed in a different way by the projection of recent changes in the level of profits, and then the model would be inherently unstable. A variety of possible growth situations were examined to illustrate some of the characteristics of growth paths that might be discerned in actual economies that are also subject to fluctuations. The nature of these paths depends on the interplay between the propensity to accumulate, the degree of thriftiness, the rate of growth of the labour force, technical progress, and institutional features, such as the organisation and attitude of labour. Not only do these factors interact to determine a series of outcomes, but their values may be interdependent. For example, a high propensity to accumulate might also be reflected in a higher rate of technical progress and in a higher degree of thriftiness.

Robinson's theory of accumulation, when attention is paid to her cautionary comments, can be seen as being faithful to Keynes's vision of the operation of capitalist economies. The present is a brief interval of time between an irrevocable past and a future that cannot be known. In such a setting, the determination of investment cannot be reduced to some formula that can be repeated over time. All that can be done is to sketch out some of the broad factors that will influence the rate of investment. Robinson's model of growth is thus open-ended. It provides a framework for examining important elements that affect the rate of accumulation over time, but the values for these elements depend on historical and institutional circumstances. Psychological factors are also relevant, since they affect the attitudes of entrepreneurs and of those who provide finance for investment. In this connection, she stated that 'there is no way (even for the purpose of our model) of reducing the complexities of the inducement to invest to a simple formula. We must be content with the conclusion that, over the long run, the rate of accumulation is likely to be whatever it is likely to be' (Robinson 1956: 244).

9

CONCLUSION

Keynes's General Theory provided a theoretical framework for the consideration of the main elements that determine the level of employment in capitalist economies. It was both an affirmation of the importance of economic theory and an indication of its limitations. An affirmation, because this theory shed light on the factors determining the level of employment and pointed to governmental policy measures that could improve an economy's economic performance. An indication of limitations, because the interplay of these factors that led to a particular level of employment was very much dependent on historical and institutional features of the economy. Keynes's General Theory shows that a situation of full employment is not the natural outcome of market forces in economies that are subject to change. Rather, there is a wide range of possible equilibrium situations, with differing degrees of unemployment. The explanation for why one of these possible equilibrium situations attracts actual values depends very much on the particular circumstances of time and place, which determine the values for the 'given' factors and the 'independent' variables of the General Theory.

The formal model to be found in the General Theory, represented by the set of equations in section 5.5 above, depicts the short-period equilibrium situation corresponding to a particular short interval in historical time. The conditions in that interval depend on decisions and actions taken in the past, and the outcomes are affected by long-term expectations about future conditions that cannot be known. The size and skills of the labour force, the quantity and nature of capital equipment and technical knowledge, the tastes and habits of consumers, attitudes to work, the social structure, and the relations between groups in the society, are all taken as given. This does not mean that these factors are constant over time – Keynes was concerned with the operation of capitalist economies that were changing over time as a result of accumulation, technical progress, and population growth – but the changes that do occur over the short interval of Keynes's formal analysis are small relative to the initial values of these factors. It is for this reason that Keynes labels these as given factors, as opposed to the independent variables whose changes in the short period can significantly affect output and employment. This distinction is admitted to be 'quite arbitrary from any absolute standpoint' (Keynes 1936: 247), but it reflects experience, the theorist's understanding of the forces at work in the economies for which this theoretical framework is relevant.

The independent variables in Keynes's analysis consist of three psychological factors and two money values. The psychological factors are the economy's propensity to consume, the long-term expectations of prospective yields from capital equipment, and the attitude to liquidity. The money values are the set of money-wage rates, as determined by wage-bargaining between firms and workers, and the quantity of money that is assumed to be determined by the central bank in the formal model. These variables can be arranged in a rather simple model to show the determination of output and employment. It is this simple model that has been taken as the core of the General Theory, even though our presentation of that theory in the preceding chapters makes clear that attention should always be paid to its specific historical context. In this analysis, effective demand is the causal factor determining the level of employment, with the investment component of that demand being given particular attention because of its volatility.

The economic policy prescriptions in *The General Theory* follow directly from this simple model. When employment is considered to be too low (unemployment too high), policies that could increase aggregate investment are suggested. These policies require intervention by government, intervention that Keynes believed was justified on the basis of his analysis, which indicated wide fluctuations in employment under conditions of *laissez-faire*. He wrote (320): 'I conclude that the duty of ordering the current volume of investment cannot safely be left in private hands'. The efficacy of such government intervention, however, depends very much on the particular circumstances of time and place. The independent variables of the analysis might also be affected by the use of these policies, and their net effects may thus not be necessarily predictable. For example, the breakdown of any policy-induced change in the value of total output into price and quantity changes, depends very much on the response of money-wage rates to changes in the demand for labour. This is an important area that was left 'open' by Keynes, except for a few observations. He recognised that an increase in the demand for labour would improve the bargaining positions of workers, and that they would be translated into increases in money-wage rates. He inferred from 'experience' that these changes in wage rates would be relatively modest, otherwise the price level would be subject to serious fluctuations (253). Robinson (1947: 1–28), in a paper written in 1936 (of which Keynes approved), pointed out that the money-wage rate changes induced by a policy of full employment might frustrate that policy. A feasible employment policy might thus have to aim at less than full employment.

This emphasis on the need to take into account the particular historical and institutional features of an economy for which policies to improve employment are developed, is implicit in a little-noticed comment made in 1937 by Keynes (1973c: 122). He noted that his 'suggestions for a cure', when unemployment is a problem, 'are on a different plane from the diagnosis'. This diagnosis is provided by his theoretical framework which explains the determination of employment in any given set of circumstances. This framework is very general, and it can be used to shed light on situations where effective demand is high and there is a potential inflationary gap, as well as when effective demand is low, and there is considerable unemployment. Keynes (1972: 367–439) used it to formulate policies that could check effective demand during wartime, and that could then provide a boost to effective demand when peace had been restored. The policy suggestions that are found scattered throughout *The General Theory* must thus be considered to be 'subject to all sorts of special assumptions and are necessarily related to the particular conditions of the time' (Keynes 1973c: 122). There is a clear warning here for all those who would use the simple model in the General Theory as a guide to policy-making without careful attention to the particular conditions of the time that will determine the effectiveness of any proposed interventions.

Keynes saw his theory as dealing with the factors determining changes in output, even though he concentrated on short-period equilibrium situations. Actual values were identified with these short-period equilibrium values because the latter were assumed to exert a strong attraction on the former. Changes in the factors determining the short-period equilibrium values, changes that always occur in capitalist economies, thus result in changing actual values. A linking of successive short periods would allow for changing output and employment to be traced out over time. It is this type of linking that underlies the notes on the trade cycle in *The General Theory*, and Keynes's consideration in chapter 18 of how his theory can explain the main features of observed changes in capitalist economies. Keynes chose this type of linking of periods over time, rather than one which was guided by some constant function over time, because of his view of the difficult 'material' that is the subject matter of economics, 'unlike the typical natural science, the material to which it is applied is, in too many respects, not homogeneous through time' (Keynes 1973c: 296). Experience showed that capitalist economies were subject to cyclical fluctuations, and Keynes believed that his General Theory, even though its formal model concentrated on short-period equilibrium, provided a basis for the examination of these fluctuations, and for the formulation of policies to mitigate them.[1]

It was not long before Harrod developed a formal model that tried to deal with accumulation over time, while observing essential aspects of Keynes's General Theory. Harrod's attempt to develop a model to deal with both trend and cycle pre-dated the General Theory, but the latter's importance for his dynamic theory should not be underestimated. Even though he labelled it as 'static', Harrod saw Keynes's theory as an essential first step in the development of dynamic theory.

> It is to be noted that for the elaboration of any such dynamic theory, a macroeconomic theory of statics was an indispensable foundation. The traditional micro theory did not provide the necessary tools.
> Thus Keynes may be truly regarded as the father of dynamic theory. And that, in the long run, will prove to have been his greatest contribution of all.
> (Harrod 1963: 140)

Our examination of the evolution of Harrod's dynamic theory has shown that his bold step of placing at the centre of his analysis a dynamic equilibrium concept could not be justified in the face of criticisms. Harrod wanted to deal with Keynes's world, a world where future conditions are unknown, and in which investment decisions are made by large numbers of entrepreneurs. A dynamic equilibrium concept for the economy as a whole, a warranted rate of growth, could be defined, but it was not possible for Harrod to justify

---

[1] Coddington (1983: 43) has pointed to what he considers to be the neglect of cyclical factors in the analytical expression of Keynesian ideas with its emphasis on '"underemployment *equilibrium*". The development of Keynesian ideas ... has accordingly resulted in "demand deficiency" becoming an essentially static idea in which the cyclical context of demand and employment fluctuations is either disregarded or, at best, is left out of focus in the middle distance.' Our interpretation of Keynes is that he implicitly saw the short-period equilibrium in his model within a cyclical context. Underemployment equilibrium was emphasised in order to contrast this theory with classical theory that considered equilibrium to be consistent only with full employment.

his initial assertion that once such a rate was achieved entrepreneurial investment decisions would keep them advancing at the same rate. There was thus the implicit admission in his 1973 book on dynamic economics, as noted in section 7.5 above, that there was no rationale for the maintenance of a line of steady advance, which had been a key element of his dynamic theory.[2] Harrod also introduced the metaphor of a 'shallow dome' to replace the 'knife-edge' previously used by others to denote the degree of instability of the equilibrium growth rate in his model. The revision of expectations that would result in a growing deviation of the rate of growth from the equilibrium rate does not necessarily result simply from any chance deviation of the actual growth rate from the equilibrium growth rate.

Robinson's extension of the General Theory to deal with accumulation over time made use of long-period equilibrium concepts, but in the end her treatment was faithful to Keynes's vision of the development of capitalist economies. Her theory of accumulation featured a large number of possible growth paths. Their relevance for any particular situation depended very much on the historical and institutional features of the economy being considered.

[2] A different interpretation of Harrod's theory is to be found in Dow (1985: 129–30). She sees Harrod's model as employing 'a mechanical time usage of equilibrium', while Keynes's model was set in historical time. Harrod's eventual retreat from the steady line of advance is consistent with the view in the present book that he wanted to deal with historical time.

REFERENCES

Akerlof, George and Janet Yellen (1985). 'A Near-Rational Model of the Business Cycle, With Wage and Price Inertia', *Quarterly Journal of Economics, 100*, Supplement, 823–38.

Alexander, S. (1950). 'Mr. Harrod's Dynamic Model', *Economic Journal, 60*, December, 724–39.

Asimakopulos, A. (1970). 'A Robinsonian Growth Model in One Sector Notation – an Amendment', *Australian Economic Papers, 9*, 171–6.

(1971). 'The Determination of Investment in Keynes's Model', *Canadian Journal of Economics, 4*, August, 382–8.

(1973). 'Keynes, Patinkin, Historical Time, and Equilibrium Analysis', *Canadian Journal of Economics, 6*, May 179–88.

(1982). 'Keynes' Theory of Effective Demand Revisited', *Australian Economic Papers, 21*, June, 18–36.

(1983a). 'Anticipations of the General Theory?', *Canadian Journal of Economics, 16*, August, 517–30.

(1983b). 'Kalecki and Keynes on Finance, Investment and Saving', *Cambridge Journal of Economics, 7*, September–December, 221–33.

(1985). 'Harrod on Harrod: the Evolution of "a line of steady growth"', *History of Political Economy, 17*, Winter, 619–35.

(1986). 'Harrod and Domar on Dynamic Economics', *Banca Nazionale del Lavoro Quarterly Review*, September, 275–98.

Asimakopulos, A. and J. C. Weldon (1963). 'The Classification of Technical Progress in Models of Economic Growth', *Economica, 30*, November, 372–86.

Baumol, William (1951). *Economic Dynamics*. New York: Macmillan.

Blinder, Alan S. (1987). 'Keynes, Lucas and Scientific Progress', *American Economic Review, 77*, May, 130–6.

(1988). 'The Challenge of High Unemployment', *American Economic Review, 78*, May, 1–15.

Bliss, C. J. (1975). 'The Reappraisal of Keynes' Economics: An Appraisal' in Parkin and Nobay (1975), 203–13.

Casarosa, C. (1981). 'The Microfoundations of Keynes's Aggregate Supply and Aggregate Demand Analysis', *Economic Journal, 91*, March, 181–93.

Chick, Victoria (1983). *Macroeconomics After Keynes: A Reconsideration of the General Theory*. Cambridge, Mass.: MIT Press.

Clower, Robert (1965). 'The Keynesian Counterrevolution: A Theoretical Appraisal', in Hahn and Brechling (1965), 103–25.

Coddington, Alan (1983). *Keynesian Economics: The Search for First Principles.* London: Allen & Unwin.

Conard, Joseph W. (1959). *An Introduction to the Theory of Interest.* Berkeley: University of California Press.

Davidson, Paul (1978). *Money and the Real World,* 2nd edn. London: Macmillan.

(1982–83). 'Rational Expectations: A Fallacious Foundation for Studying Crucial Decision-making Processes', *Journal of Post Keynesian Economics, 5,* Winter, 182–98.

Dow, Sheila C. (1985). *Macroeconomic Thought: A Methodological Approach.* Oxford: Basil Blackwell.

Dunlop, John T. (1938). 'The Movement of Real and Money Wage Rates', *Economic Journal, 48,* September, 413–34.

Fender, John (1981). *Understanding Keynes: An Analysis of 'The General Theory'.* New York: John Wiley & Sons.

Friedman, M. (1957). *A Theory of the Consumption Function.* Princeton: Princeton University Press.

(1968). 'The Role of Monetary Policy', *American Economic Review, 78,* March, 1–17.

Frisch, Ragnar (1933). 'Propagation Problems and Impulse Problems in Dynamic Economics', in *Economic Essays in Honour of Gustav Cassel.* London: Allen & Unwin, 171–205.

Geary, P. T. and J. Kennan (1982). 'The Employment-Real Wage Relationship: An International Study', *Journal of Political Economy, 90,* August, 854–71.

Hahn, F. H. and F.P.R. Brechling (1965). *The Theory of Interest Rates.* London: Macmillan.

Hamouda, Omar F. and John N. Smithin (eds.) (1988). *Keynes and Public Policy After Fifty Years,* volume 2. Aldershot: Edward Elgar.

Hansen, Bent (1970). *A Survey of General Equilibrium Systems.* New York: McGraw-Hill.

Harrod, R. F. (1936). *The Trade Cycle: An Essay.* London: Macmillan.

(1937). 'Mr. Keynes and Traditional Theory', *Econometrica, 5,* January, 74–86.

(1939). 'An Essay in Dynamic Theory', *Economic Journal, 49,* March, 14–33.

(1948). *Towards a Dynamic Economics.* London: Macmillan.

(1951). 'Notes on Trade Cycle Theory', *Economic Journal, 61,* June, 261–75.

(1959). 'Domar and Dynamic Economics', *Economic Journal, 69,* September, 451–64.

(1960). 'Second Essay in Dynamic Theory', *Economic Journal, 70,* June, 277–93.

(1963). 'Retrospect on Keynes', in Lekachman (1964), 139–52.

(1964). 'Are Monetary and Fiscal Policies Enough?', *Economic Journal, 74,* December, 903–15.

(1969). *Money.* London: Macmillan.

(1970). 'Harrod After Twenty-One Years: a Comment', *Economic Journal, 80,* September, 737–41.

(1973). *Economic Dynamics*. London: Macmillan.

Hawtrey, R. G. (1937a). *Capital and Employment*. London: Longmans.

(1937b). 'Alternative Theories of the Rate of Interest: III', *Economic Journal*, 47, September, 437–43.

Hicks, J. R. (1936). 'Mr. Keynes's Theory of Employment', *Economic Journal*, 46, June, 238–53.

(1937). 'Mr. Keynes and the "Classics"': A Suggested Interpretation', *Econometrica*, 5, April, 147–59.

(1965). *Capital and Growth*. Oxford: Oxford University Press.

(1974). *The Crisis in Keynesian Economics*. Oxford: Basil Blackwell.

(1985). *Methods of Dynamic Economics*. Oxford: Clarendon Press.

Kahn, Richard (1931). 'The Relation of Home Investment to Unemployment', *Economic Journal*, 41, June, 173–98. All page references are to the reprinting in Kahn (1972), 1–27.

(1954). 'Some Notes on Liquidity Preference', *Manchester School of Economics and Social Studies*, 22, September, 229–57. All page references are to the reprinting in Kahn (1972), 72–96.

(1959). 'Exercises in the Analysis of Growth', *Oxford Economic Papers*, 11, June, 143–56. All page references are to the reprinting in Kahn (1972), 192–207.

(1972). *Selected Essays on Employment and Growth*. Cambridge: Cambridge University Press.

(1984). *The Making of Keynes' General Theory*. Cambridge: Cambridge University Press.

Kaldor, N. (1939). 'Speculation and Economic Stability', *Review of Economic Studies*, 6, October, 1–27. All page references are to the reprinting in Kaldor (1960), 17–58.

(1957). 'A Model of Economic Growth', *Economic Journal*, 67, September, 591–624.

(1960). *Essays in Economic Stability and Growth*. London: Duckworth.

Kalecki, Michal (1935). 'A Macrodynamic Theory of Business Cycles', *Econometrica*, 3, July, 327–44.

(1937a). 'A Theory of the Business Cycle', *Review of Economic Studies*, 4, February, 77–87.

(1937b). 'A Theory of Commodity, Income and Capital Taxation', *Economic Journal*, 47, September, 444–50. All page references are to the reprinting in Kalecki (1971), 35–42.

(1944). 'Professor Pigou on the "Classical Stationary State" – A Comment', *Economic Journal*, 54, April, 131–2.

(1971). *Selected Essays on the Dynamics of the Capitalist Economy: 1933–1970*. Cambridge: Cambridge University Press.

Keynes, John Maynard (1930a). *A Treatise on Money*, vol. 1: *The Pure Theory of Money*. London: Macmillan.

(1930b). *A Treatise on Money*, vol. 2: *The Applied Theory of Money*. London: Macmillan.

(1936). *The General Theory of Employment, Interest and Money*. London: Macmillan.

(1937a). 'The General Theory of Unemployment', *Quarterly Journal of*

Economics, *51*, February. All page references are to the reprinting in Keynes (1973c), 109–23.

(1937b). 'Alternative Theories of the Rate of Interest', *Economic Journal*, *47*, June, 241–52. All page references are to the reprinting in Keynes (1973c), 205–15.

(1937c). 'The "Ex-Ante" Theory of the Rate of Interest', *Economic Journal*, *47*, December, 663–9. All page references are to the reprinting in Keynes (1973c), 215–23.

(1938). 'Mr. Keynes on "Finance"', *Economic Journal*, *48*, 318–22. All page references are to the reprinting in Keynes (1973c), 229–33.

(1939). 'Relative Movements of Real Wages and Output', *Economic Journal*, *49*, March, 34–51. All page references are to the reprinting in Keynes (1973a), 394–412.

(1971). *A Tract on Monetary Reform*, edited by Donald Moggridge. Vol. 4 of the *Collected Writings*. London: Macmillan for the Royal Economic Society.

(1972). *Essays in Persuasion*, edited by Donald Moggridge. Vol. 9 of the *Collected Writings*. London: Macmillan for the Royal Economic Society.

(1973a). *The General Theory of Employment, Interest and Money*, edited by Donald Moggridge. Vol. 7 of the *Collected Writings*. London: Macmillan for the Royal Economic Society.

(1973b). *The General Theory and After: Part I Preparation*, edited by Donald Moggridge. Vol. 13 of the *Collected Writings*. London: Macmillan for the Royal Economic Society.

(1973c). *The General Theory and After: Part II Defence and Development*, edited by Donald Moggridge. Vol. 14 of the *Collected Writings*. London: Macmillan for the Royal Economic Society.

(1979). *The General Theory and After: A Supplement*, edited by Donald Moggridge. Vol. 29 of the *Collected Writings*. London: Macmillan for the Royal Economic Society.

(1983). *Articles and Correspondence: Investment and Editorial*, edited by Donald Moggridge. Vol. 12 of the *Collected Writings*. London: Macmillan for the Royal Economic Society.

Kowalik, T. et al. (1964). *Problems of Economic Dynamics and Planning: Essays in Honour of Michal Kalecki*. Warsaw: PWN – Polish Scientific Publishers.

Kregel, J. A. (1976). 'Economic Methodology in the Face of Uncertainty', *Economic Journal*, *86*, June, 209–25.

(1980). 'Economic Dynamics and the Theory of Steady Growth: An Historical Essay on Harrod's "Knife-Edge"', *History of Political Economy*, *12*, Spring, 97–123.

Kurihara, Kenneth K. (ed.) (1954). *Post Keynesian Economics*. New Brunswick, N.J.: Rutgers University Press.

Kuznets, Simon (1946). *National Income, a Summary of Findings*. New York: National Bureau of Economic Research.

Leijonhufvud, Axel (1968). *On Keynesian Economics and the Economics of Keynes*. London: Oxford University Press.

(1969). *Keynes and the Classics: Two Lectures on Keynes' Contribution to Economic Theory*. London: Institute of Economic Affairs, Occasional Paper, 30.

Lekachman, Robert (ed.) (1964). *Keynes' General Theory: Reports of Three Decades*. New York: St Martins Press.

Lerner, Abba P. (1952). 'The Essential Properties of Interest and Money', *Quarterly Journal of Economics*, 66, May, 173–93.

Leroy, Stephen F. (1983). 'Keynes's theory of investment', *History of Political Economy*, 15, Fall, 397–421.

Little, I. M. D. (1957). 'Classical Growth', *Oxford Economic Papers*, 9, June, 152–77.

Lucas, Robert E. Jr. (1981). *Studies in Business – Cycle Theory*. Cambridge, Mass.: MIT Press.

Lutz, Friedrich A. and Lloyd W. Mints (1951). *Readings in Monetary Theory*. Homewood, Ill.: Richard D. Irwin.

Malinvaud, E. (1977). *The Theory of Unemployment Reconsidered*. Oxford: Basil Blackwell.

Mankiw, N. Gregory (1985). 'Small Menu Costs and Large Business Cycles: A Macroeconomic Model of Monopoly', *Quarterly Journal of Economics*, 100, May, 529–37.

Marshall, Alfred (1920). *Principles of Economics*, 8th edn. London: Macmillan.

Minsky, Hyman P. (1975). *John Maynard Keynes*. New York: Columbia University Press.

Modigliani, Franco (1944). 'Liquidity Preference and the Theory of Interest and Money', *Econometrica*, 12, January, 45–88. All page references are to Lutz and Mints (1951).

Modigliani, Franco and Richard Brumberg (1954). 'Utility Analysis and the Consumption Function: An Interpretation of Cross-Section Data', in Kurihara (1954), 388–436.

Ohlin, B. (1937a). 'Some Notes on the Stockholm Theory of Saving and Investment', *Economic Journal*, 47, March, 53–69, and June, 221–40.

  (1937b). 'Alternative Theories of the Rate of Interest: Rejoinder I', *Economic Journal*, 47, September, 423–27.

Parkin, Michael and A. R. Nobay (1975). *Current Economic Problems*. Cambridge: Cambridge University Press.

Parrinello, Sergio (1980). 'The Price Level in Keynes' Effective Demand', *Journal of Post Keynesian Economics*, 3, 63–78.

Pasinetti, Luigi (1974). *Growth and Income Distribution: Essays in Economic Theory*. Cambridge: Cambridge University Press.

Patinkin, Don (1965). *Money, Interest, and Prices*, 2nd edn. New York: Harper & Row.

  (1982). *Anticipations of the General Theory?: And Other Essays on Keynes*. Chicago: University of Chicago Press.

Potestio, Paola (1986). 'Equilibrium and Employment in "The General Theory"', *Giornale degli economisti e annali di economia*, Luglio-Agosto, 363–88.

Reddaway, W. B. (1964). 'Keynesian Analysis and a Managed Economy', in Lekachman (1964), 108–23.

Robertson, Dennis H. (1936). 'Some Notes on Mr. Keynes' General Theory of Employment', *Quarterly Journal of Economics*, 51, November, 168–91.

(1937). 'Alternative Theories of the Rate of Interest: Rejoinder II', *Economic Journal*, 47, September, 428–36.

(1938). 'Mr. Keynes and "Finance"', *Economic Journal*, 48, June, 314–18.

Robinson, E. A. G. (1964). 'Could There Have Been a "General Theory" Without Keynes?', in Lekachman (1964), 87–95.

Robinson, Joan (1933). 'A Parable on Savings and Investment', *Economica*, 13, February, 75–84.

(1937). 'Full Employment', in Robinson (1947), 1–28.

(1947). *Essays in the Theory of Employment*, 2nd edn. Oxford: Basil Blackwell.

(1952). 'The Generalisation of the General Theory', in *The Rate of Interest and Other Essays*. London: Macmillan. All page references are to Robinson (1979).

(1956). *The Accumulation of Capital*. London: Macmillan.

(1960). 'Accumulation and the Production Function', in *Collected Economic Papers*, vol. 2. Oxford: Basil Blackwell, 132–44.

(1962). *Essays in the Theory of Economic Growth*. London: Macmillan.

(1963). 'Findlay's Robinsonian Model of Accumulation: A Comment', *Economica*, 30, November, 408–11.

(1964). 'Kalecki and Keynes' in Kowalik et al. (1964). Reprinted in Robinson (1965), 92–9.

(1965). *Collected Economic Papers*, vol. 3. Oxford: Basil Blackwell.

(1969). 'A Further Note', *Review of Economic Studies*, 36, April, 260–2.

(1970). 'Harrod after Twenty-One Years', *Economic Journal*, 80, September, 731–7.

(1971). *Economic Heresies*. New York: Basic Books.

(1975). 'The Unimportance of Reswitching', *Quarterly Journal of Economics*, 89, February, 32–9.

(1979). *The Generalisation of the General Theory and Other Essays*, 2nd edn. of Robinson (1952). London: Macmillan.

Rowley, J. C. R. (1988). 'The Keynes–Tinbergen Exchange in Retrospect', in Hamouda and Smithin (1988), 23–31.

Samuelson, Paul A. (1939). 'Interactions Between the Multiplier Analysis and the Principle of Acceleration', *Review of Economic Statistics*, 21, May, 75–8.

(1968). 'What Classical and Neoclassical Monetary Theory Really Was', *Canadian Journal of Economics*, 1, February, 1–15.

Shackle, G. L. S. (1967). *The Years of High Theory*. Cambridge: Cambridge University Press.

Solow, R. (1956). 'A Contribution to the Theory of Economic Growth', *Quarterly Journal of Economics*, 70, February, 65–94.

Targetti, F. and B. Kinda-Hass (1982). 'Kalecki's Review of Keynes' *General Theory*', *Australian Economic Papers*, 21, December, 244–60.

Tarshis, Lorie (1939). 'Changes in Real and Money Wages', *Economic Journal*, 49, March, 150–54.

Tinbergen, J. (1939). *A Method and its Application to Investment Activity*; Statistical Testing of Business-Cycle Theories I. Geneva: League of Nations.

Townshend, Hugh (1937a). 'Liquidity-Premium and the Theory of Value', *Economic Journal*, 47, March, 157—69.

(1937b). 'Review of *Capital and Employment*', *Economic Journal*, *47*, June, 321–26.

Trevithick, J. (1976). 'Money Wage Inflexibility and the Keynesian Labour Supply Function', *Economic Journal*, *86*, June, 327–32.

Vicarelli, Fausto (1984). *Keynes: The Instability of Capitalism*. Philadelphia: University of Pennsylvania Press.

Viner, Jacob (1936). 'Mr. Keynes on the Causes of Unemployment', *Quarterly Journal of Economics*, *51*, November, 147–67.

AUTHOR INDEX

SUBJECT INDEX

acceleration principle, 138–40,
142–3, 146
accelerator *see* acceleration
principle
accumulation, 9, 106, 137–8, 151,
167–8, 171, 177n, 178–9, 181n,
188, 191–2
rate of, 135, 169–71, 174–88
theory of, 9, 51, 117, 135, 156,
168, 171, 186, 192
actual investment *see* investment,
expenditures
actual prices *see* prices, market
actual rate of accumulation, 178,
183, 186
actual rate of growth, 147–8, 161–3,
192
aggregate demand, 6, 21, 47, 57,
67, 102
aggregate demand function, 20–2,
24–5, 39, 43–7, 49, 51–2, 55–8,
60–1, 63, 65, 120
aggregate demand price *see*
aggregate demand function
aggregate income, 19, 63
aggregate investment, 67–8, 110,
189
aggregate proceeds function, 57
aggregate supply function, 19–22,
39, 42–3, 45–7, 49, 51–7, 120
aggregate supply price *see* aggregate
supply function
animal spirits, 81, 117, 156n, 168,
170, 177–80, 182, 185
average propensity to consume,
59n, 63–4, 125, 172

banking system, 8, 13, 15, 87–8,
93n, 109, 112–13, 170
bastard golden age, 181
bears, 92
bonds *see* long-term securities
bulls, 91–2
business cycle, 5, 8–9, 67, 74–5, 79,
83n, 84, 121–2, 131–4, 136,
138–40, 142–5, 148, 151, 155,
158, 160, 162, 164–5, 174,
183n, 190
capital coefficient, 148, 153, 155
required, 148
capital-saving technical progress,
153n, 154n
capitalists' expenditures, 78, 173–4
central bank, 8, 88, 90, 189
central message, 102, 139
centrifugal forces, 159, 161–2
Circus, 16, 17n, 18, 166
classical theory, 7, 20–1, 26, 28, 31,
38, 47, 49, 52, 86, 120–1, 131n,
135, 162, 191n
of interest, 23, 72n, 96–7, 99
closed economy, 3, 58, 116, 127,
173
commodity markets, 28, 31, 35, 37,
45, 49, 52, 111n
competitive firms, 20–2, 34, 40–3,
52, 55, 57
competitive markets, 5, 19, 49, 170
consumption expenditures, 3, 7, 13,
15, 17, 21–2, 27, 44, 47, 58,
60–1, 63, 65–6, 69–70, 82, 102,
129, 134, 159n, 172, 184
consumption function, 45–6, 50, 52,